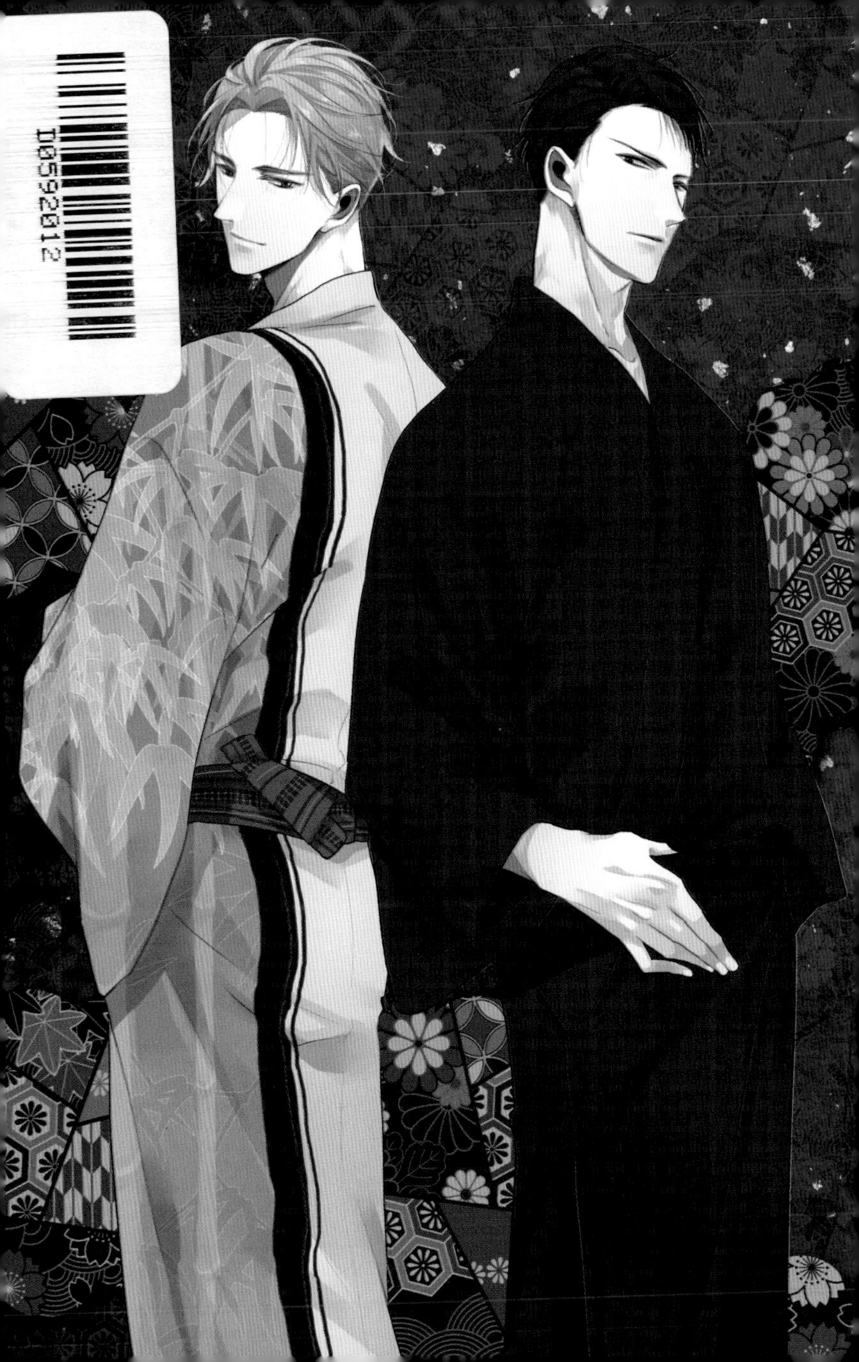

Contents

Black or White

2

SACHIMO

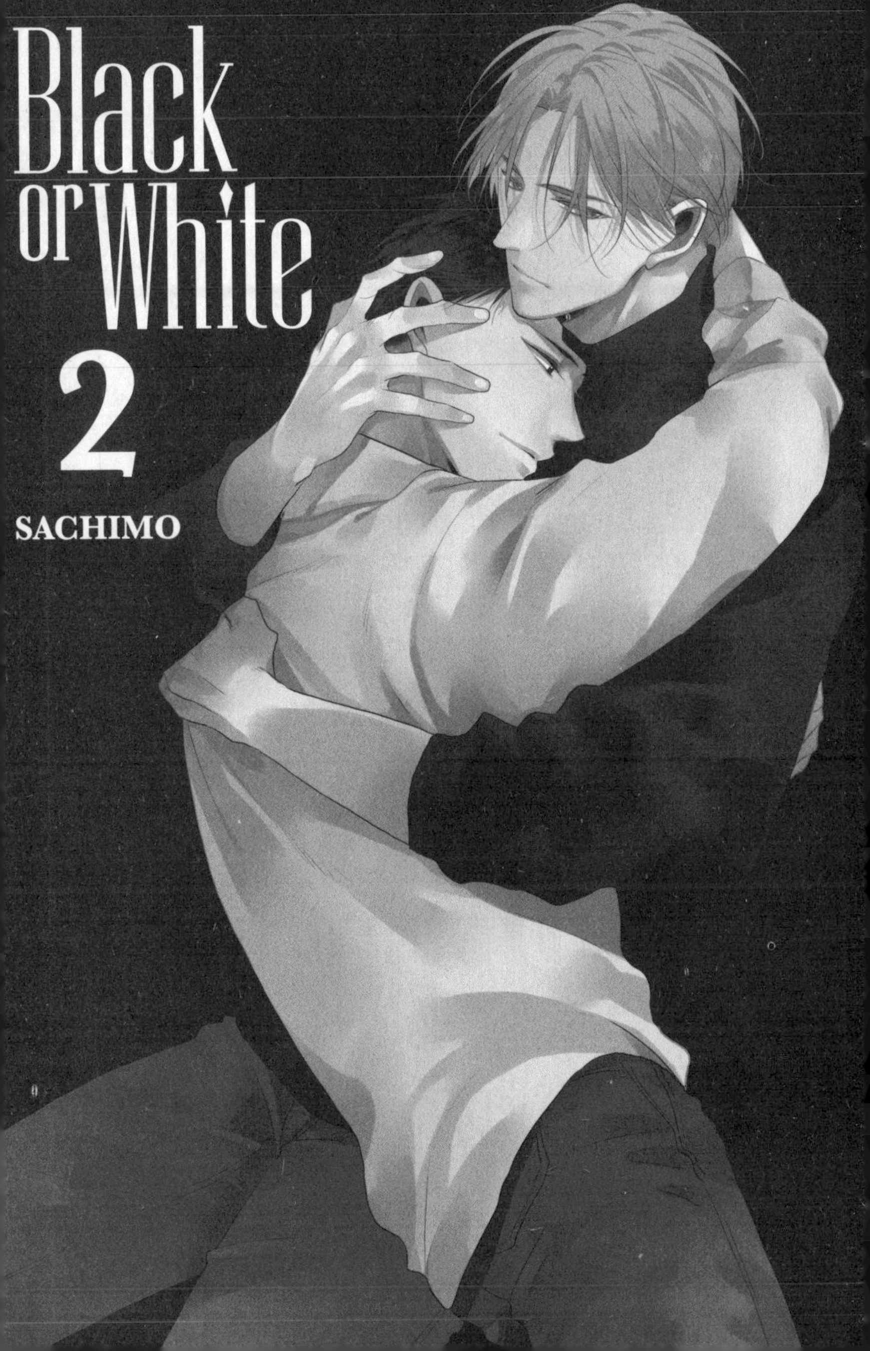

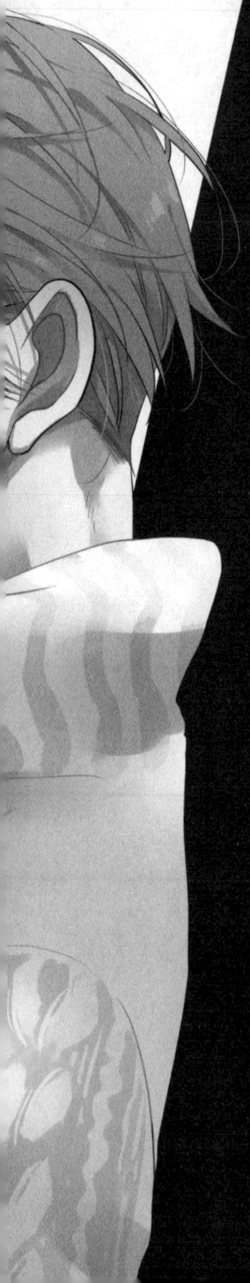

Black or White

ACT 4

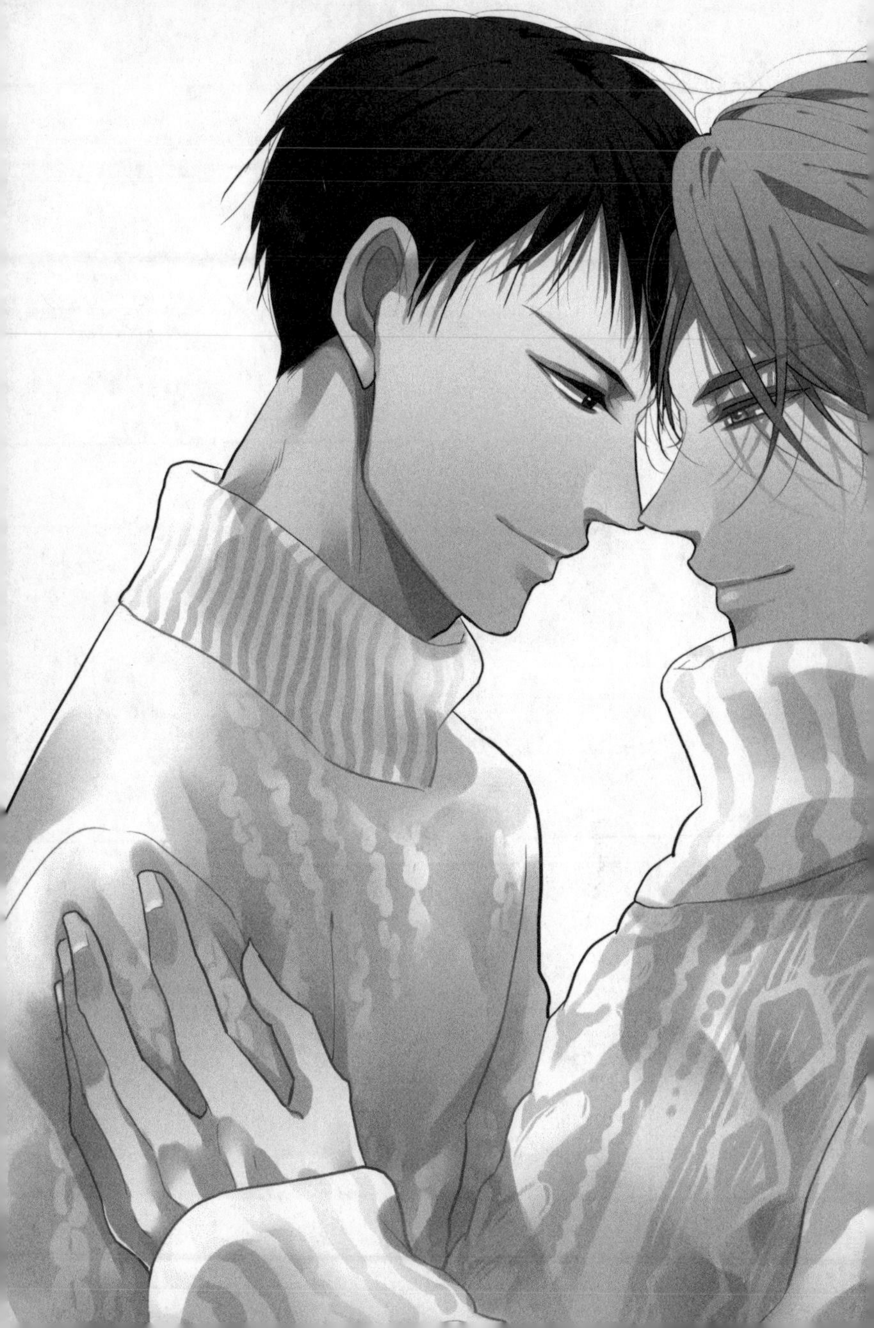

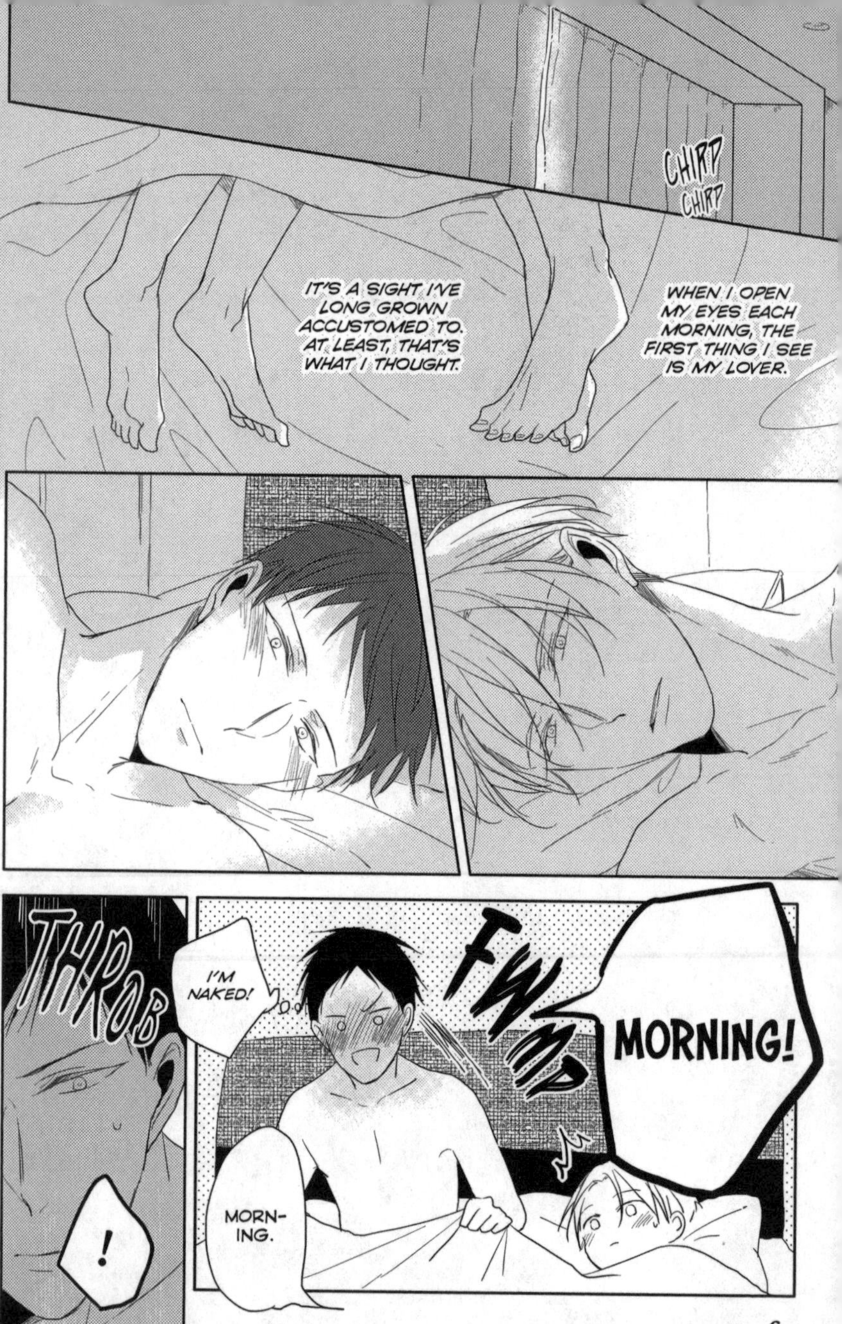
CHIRP
CHIRP
WHEN I OPEN MY EYES EACH MORNING, THE FIRST THING I SEE IS MY LOVER.
IT'S A SIGHT I'VE LONG GROWN ACCUSTOMED TO. AT LEAST, THAT'S WHAT I THOUGHT.
MORNING!
FWMP
I'M NAKED!
MORN-ING.
THROB
!

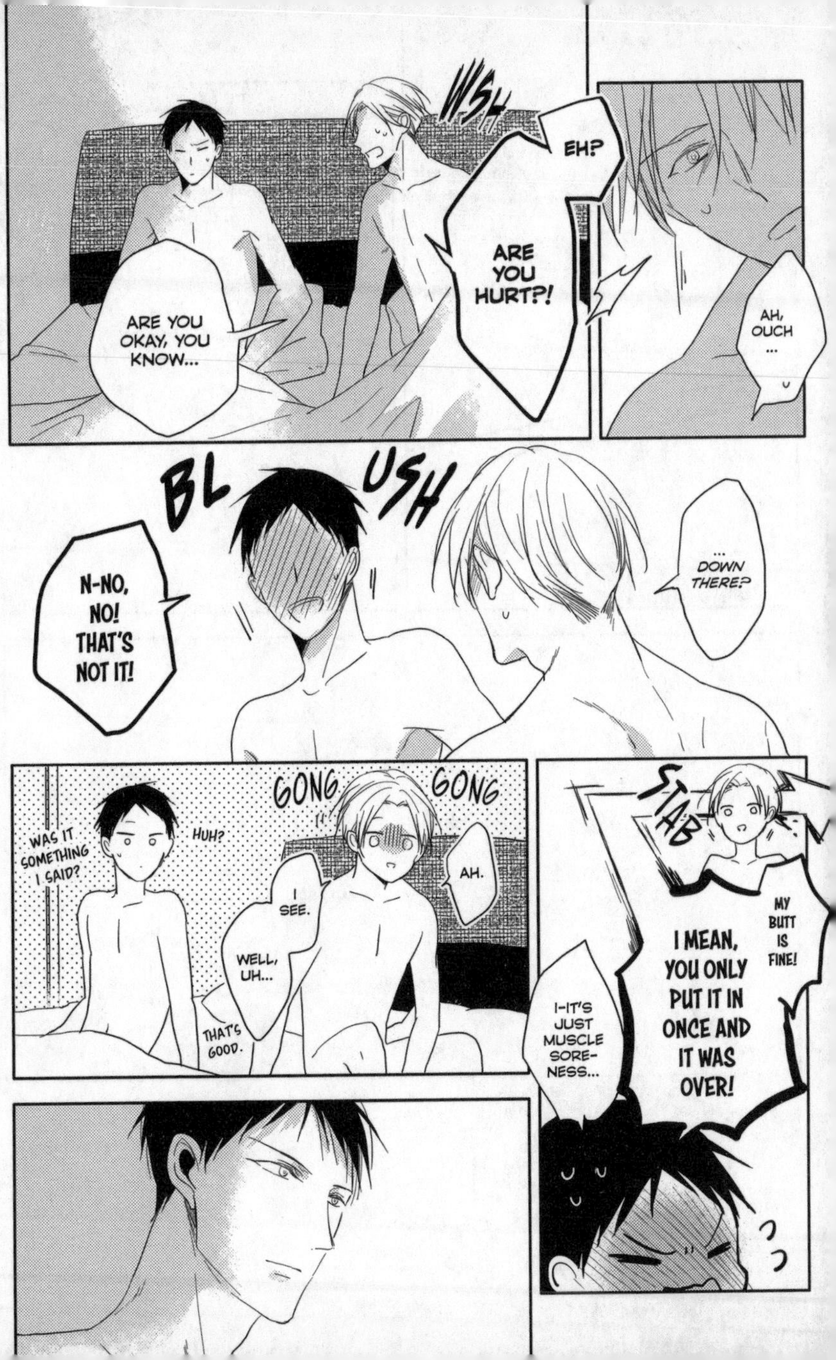
AH, OUCH ...
WSH
EH?
ARE YOU HURT?!
ARE YOU OKAY, YOU KNOW...
... DOWN THERE?
BLUSH
N-NO, NO! THAT'S NOT IT!
STAB
MY BUTT IS FINE!
I MEAN, YOU ONLY PUT IT IN ONCE AND IT WAS OVER!
I-IT'S JUST MUSCLE SORE-NESS...
GONG GONG
AH.
HUH?
WAS IT SOMETHING I SAID?
I SEE.
WELL, UH...
THAT'S GOOD.

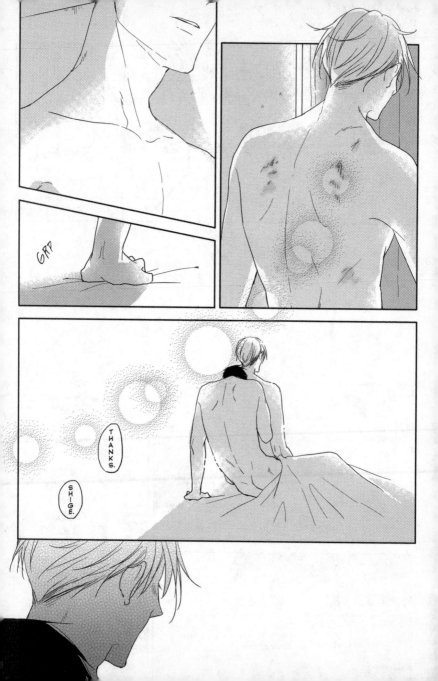

GRP

THANKS.

SHIGE.

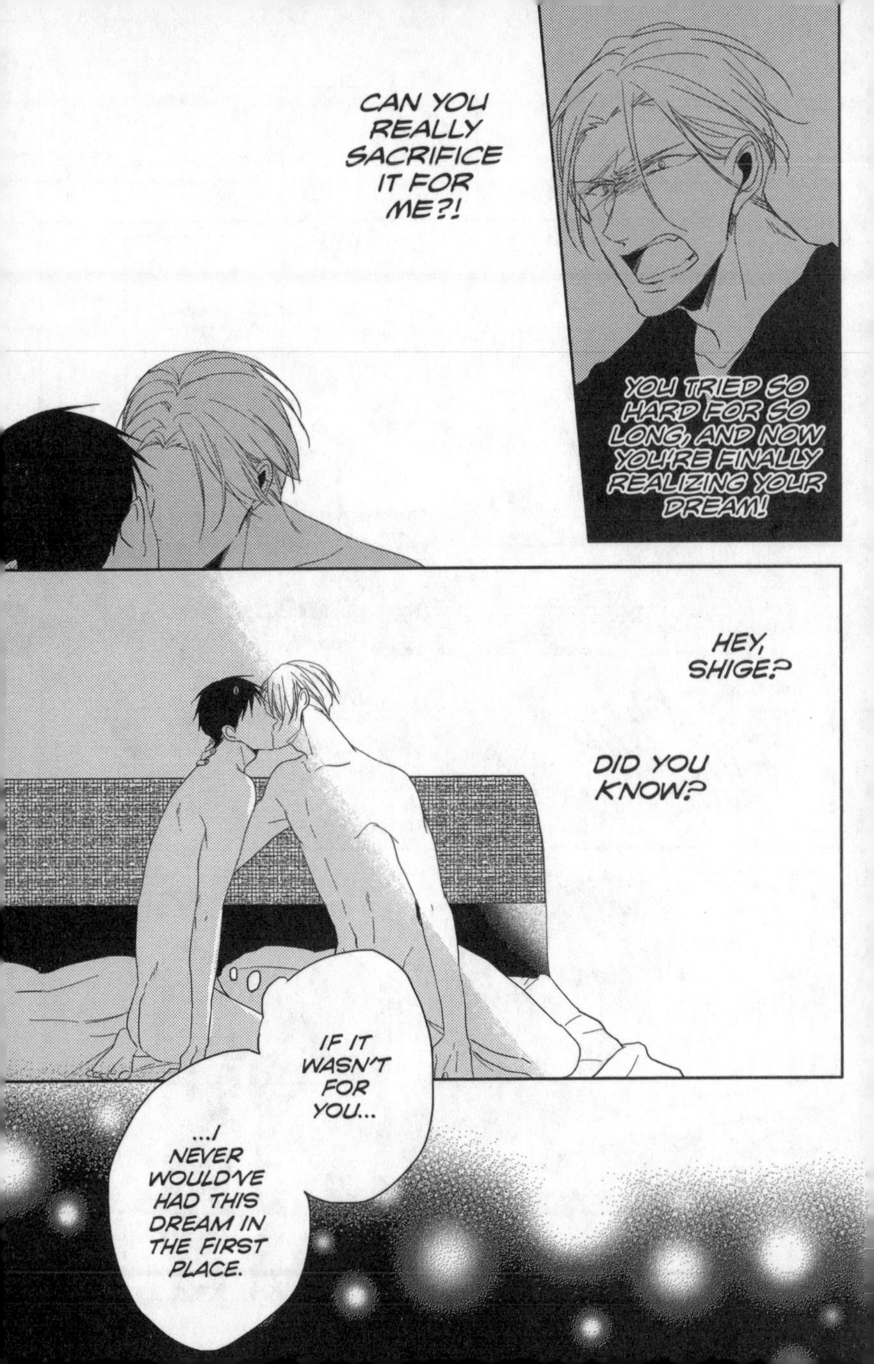
YOU TRIED SO HARD FOR SO LONG, AND NOW YOU'RE FINALLY REALIZING YOUR DREAM!
CAN YOU REALLY SACRIFICE IT FOR ME?!
HEY, SHIGE?
DID YOU KNOW?
IF IT WASN'T FOR YOU...
...I NEVER WOULD'VE HAD THIS DREAM IN THE FIRST PLACE.

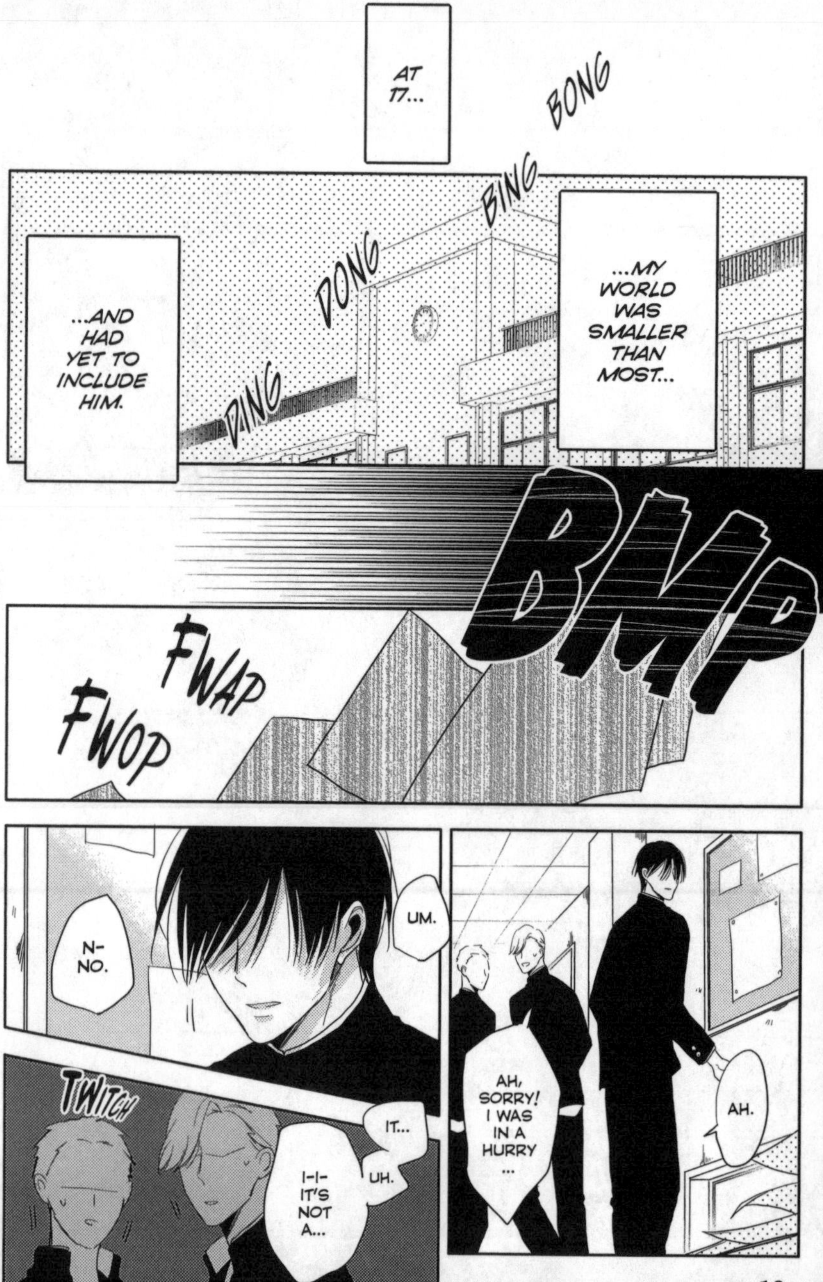
AT 17...
...MY WORLD WAS SMALLER THAN MOST...
BONG
BING
DONG
DING
...AND HAD YET TO INCLUDE HIM.
BMP
FWAP
FWOP
AH.
AH, SORRY! I WAS IN A HURRY ...
UM.
N-NO.
IT...
UH.
I-I-IT'S NOT A...
TWITCH

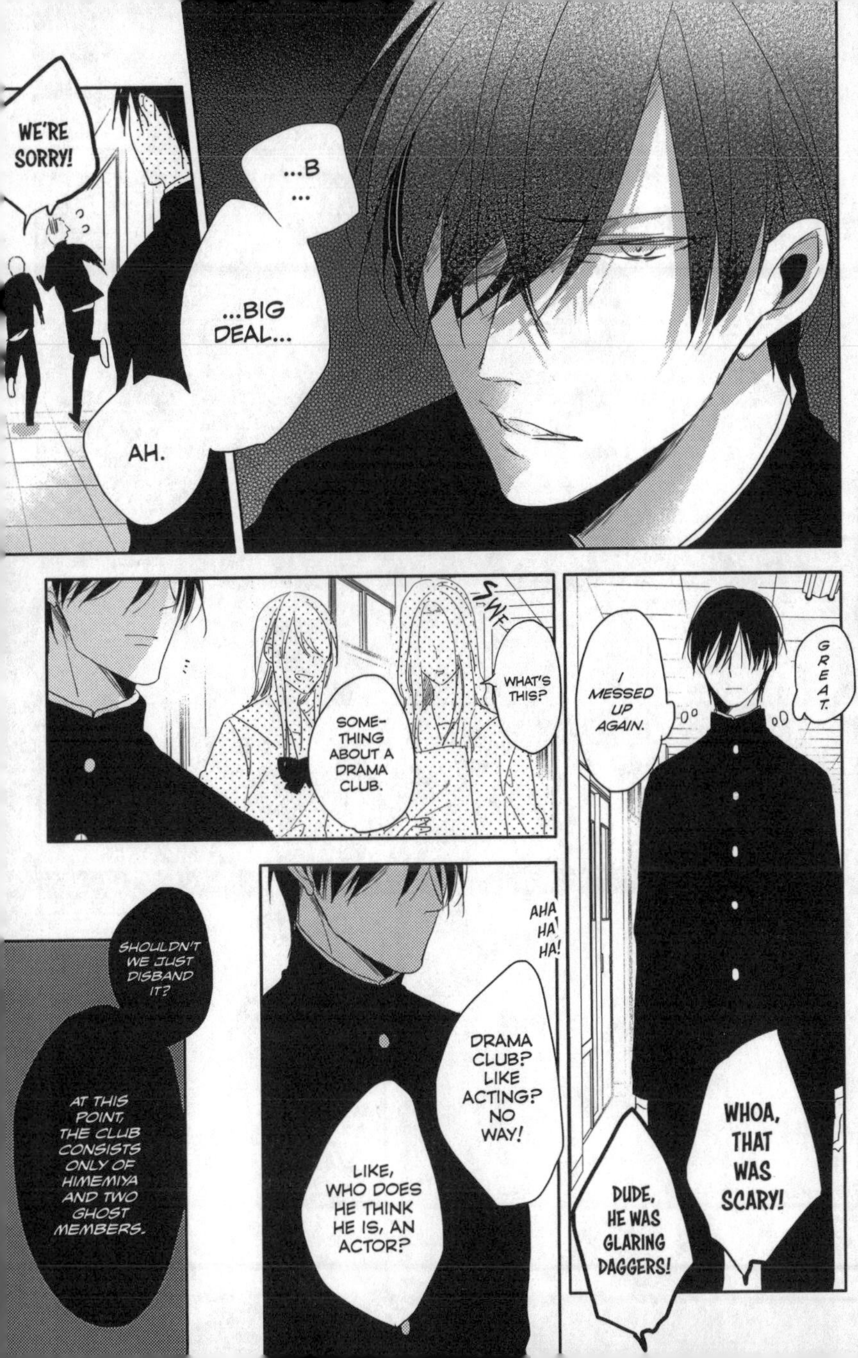
...B
...
...BIG DEAL...
AH.
WE'RE SORRY!
GREAT.
I MESSED UP AGAIN.
WHOA, THAT WAS SCARY!
DUDE, HE WAS GLARING DAGGERS!
SWF
WHAT'S THIS?
SOME-THING ABOUT A DRAMA CLUB.
AHA HA HA!
DRAMA CLUB? LIKE ACTING? NO WAY!
LIKE, WHO DOES HE THINK HE IS, AN ACTOR?
SHOULDN'T WE JUST DISBAND IT?
AT THIS POINT, THE CLUB CONSISTS ONLY OF HIMEMIYA AND TWO GHOST MEMBERS.

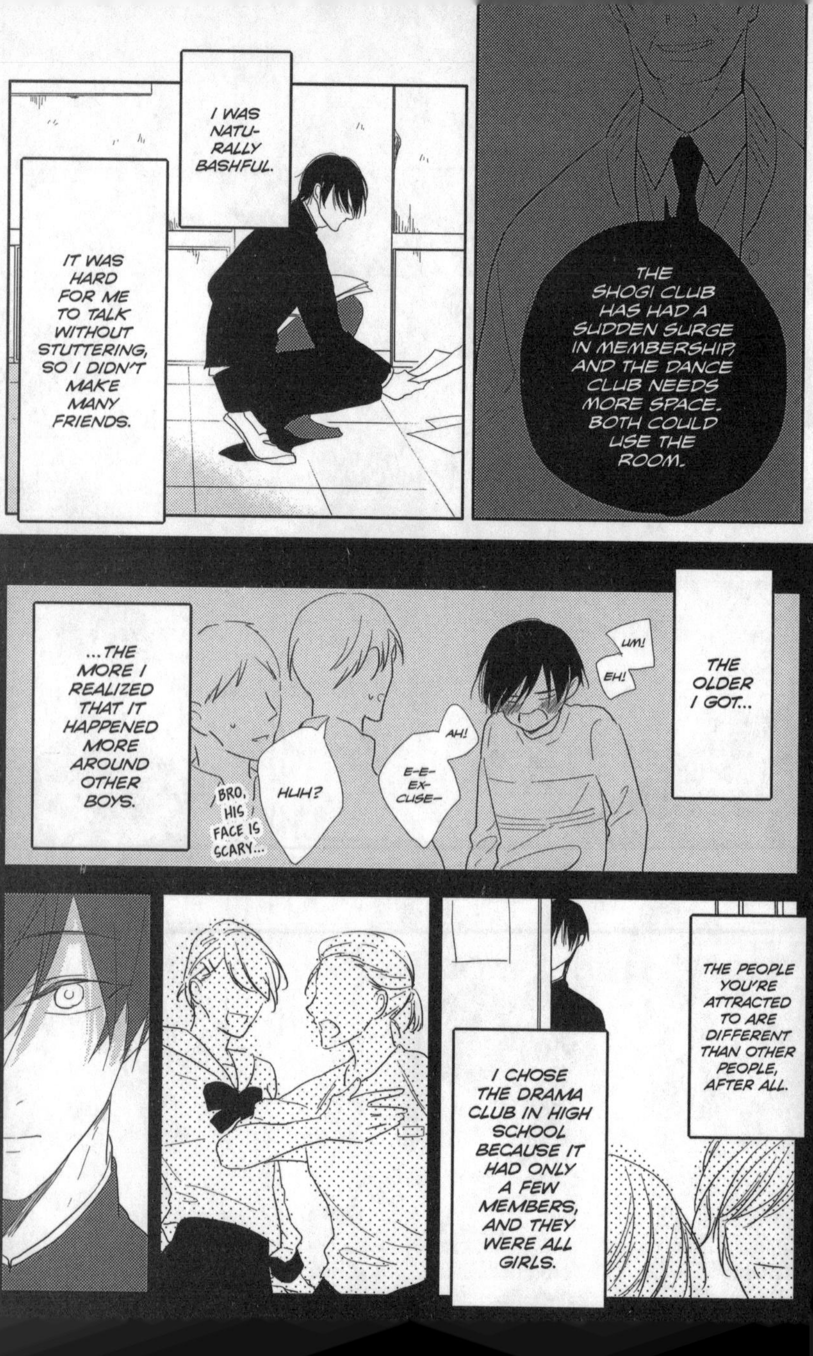
THE SHOGI CLUB HAS HAD A SUDDEN SURGE IN MEMBERSHIP, AND THE DANCE CLUB NEEDS MORE SPACE. BOTH COULD USE THE ROOM.
I WAS NATU-RALLY BASHFUL.
IT WAS HARD FOR ME TO TALK WITHOUT STUTTERING, SO I DIDN'T MAKE MANY FRIENDS.
THE OLDER I GOT...
UM!
EH!
AH!
E-E-EX-CUSE—
HUH?
BRO, HIS FACE IS SCARY...
...THE MORE I REALIZED THAT IT HAPPENED MORE AROUND OTHER BOYS.
THE PEOPLE YOU'RE ATTRACTED TO ARE DIFFERENT THAN OTHER PEOPLE, AFTER ALL.
I CHOSE THE DRAMA CLUB IN HIGH SCHOOL BECAUSE IT HAD ONLY A FEW MEMBERS, AND THEY WERE ALL GIRLS.

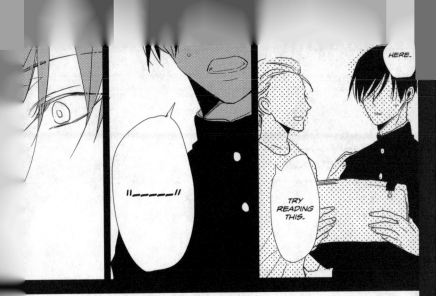

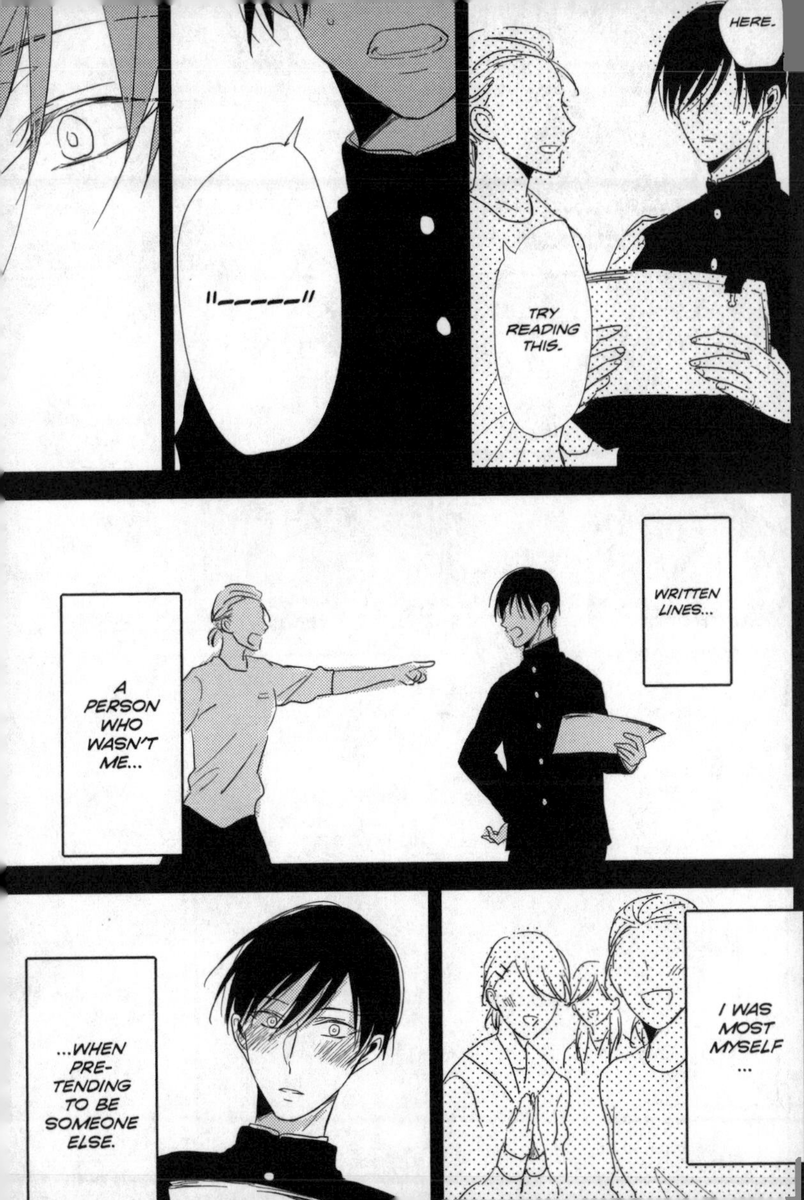
HERE.
TRY READING THIS.
"------"
WRITTEN LINES...
A PERSON WHO WASN'T ME...
I WAS MOST MYSELF ...
...WHEN PRE-TENDING TO BE SOMEONE ELSE.

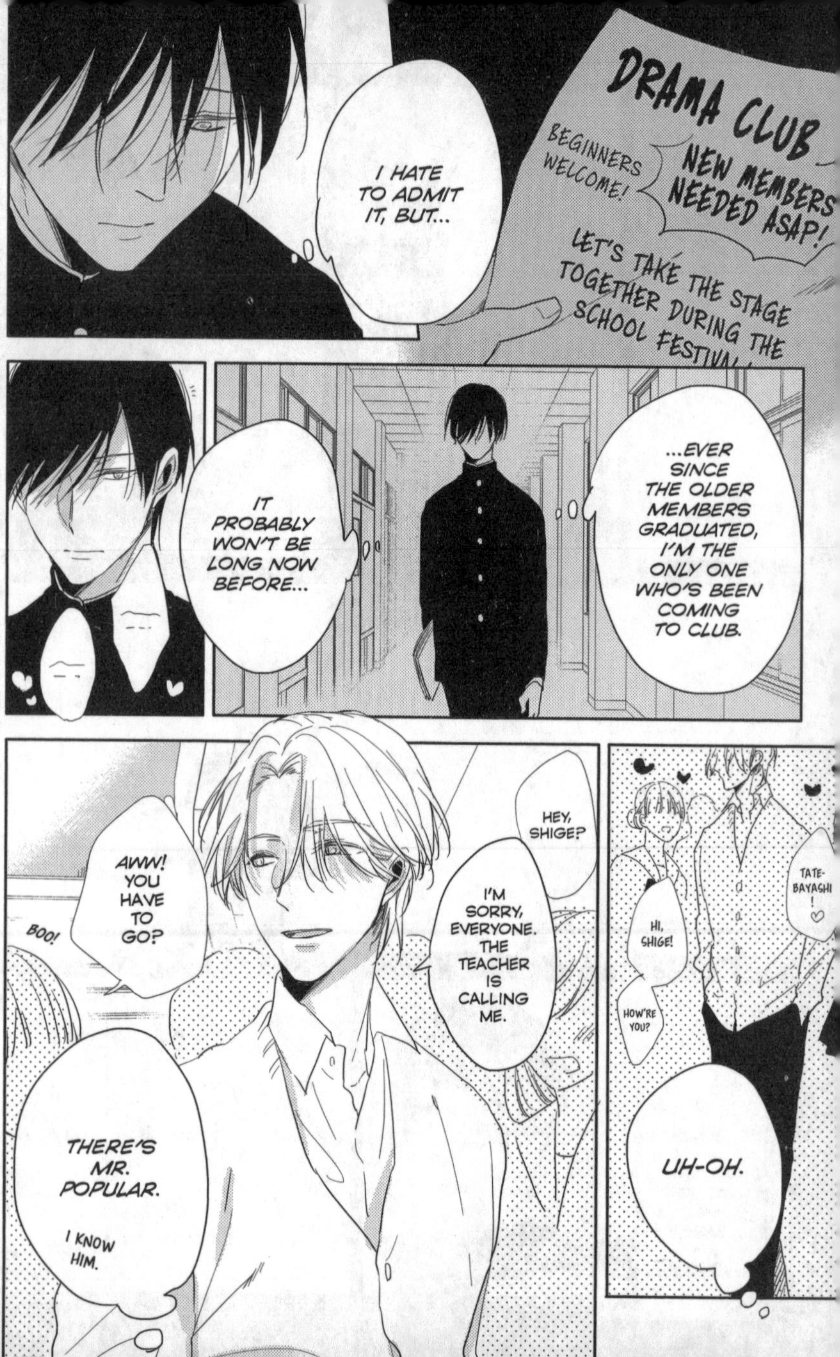
DRAMA CLUB
NEW MEMBERS NEEDED ASAP!
BEGINNERS WELCOME!
LET'S TAKE THE STAGE TOGETHER DURING THE SCHOOL FESTIVAL
I HATE TO ADMIT IT, BUT...
...EVER SINCE THE OLDER MEMBERS GRADUATED, I'M THE ONLY ONE WHO'S BEEN COMING TO CLUB.
IT PROBABLY WON'T BE LONG NOW BEFORE...
TATE-BAYASHI! ♡
HI, SHIGE!
HOW'RE YOU?
UH-OH.
HEY, SHIGE?
I'M SORRY, EVERYONE. THE TEACHER IS CALLING ME.
AWW! YOU HAVE TO GO?
BOO!
THERE'S MR. POPULAR.
I KNOW HIM.

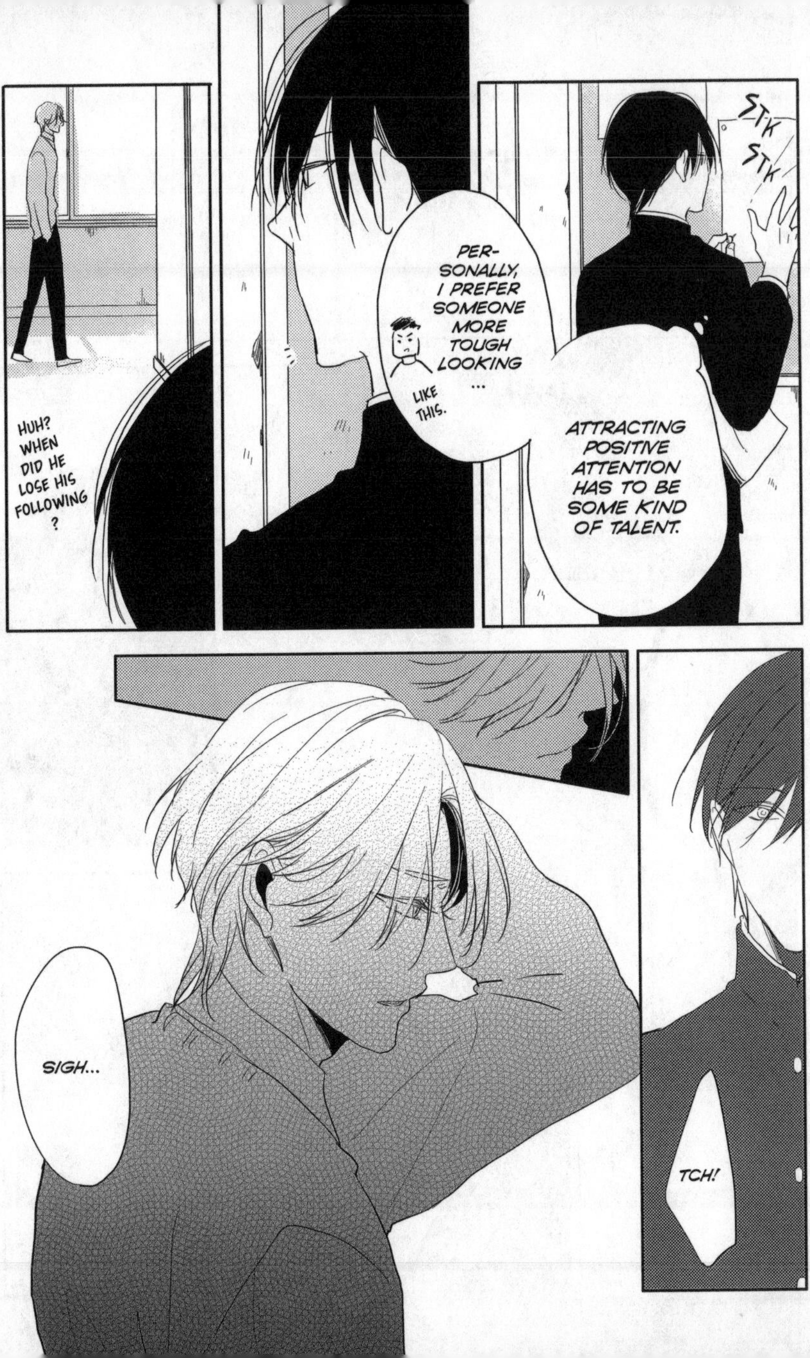
STK STK
ATTRACTING POSITIVE ATTENTION HAS TO BE SOME KIND OF TALENT.
PER-SONALLY, I PREFER SOMEONE MORE TOUGH LOOKING ...
LIKE THIS.
HUH? WHEN DID HE LOSE HIS FOLLOWING ?
TCH!
SIGH...

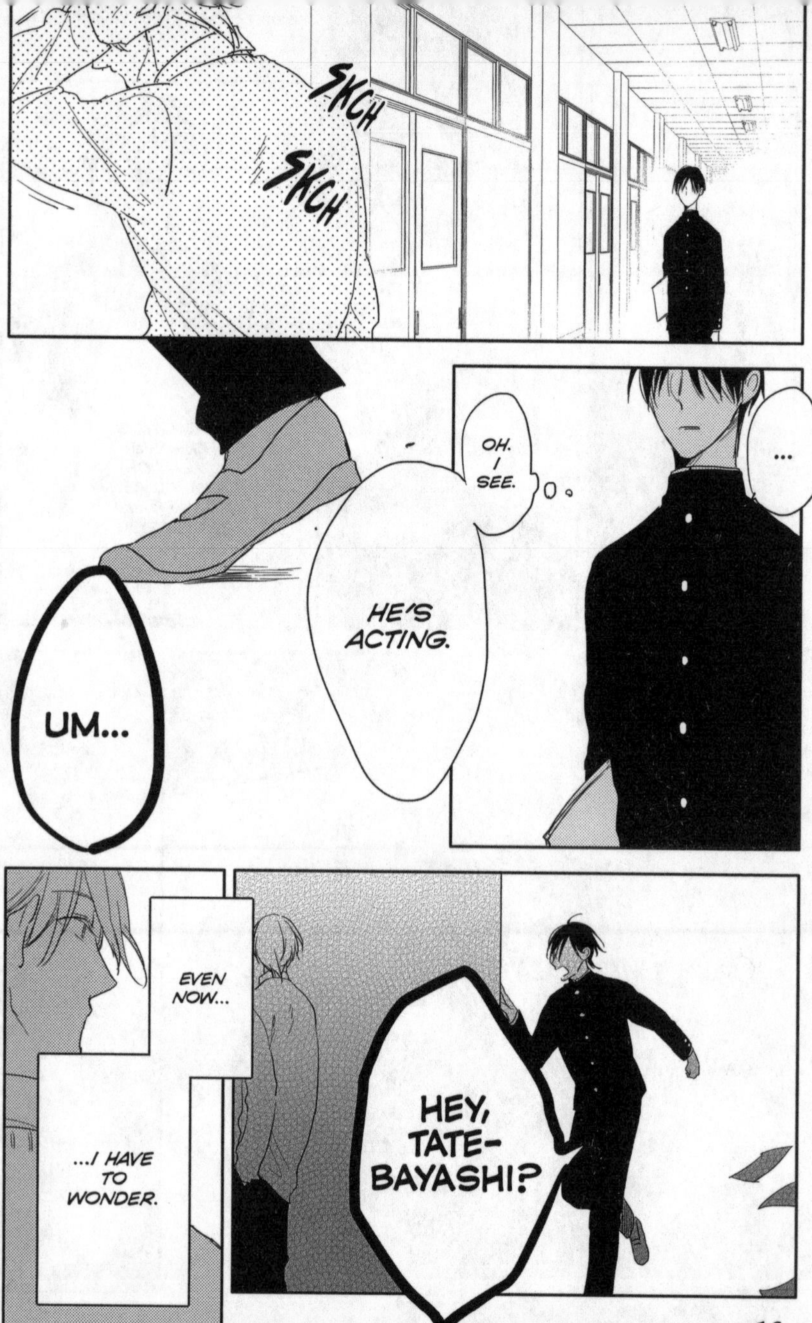
SKCH
SKCH
...
OH. I SEE.
HE'S ACTING.
UM...
HEY, TATE-BAYASHI?
EVEN NOW...
...I HAVE TO WONDER.

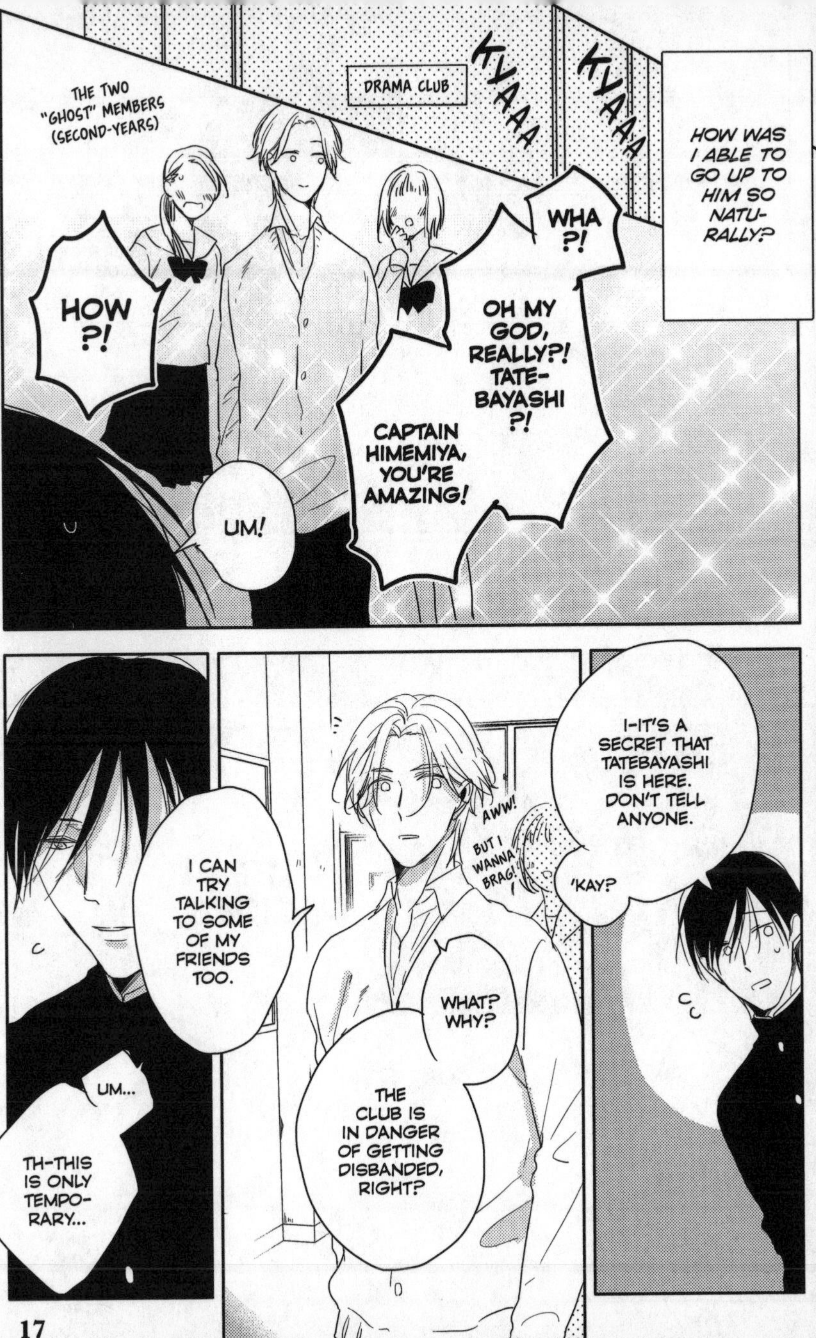
HOW WAS I ABLE TO GO UP TO HIM SO NATU-RALLY?
KYAAA
KYAAA
DRAMA CLUB
WHA ?!
OH MY GOD, REALLY?! TATE-BAYASHI ?!
CAPTAIN HIMEMIYA, YOU'RE AMAZING!
THE TWO "GHOST" MEMBERS (SECOND-YEARS)
HOW ?!
UM!
I-IT'S A SECRET THAT TATEBAYASHI IS HERE. DON'T TELL ANYONE.
'KAY?
AWW!
BUT I WANNA BRAG!
WHAT? WHY?
THE CLUB IS IN DANGER OF GETTING DISBANDED, RIGHT?
I CAN TRY TALKING TO SOME OF MY FRIENDS TOO.
UM...
TH-THIS IS ONLY TEMPO-RARY...

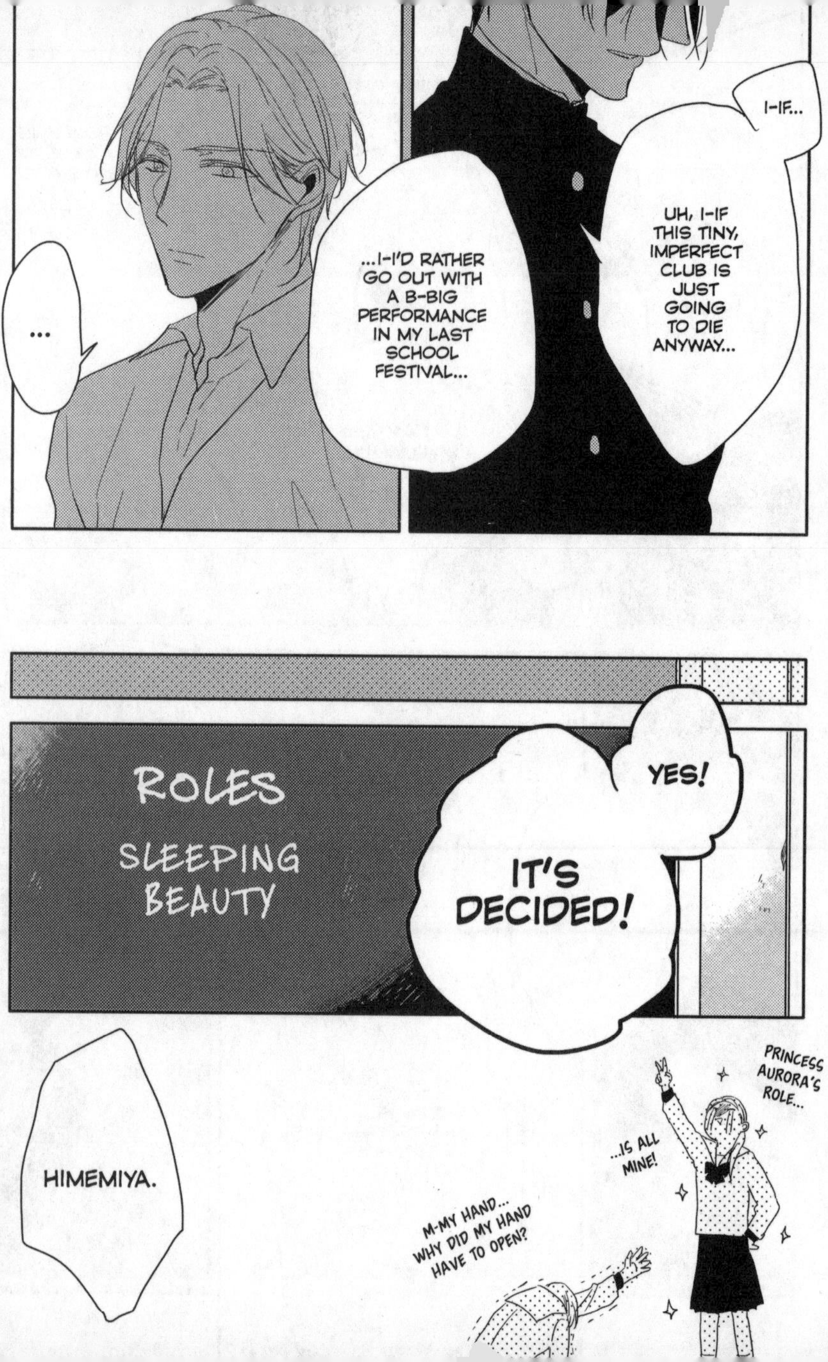

I-IF...
UH, I-IF THIS TINY, IMPERFECT CLUB IS JUST GOING TO DIE ANYWAY...
...I-I'D RATHER GO OUT WITH A B-BIG PERFORMANCE IN MY LAST SCHOOL FESTIVAL...
...
YES! IT'S DECIDED!
ROLES
SLEEPING BEAUTY
PRINCESS AURORA'S ROLE...
...IS ALL MINE!
M-MY HAND... WHY DID MY HAND HAVE TO OPEN?
HIMEMIYA.

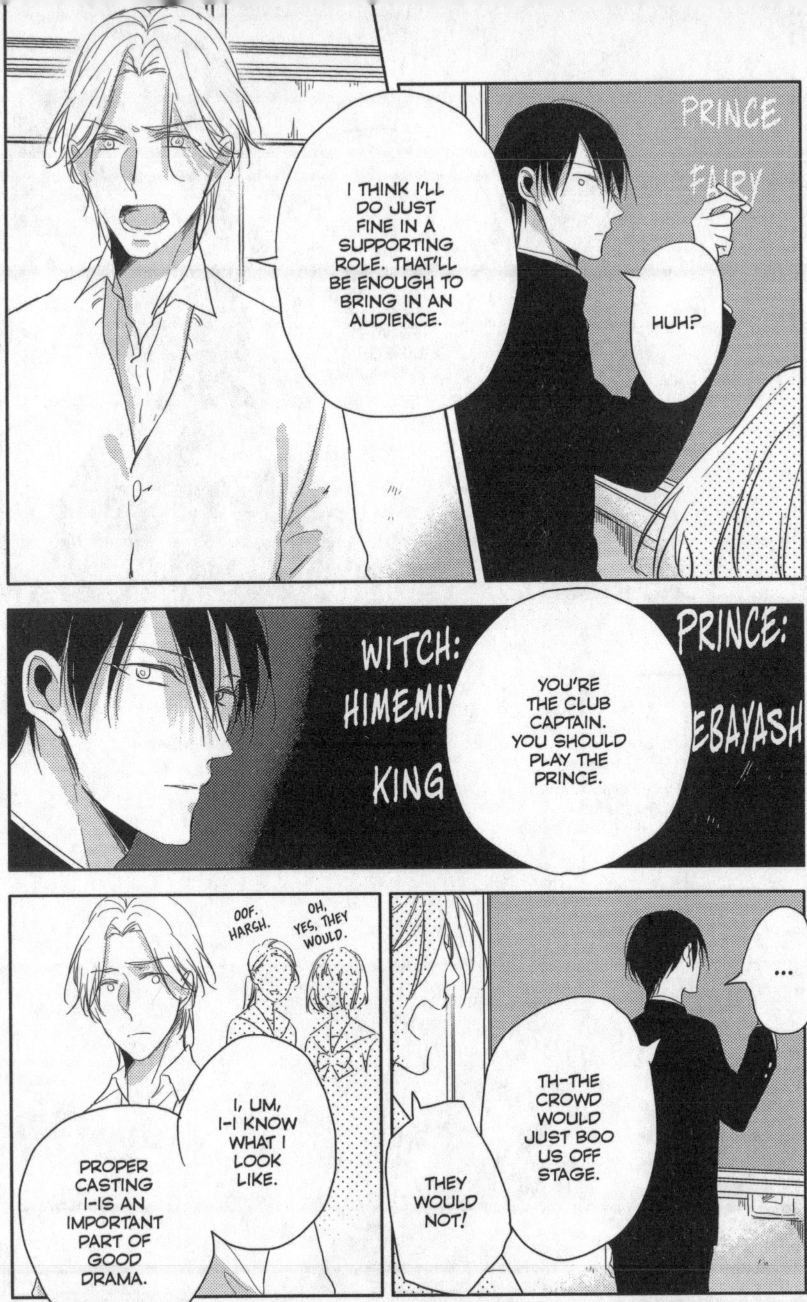
PRINCE
FAIRY
I THINK I'LL DO JUST FINE IN A SUPPORTING ROLE. THAT'LL BE ENOUGH TO BRING IN AN AUDIENCE.
HUH?
PRINCE:
EBAYASH
YOU'RE THE CLUB CAPTAIN. YOU SHOULD PLAY THE PRINCE.
WITCH:
HIMEMIY
KING
...
TH-THE CROWD WOULD JUST BOO US OFF STAGE.
THEY WOULD NOT!
OH, YES, THEY WOULD.
OOF. HARSH.
I, UM, I-I KNOW WHAT I LOOK LIKE.
PROPER CASTING I-IS AN IMPORTANT PART OF GOOD DRAMA.

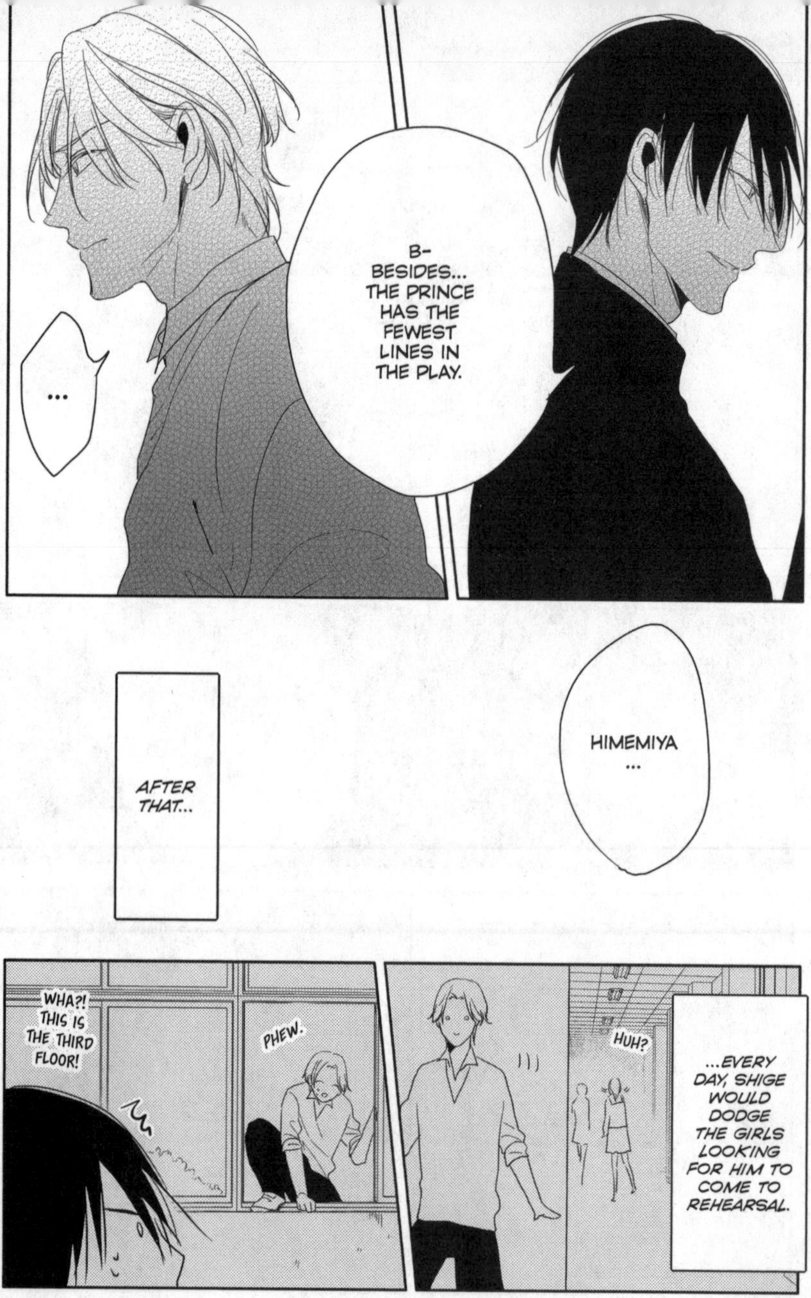
B-BESIDES... THE PRINCE HAS THE FEWEST LINES IN THE PLAY.
...
HIMEMIYA...
AFTER THAT...
...EVERY DAY, SHIGE WOULD DODGE THE GIRLS LOOKING FOR HIM TO COME TO REHEARSAL.
HUH?
PHEW.
WHA?! THIS IS THE THIRD FLOOR!

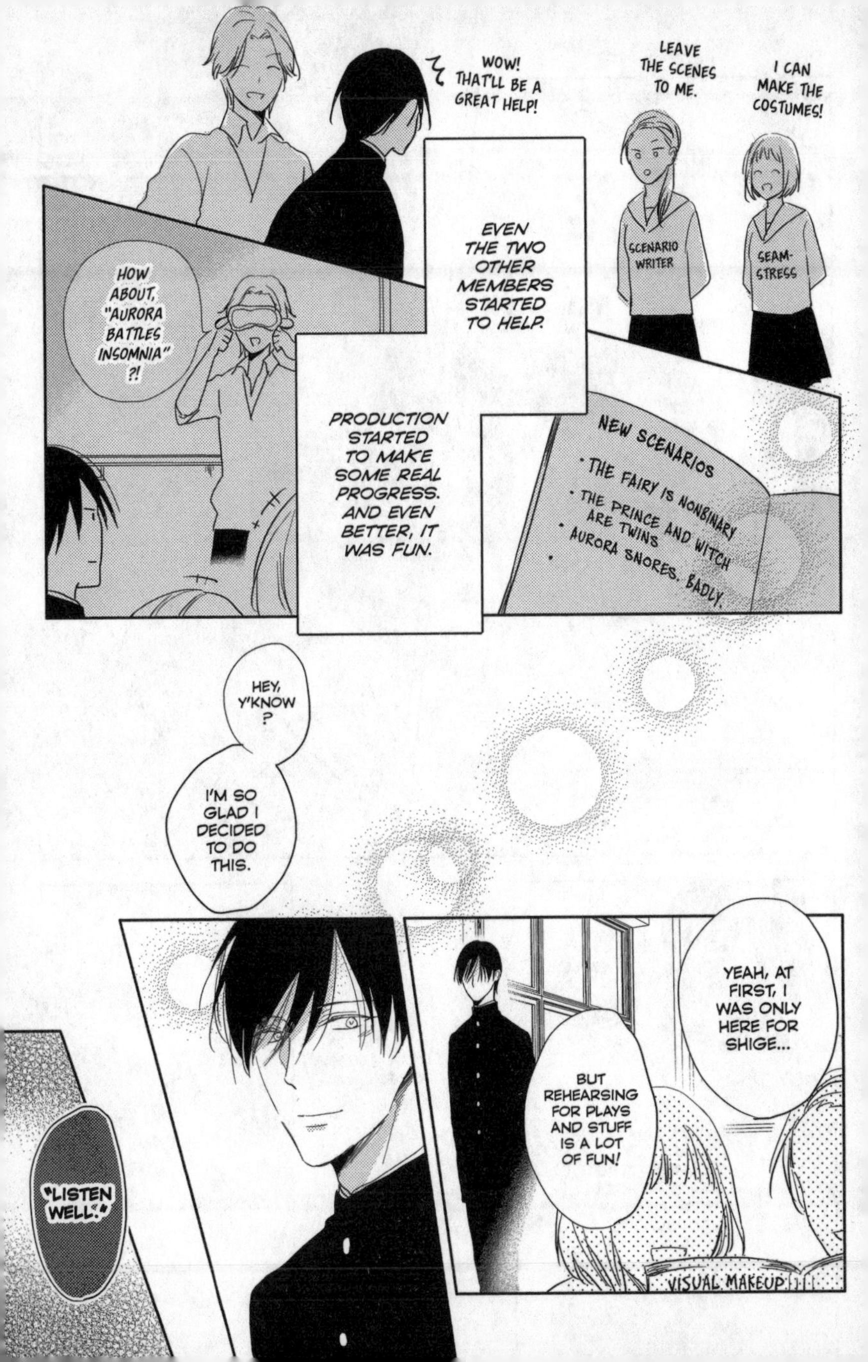

I CAN MAKE THE COSTUMES!
SEAM-STRESS
LEAVE THE SCENES TO ME.
SCENARIO WRITER
WOW! THAT'LL BE A GREAT HELP!
EVEN THE TWO OTHER MEMBERS STARTED TO HELP.
NEW SCENARIOS
• THE FAIRY IS NONBINARY
• THE PRINCE AND WITCH ARE TWINS
• AURORA SNORES. BADLY.
•
PRODUCTION STARTED TO MAKE SOME REAL PROGRESS. AND EVEN BETTER, IT WAS FUN.
HOW ABOUT, "AURORA BATTLES INSOMNIA"?!
HEY, Y'KNOW?
I'M SO GLAD I DECIDED TO DO THIS.
YEAH, AT FIRST, I WAS ONLY HERE FOR SHIGE...
BUT REHEARSING FOR PLAYS AND STUFF IS A LOT OF FUN!
VISUAL MAKEUP
"LISTEN WELL."

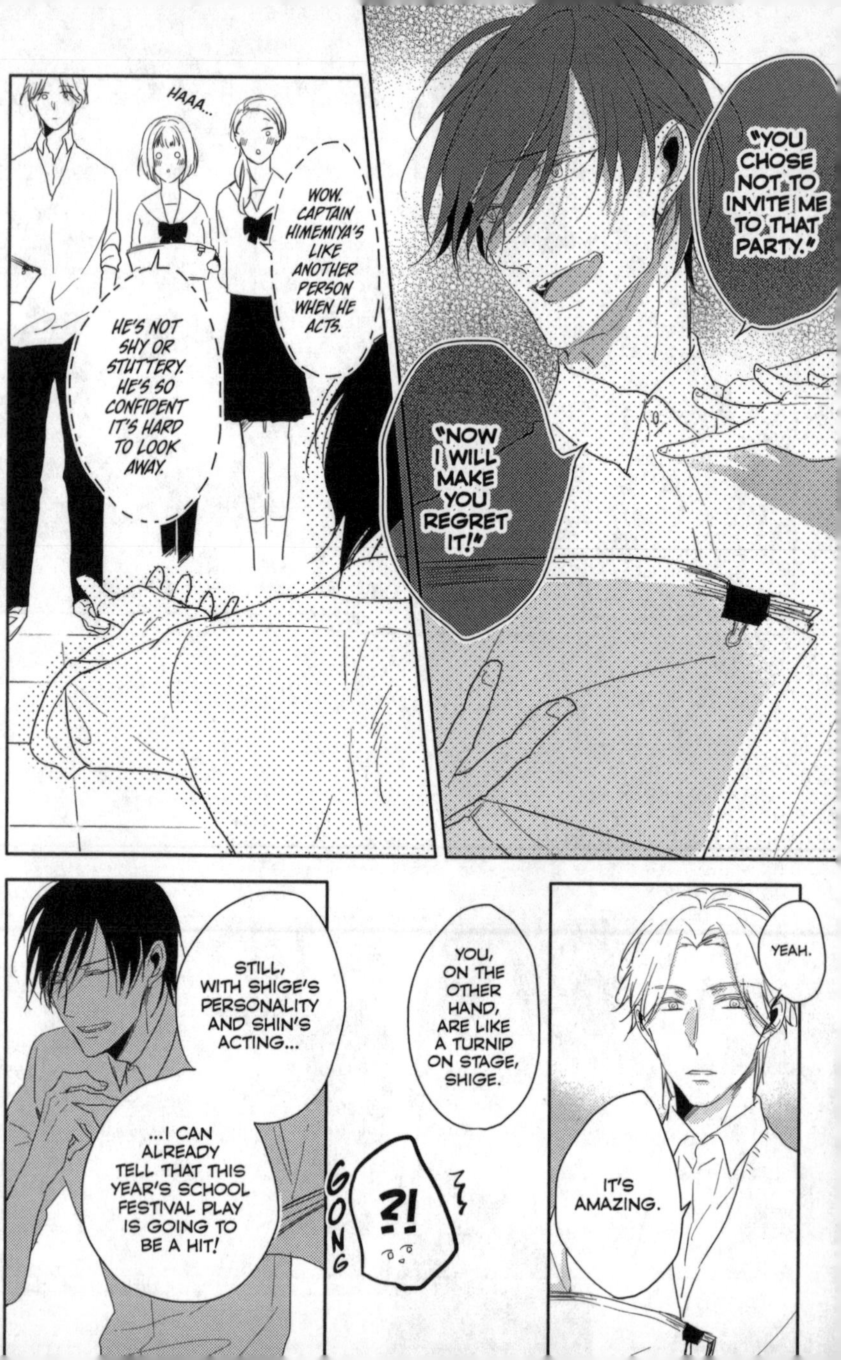
"YOU CHOSE NOT TO INVITE ME TO THAT PARTY."
"NOW I WILL MAKE YOU REGRET IT!"
HAAA...
WOW. CAPTAIN HIMEMIYA'S LIKE ANOTHER PERSON WHEN HE ACTS.
HE'S NOT SHY OR STUTTERY. HE'S SO CONFIDENT IT'S HARD TO LOOK AWAY.
YEAH.
IT'S AMAZING.
YOU, ON THE OTHER HAND, ARE LIKE A TURNIP ON STAGE, SHIGE.
STILL, WITH SHIGE'S PERSONALITY AND SHIN'S ACTING...
...I CAN ALREADY TELL THAT THIS YEAR'S SCHOOL FESTIVAL PLAY IS GOING TO BE A HIT!
GONG
?!

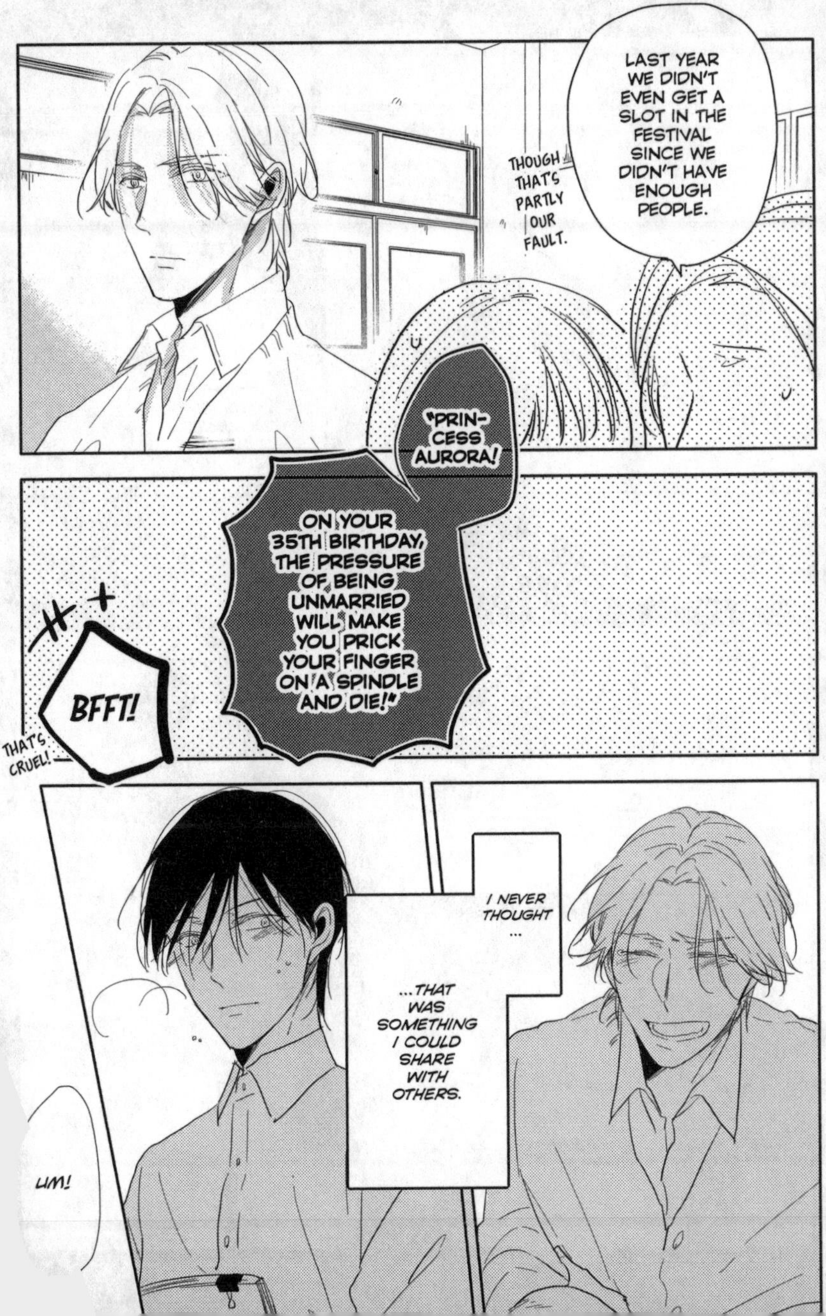
LAST YEAR WE DIDN'T EVEN GET A SLOT IN THE FESTIVAL SINCE WE DIDN'T HAVE ENOUGH PEOPLE.
THOUGH THAT'S PARTLY OUR FAULT.
"PRIN-CESS AURORA!
ON YOUR 35TH BIRTHDAY, THE PRESSURE OF BEING UNMARRIED WILL MAKE YOU PRICK YOUR FINGER ON A SPINDLE AND DIE!"
BFFT!
THAT'S CRUEL!
I NEVER THOUGHT...
...THAT WAS SOMETHING I COULD SHARE WITH OTHERS.
UM!

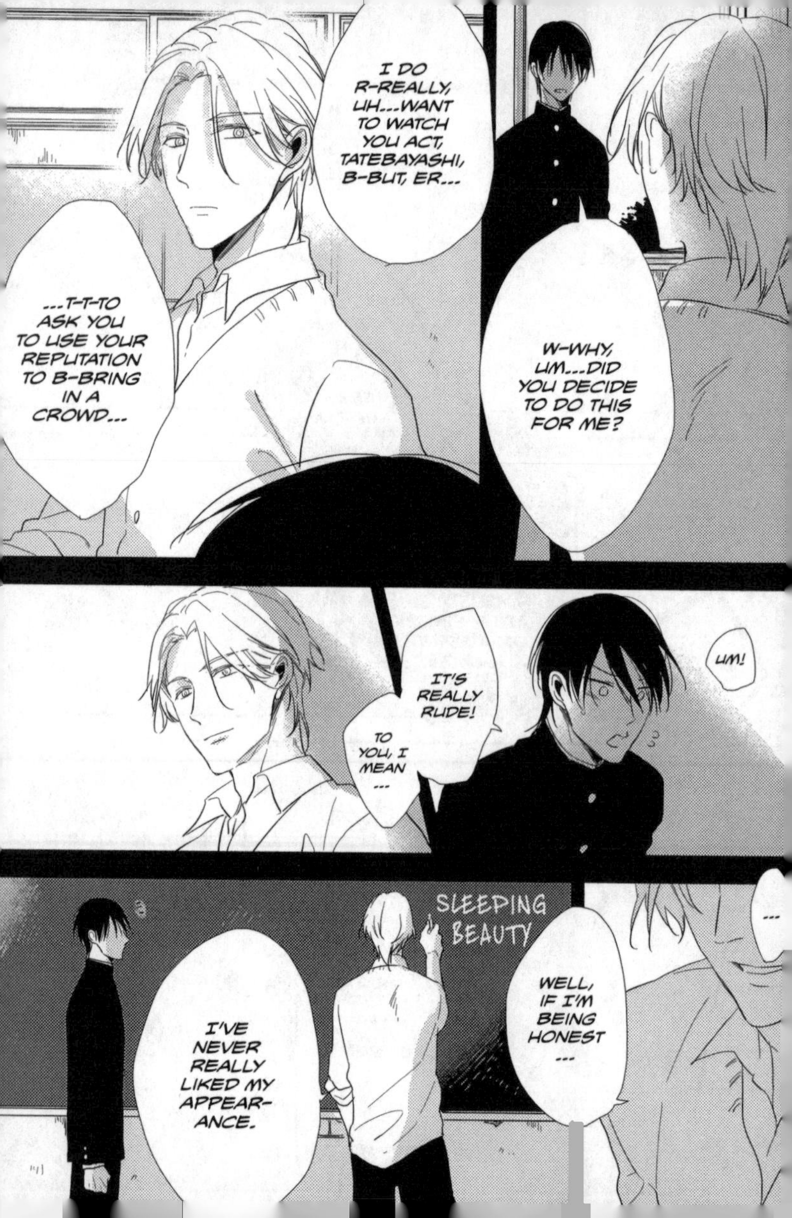
W-WHY, UM...DID YOU DECIDE TO DO THIS FOR ME?
I DO R-REALLY, UH...WANT TO WATCH YOU ACT, TATEBAYASHI, B-BUT, ER...
...T-T-TO ASK YOU TO USE YOUR REPUTATION TO B-BRING IN A CROWD...
UM!
IT'S REALLY RUDE!
TO YOU, I MEAN ...
...
WELL, IF I'M BEING HONEST ...
SLEEPING BEAUTY
I'VE NEVER REALLY LIKED MY APPEAR-ANCE.

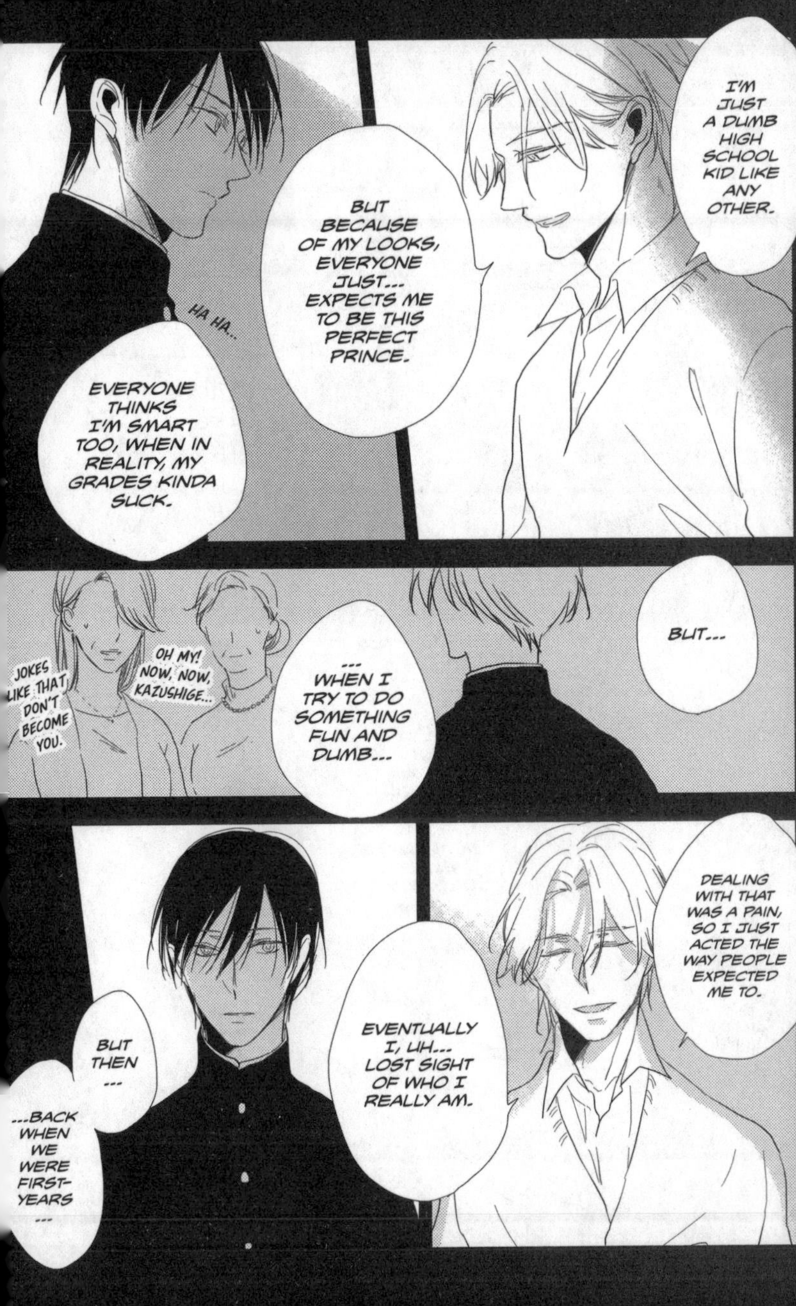
I'M JUST A DUMB HIGH SCHOOL KID LIKE ANY OTHER.
BUT BECAUSE OF MY LOOKS, EVERYONE JUST... EXPECTS ME TO BE THIS PERFECT PRINCE.
HA HA...
EVERYONE THINKS I'M SMART TOO, WHEN IN REALITY, MY GRADES KINDA SUCK.
BUT...
...WHEN I TRY TO DO SOMETHING FUN AND DUMB...
OH MY! NOW, NOW, KAZUSHIGE...
JOKES LIKE THAT DON'T BECOME YOU.
DEALING WITH THAT WAS A PAIN, SO I JUST ACTED THE WAY PEOPLE EXPECTED ME TO.
EVENTUALLY I, UH... LOST SIGHT OF WHO I REALLY AM.
BUT THEN...
...BACK WHEN WE WERE FIRST-YEARS...

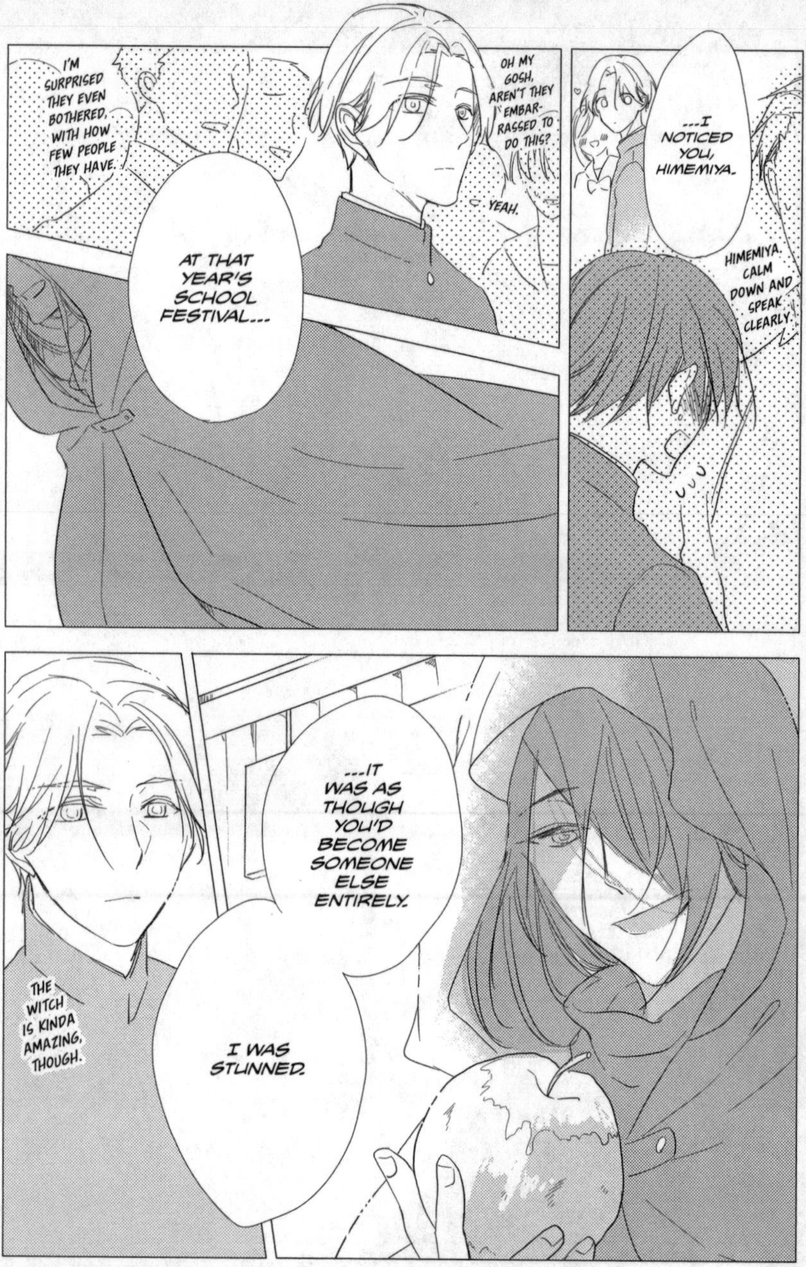
...I NOTICED YOU, HIMEMIYA.
HIMEMIYA. CALM DOWN AND SPEAK CLEARLY.
OH MY GOSH, AREN'T THEY EMBARRASSED TO DO THIS?
YEAH.
I'M SURPRISED THEY EVEN BOTHERED, WITH HOW FEW PEOPLE THEY HAVE.
AT THAT YEAR'S SCHOOL FESTIVAL...
...IT WAS AS THOUGH YOU'D BECOME SOMEONE ELSE ENTIRELY.
I WAS STUNNED.
THE WITCH IS KINDA AMAZING, THOUGH.

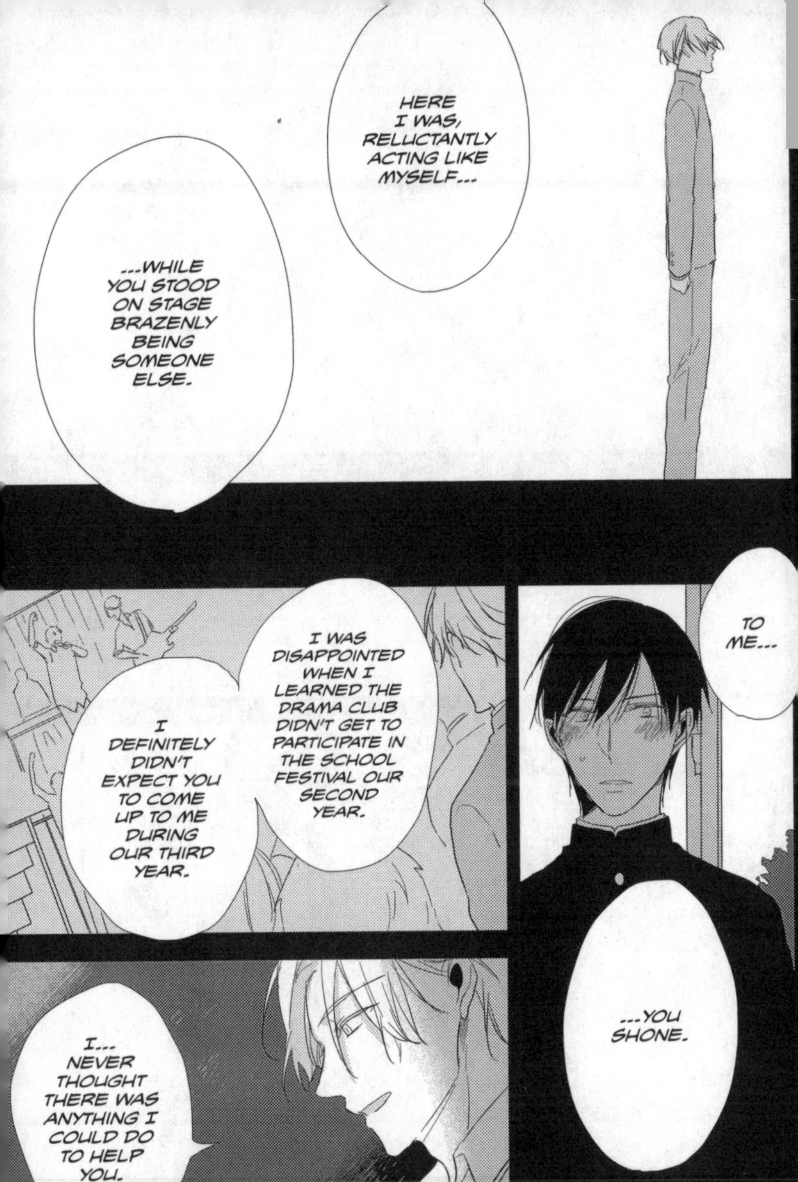
HERE I WAS, RELUCTANTLY ACTING LIKE MYSELF...
...WHILE YOU STOOD ON STAGE BRAZENLY BEING SOMEONE ELSE.
TO ME...
...YOU SHONE.
I WAS DISAPPOINTED WHEN I LEARNED THE DRAMA CLUB DIDN'T GET TO PARTICIPATE IN THE SCHOOL FESTIVAL OUR SECOND YEAR.
I DEFINITELY DIDN'T EXPECT YOU TO COME UP TO ME DURING OUR THIRD YEAR.
I... NEVER THOUGHT THERE WAS ANYTHING I COULD DO TO HELP YOU.

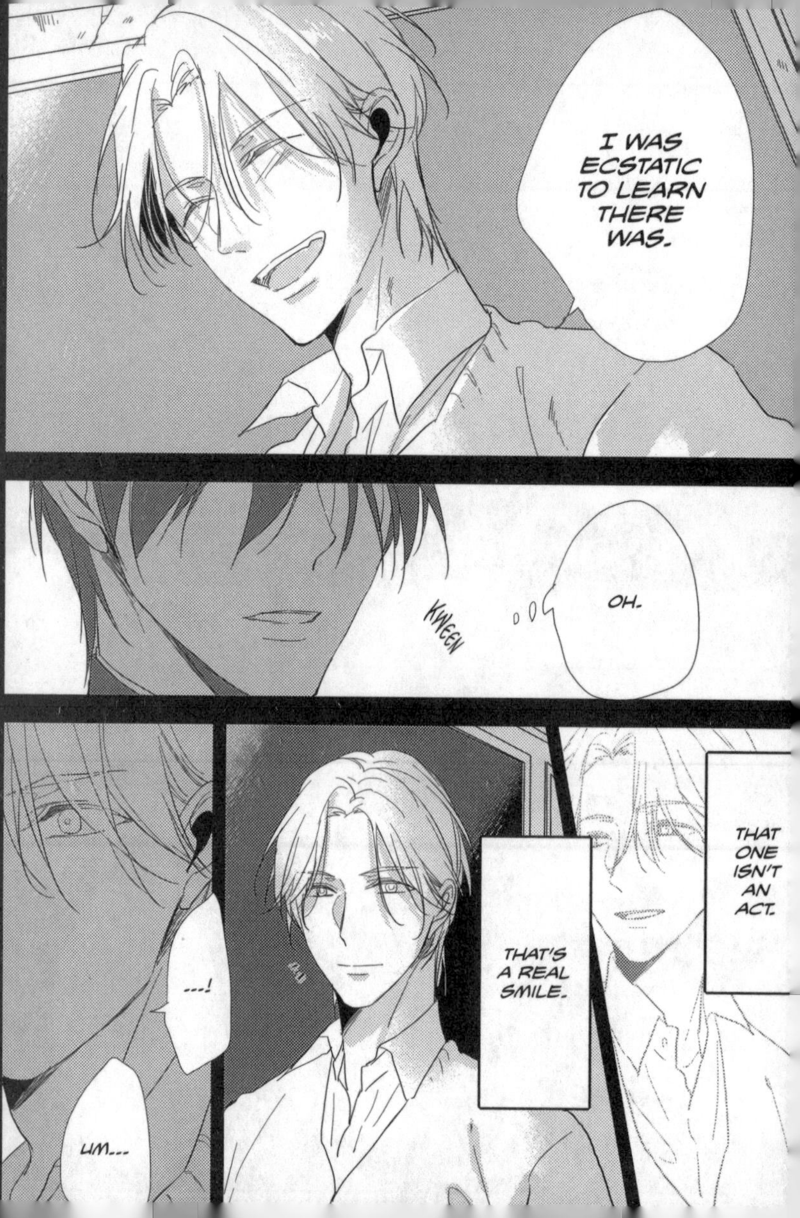
I WAS ECSTATIC TO LEARN THERE WAS.
OH.
KWEEN
THAT ONE ISN'T AN ACT.
THAT'S A REAL SMILE.
...!
UM...

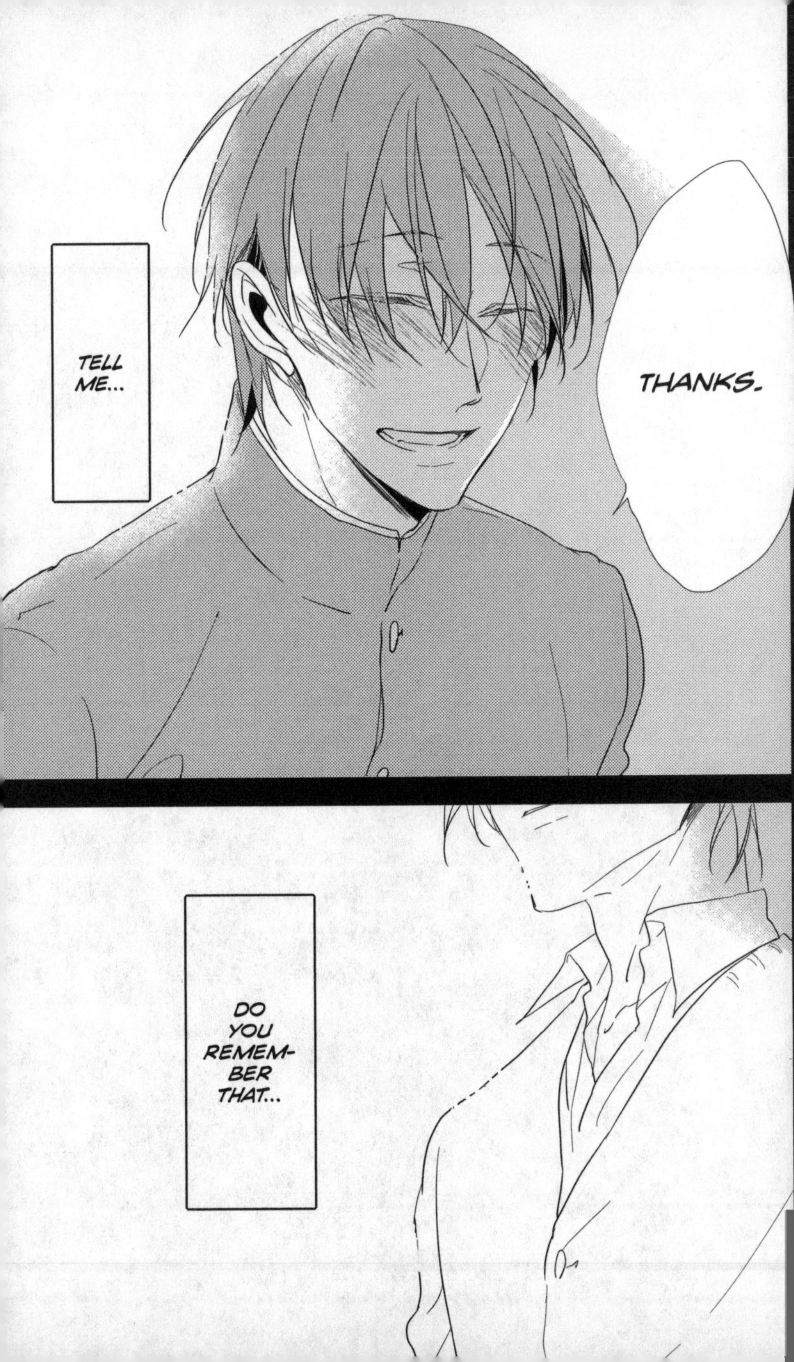
THANKS.
TELL ME...
DO YOU REMEMBER THAT...

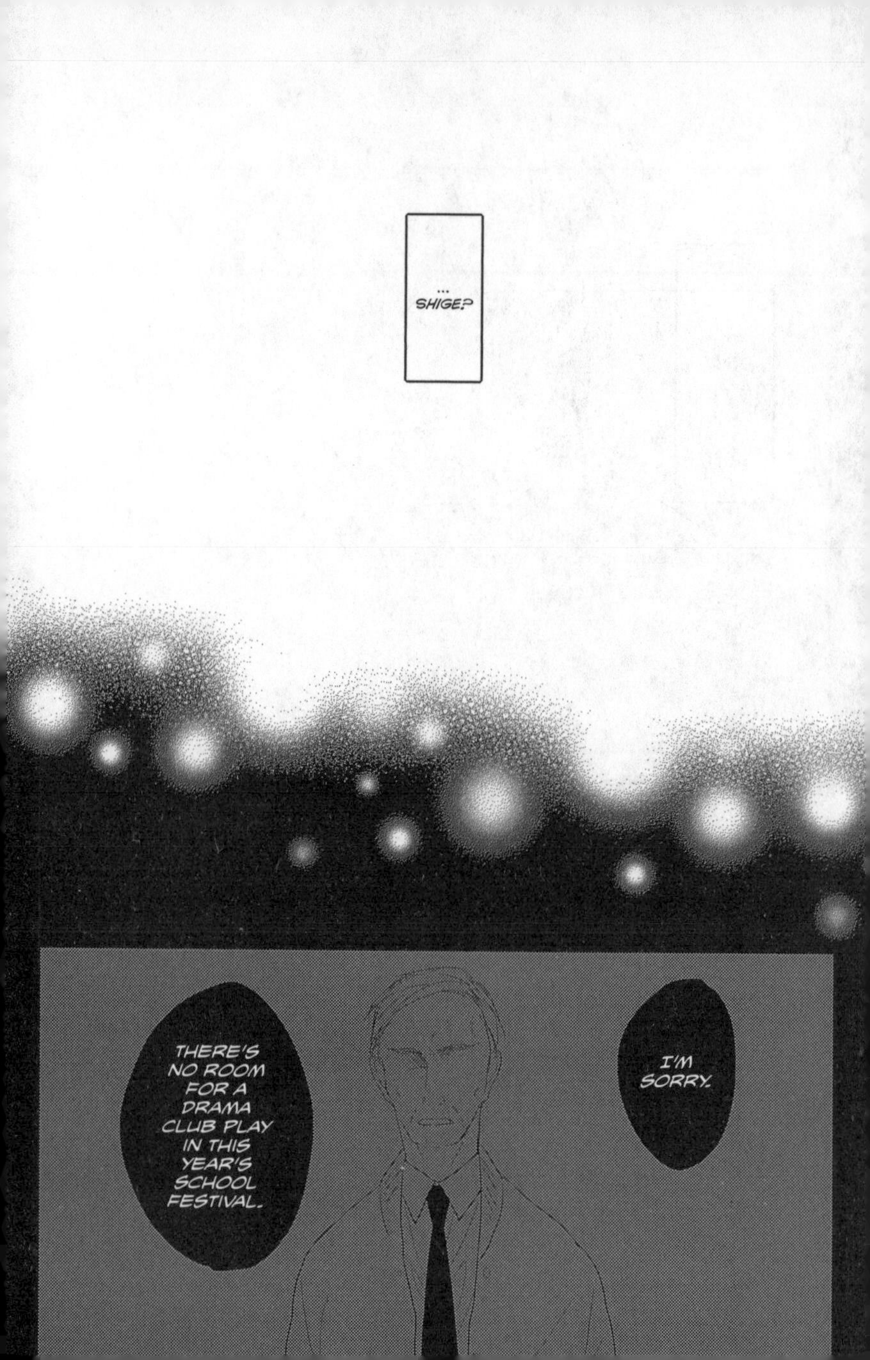
...SHIGE?
I'M SORRY.
THERE'S NO ROOM FOR A DRAMA CLUB PLAY IN THIS YEAR'S SCHOOL FESTIVAL.

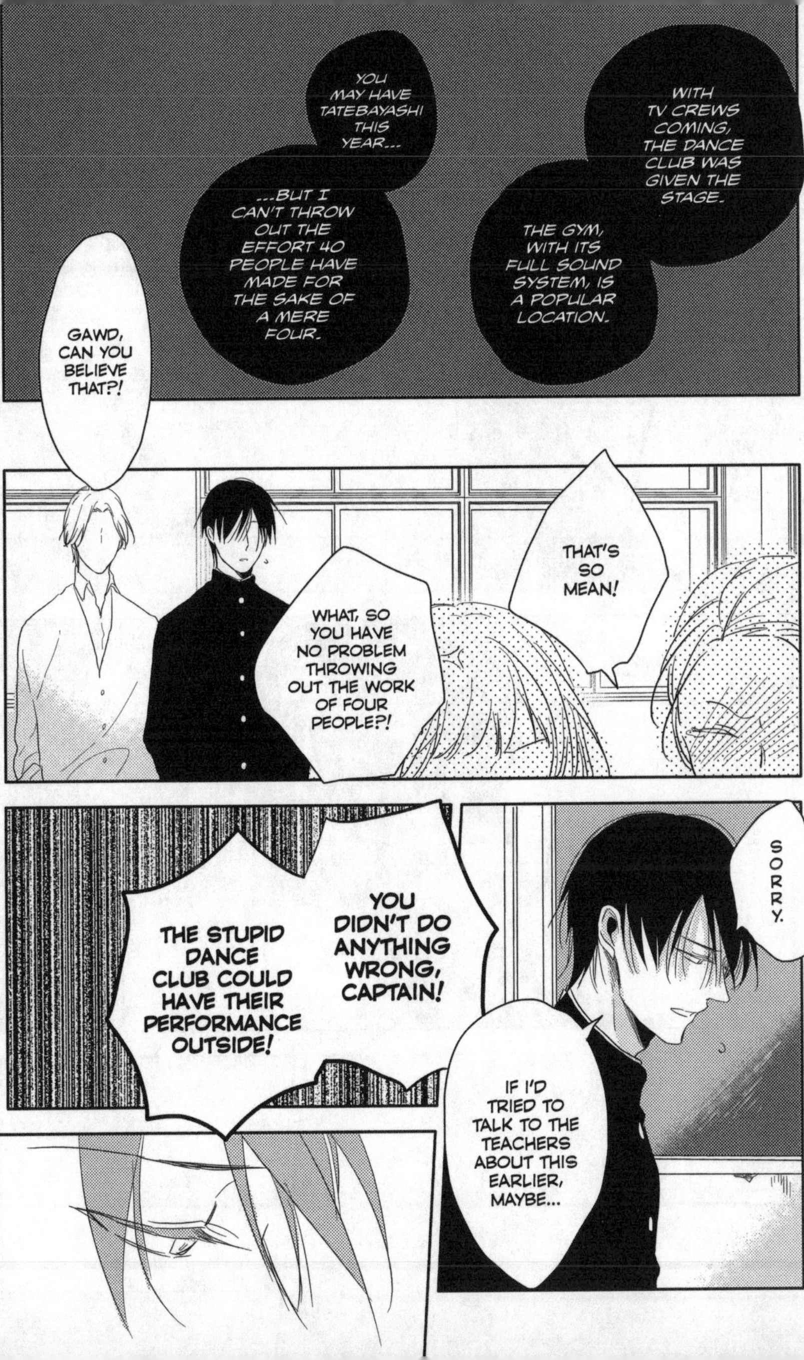
WITH TV CREWS COMING, THE DANCE CLUB WAS GIVEN THE STAGE.
THE GYM, WITH ITS FULL SOUND SYSTEM, IS A POPULAR LOCATION.
YOU MAY HAVE TATEBAYASHI THIS YEAR...
...BUT I CAN'T THROW OUT THE EFFORT 40 PEOPLE HAVE MADE FOR THE SAKE OF A MERE FOUR.
GAWD, CAN YOU BELIEVE THAT?!
THAT'S SO MEAN!
WHAT, SO YOU HAVE NO PROBLEM THROWING OUT THE WORK OF FOUR PEOPLE?!
SORRY.
IF I'D TRIED TO TALK TO THE TEACHERS ABOUT THIS EARLIER, MAYBE...
YOU DIDN'T DO ANYTHING WRONG, CAPTAIN!
THE STUPID DANCE CLUB COULD HAVE THEIR PERFORMANCE OUTSIDE!

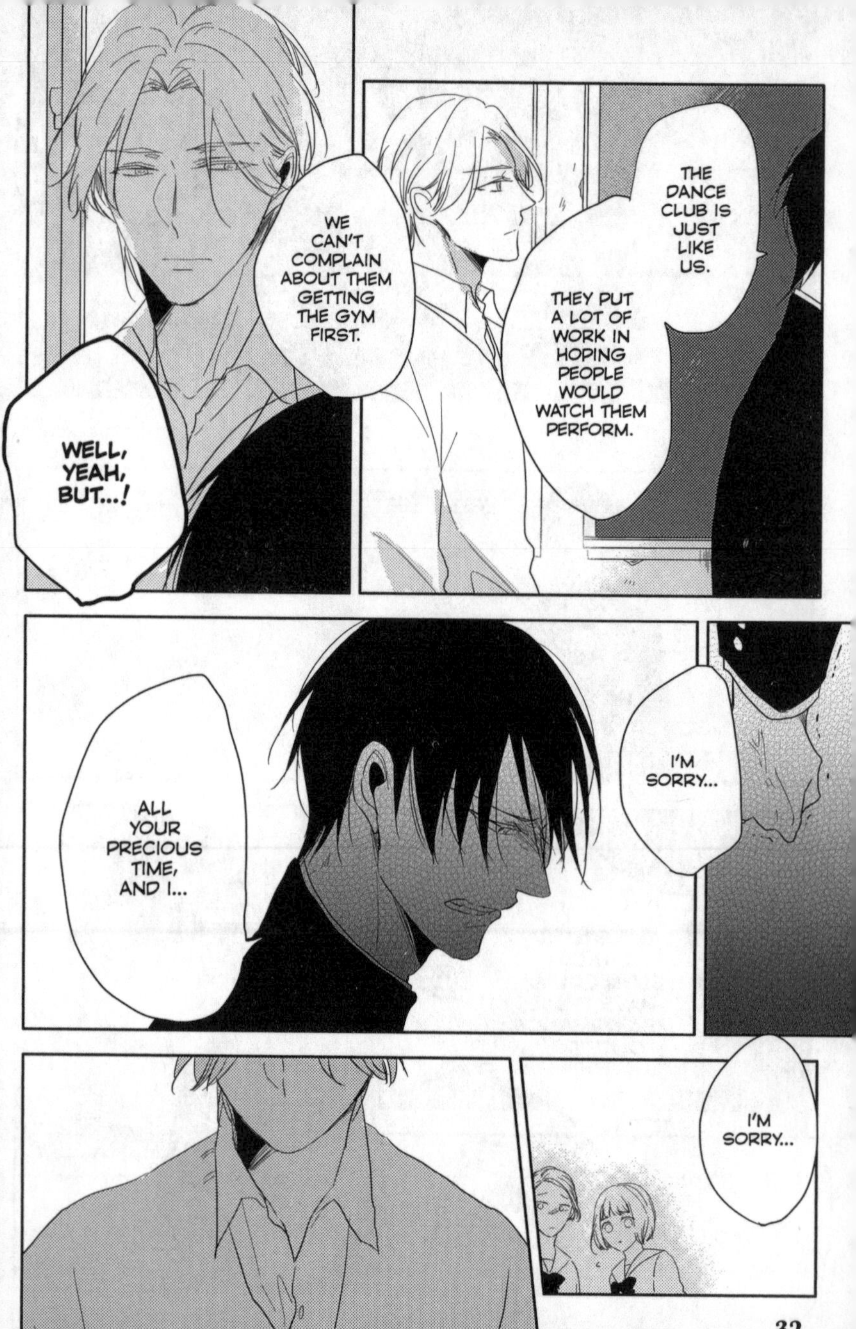
THE DANCE CLUB IS JUST LIKE US.
THEY PUT A LOT OF WORK IN HOPING PEOPLE WOULD WATCH THEM PERFORM.
WE CAN'T COMPLAIN ABOUT THEM GETTING THE GYM FIRST.
WELL, YEAH, BUT...!
I'M SORRY...
ALL YOUR PRECIOUS TIME, AND I...
I'M SORRY...

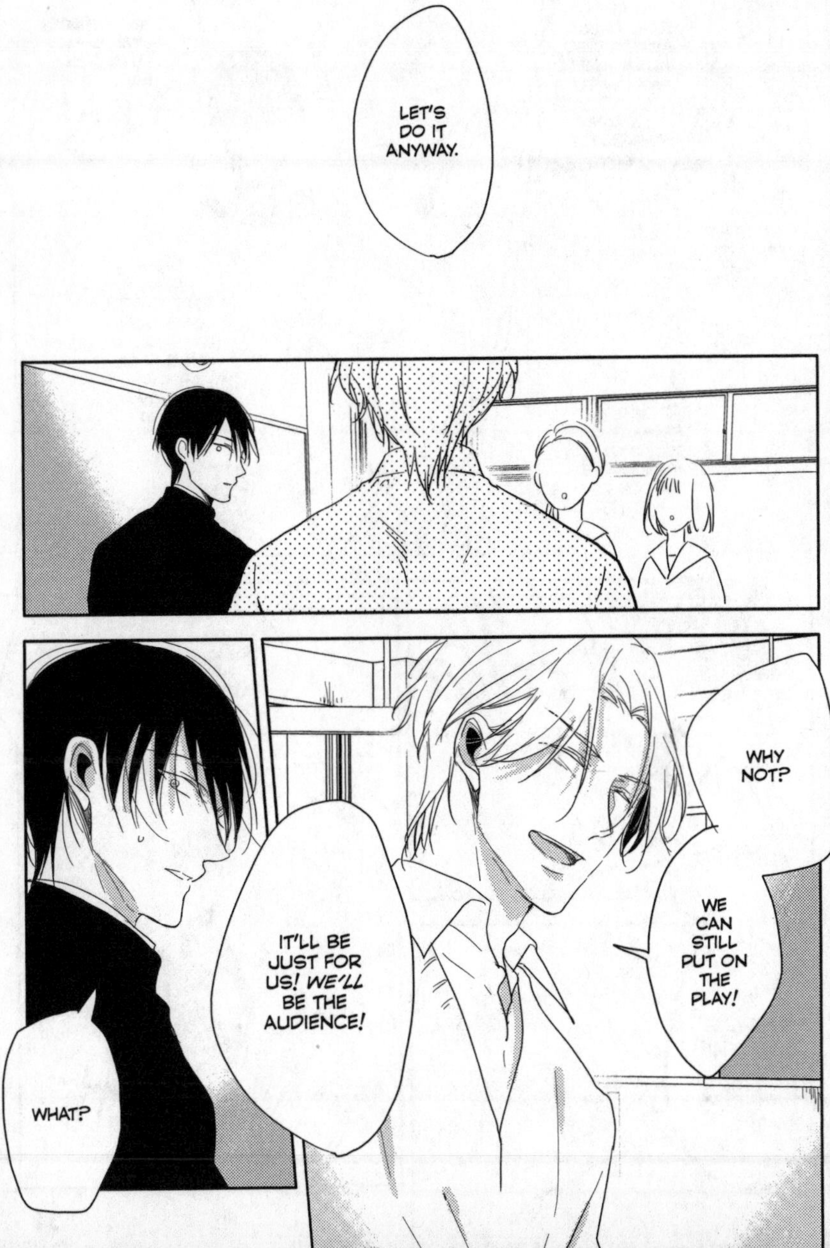
LET'S DO IT ANYWAY.
WHY NOT?
WE CAN STILL PUT ON THE PLAY!
IT'LL BE JUST FOR US! *WE'LL* BE THE AUDIENCE!
WHAT?

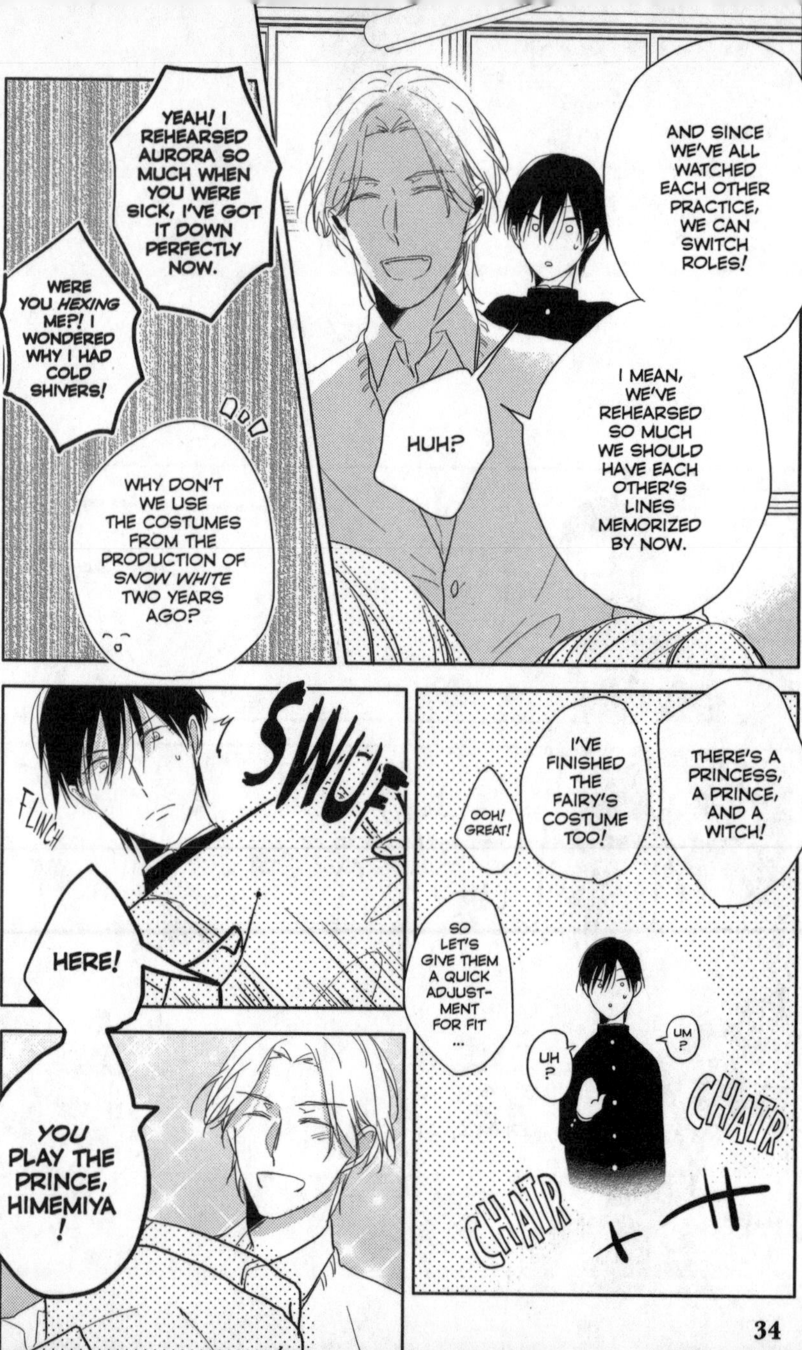
AND SINCE WE'VE ALL WATCHED EACH OTHER PRACTICE, WE CAN SWITCH ROLES!
HUH?
I MEAN, WE'VE REHEARSED SO MUCH WE SHOULD HAVE EACH OTHER'S LINES MEMORIZED BY NOW.
YEAH! I REHEARSED AURORA SO MUCH WHEN YOU WERE SICK, I'VE GOT IT DOWN PERFECTLY NOW.
WERE YOU *HEXING* ME?! I WONDERED WHY I HAD COLD SHIVERS!
WHY DON'T WE USE THE COSTUMES FROM THE PRODUCTION OF *SNOW WHITE* TWO YEARS AGO?
THERE'S A PRINCESS, A PRINCE, AND A WITCH!
I'VE FINISHED THE FAIRY'S COSTUME TOO!
OOH! GREAT!
SO LET'S GIVE THEM A QUICK ADJUSTMENT FOR FIT ...
UM?
UH?
CHATR
CHATR
SWUF
FLINCH
HERE!
YOU PLAY THE PRINCE, HIMEMIYA!

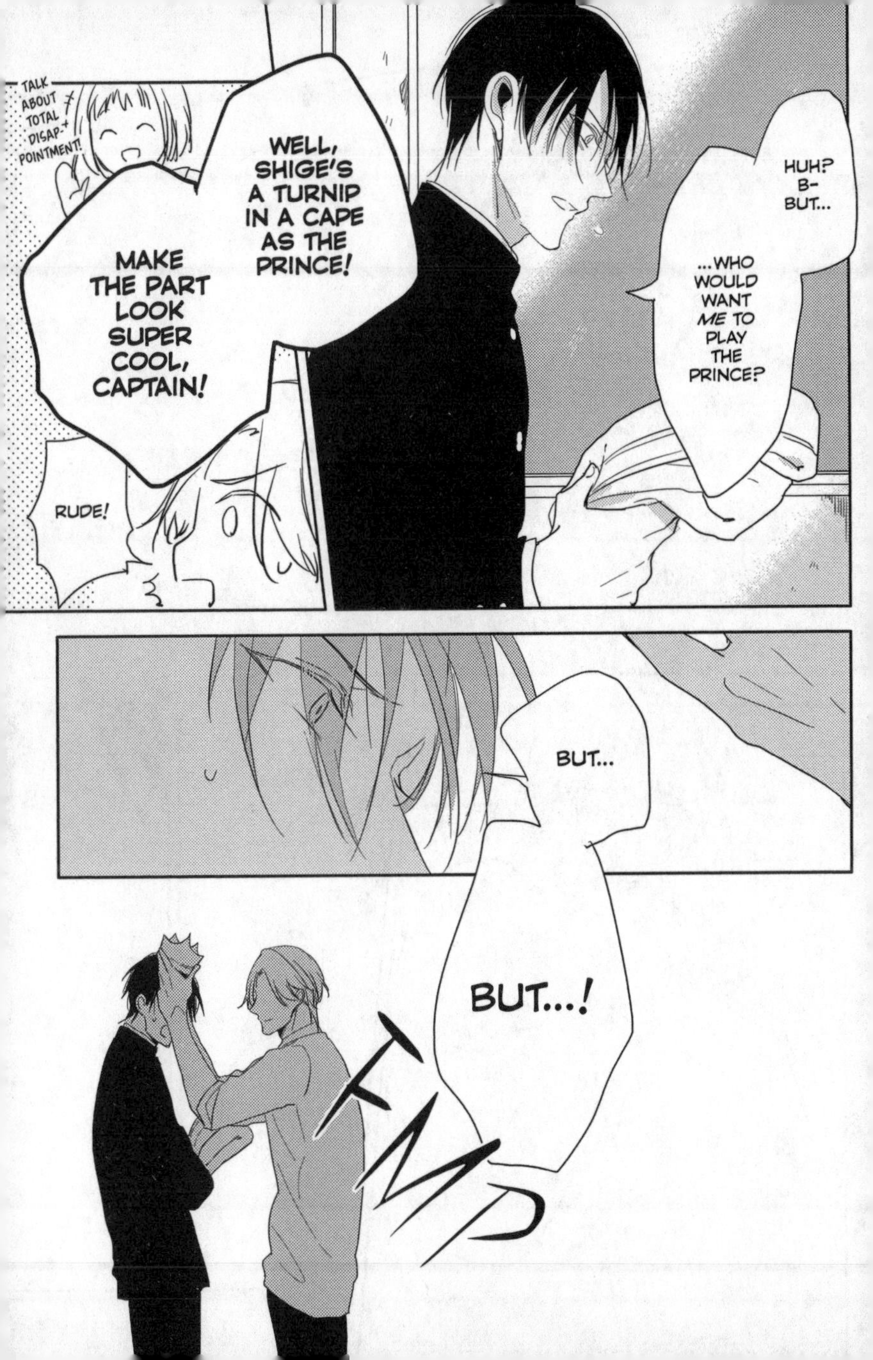
HUH? B-BUT...
...WHO WOULD WANT *ME* TO PLAY THE PRINCE?
WELL, SHIGE'S A TURNIP IN A CAPE AS THE PRINCE!
MAKE THE PART LOOK SUPER COOL, CAPTAIN!
TALK ABOUT TOTAL DISAP-POINTMENT!
RUDE!
BUT...
BUT...!

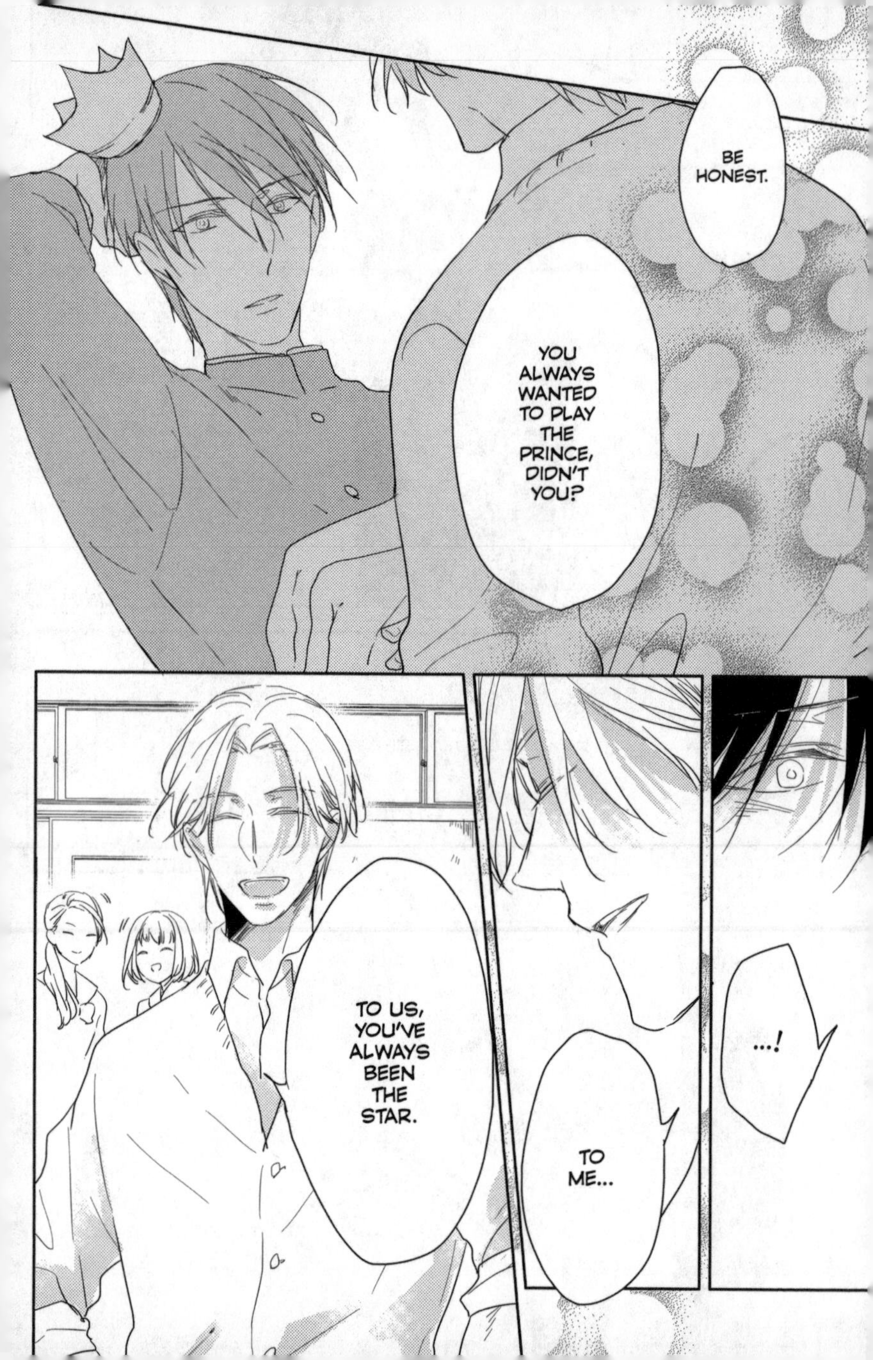
BE HONEST.
YOU ALWAYS WANTED TO PLAY THE PRINCE, DIDN'T YOU?
...!
TO ME...
TO US, YOU'VE ALWAYS BEEN THE STAR.

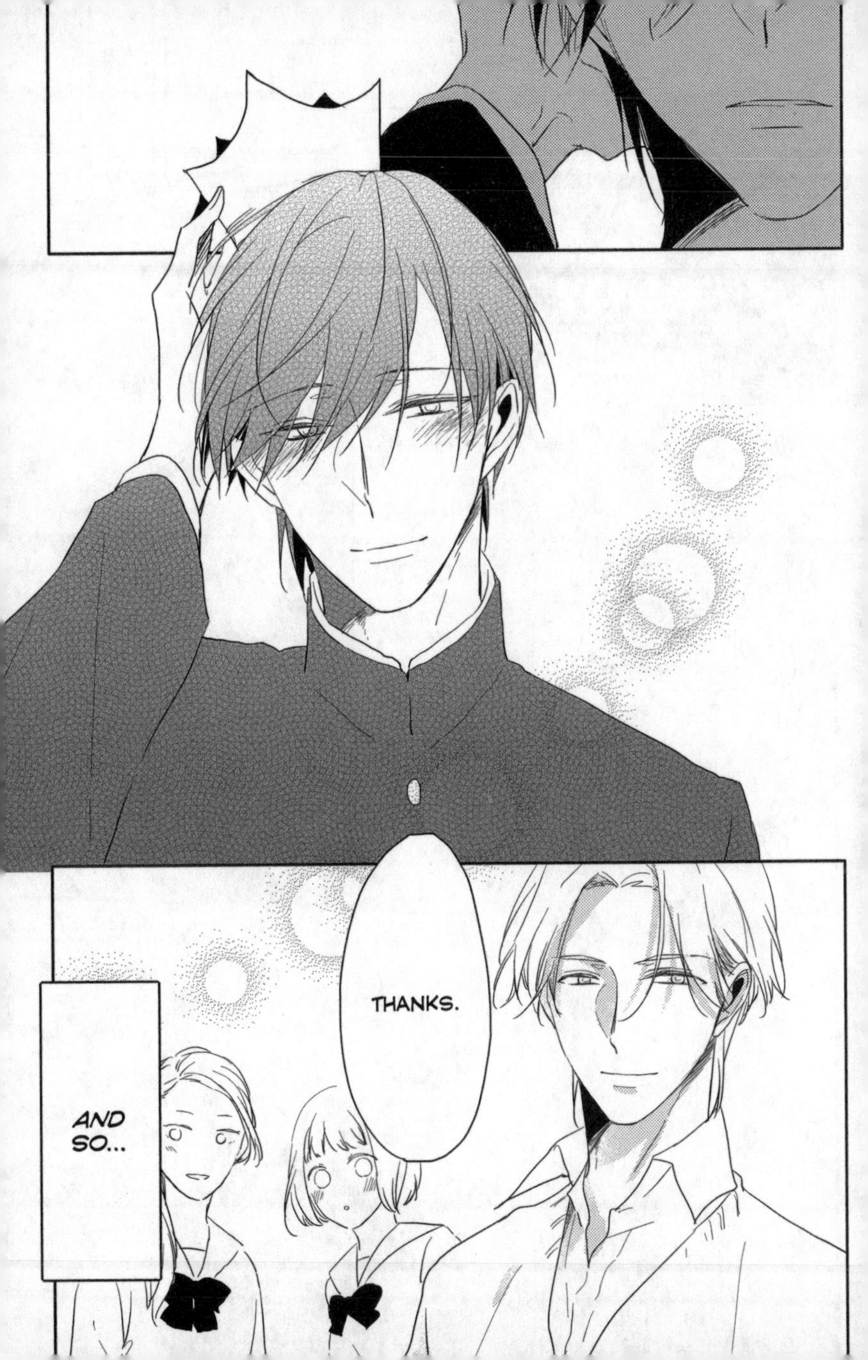
THANKS.
AND SO...

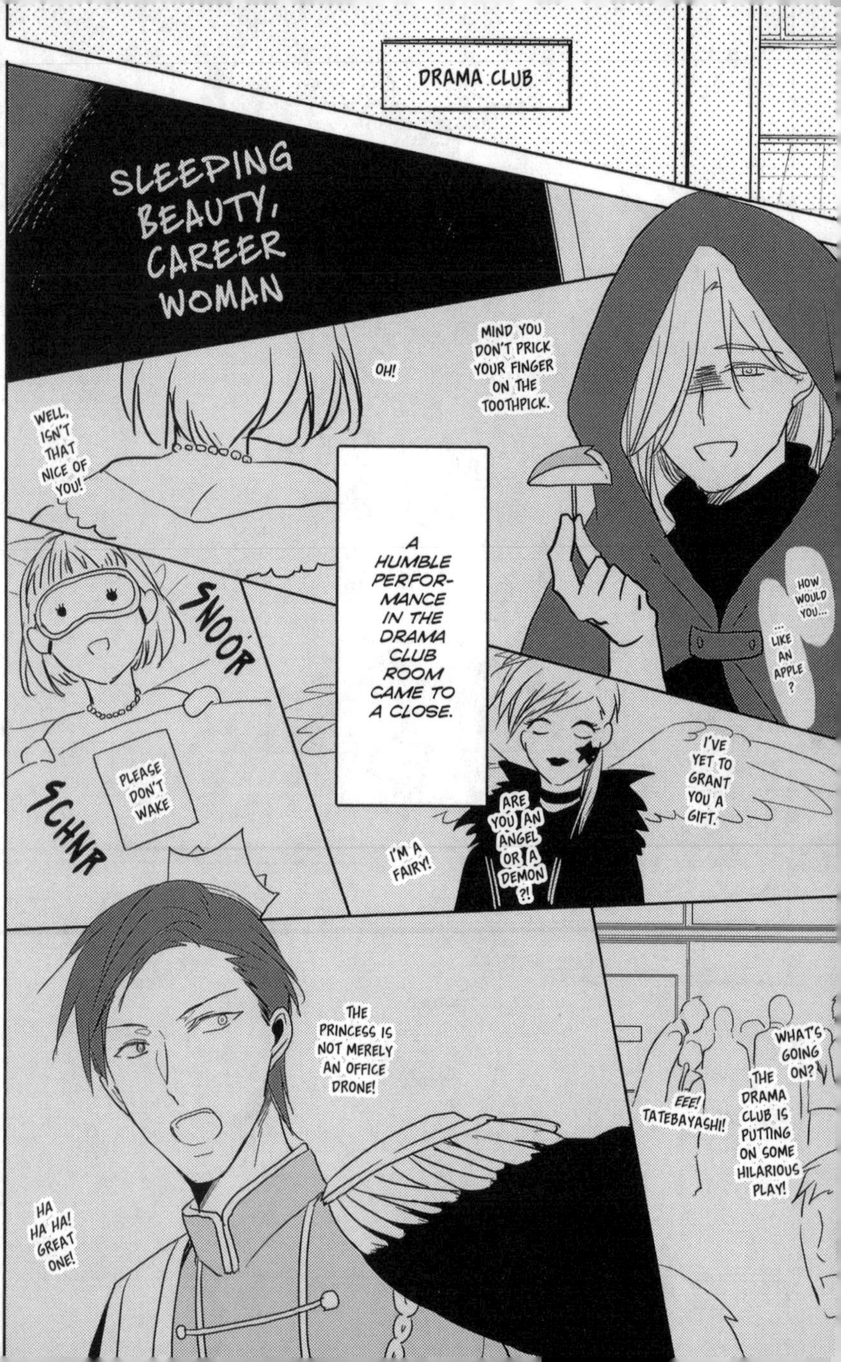
DRAMA CLUB
SLEEPING BEAUTY, CAREER WOMAN
MIND YOU DON'T PRICK YOUR FINGER ON THE TOOTHPICK.
OH!
WELL, ISN'T THAT NICE OF YOU!
HOW WOULD YOU...
...LIKE AN APPLE?
I'VE YET TO GRANT YOU A GIFT.
ARE YOU AN ANGEL OR A DEMON?!
I'M A FAIRY!
SNOOR
PLEASE DON'T WAKE
SCHNR
A HUMBLE PERFORMANCE IN THE DRAMA CLUB ROOM CAME TO A CLOSE.
WHAT'S GOING ON?
THE DRAMA CLUB IS PUTTING ON SOME HILARIOUS PLAY!
EEE! TATEBAYASHI!
THE PRINCESS IS NOT MERELY AN OFFICE DRONE!
HA HA HA! GREAT ONE!

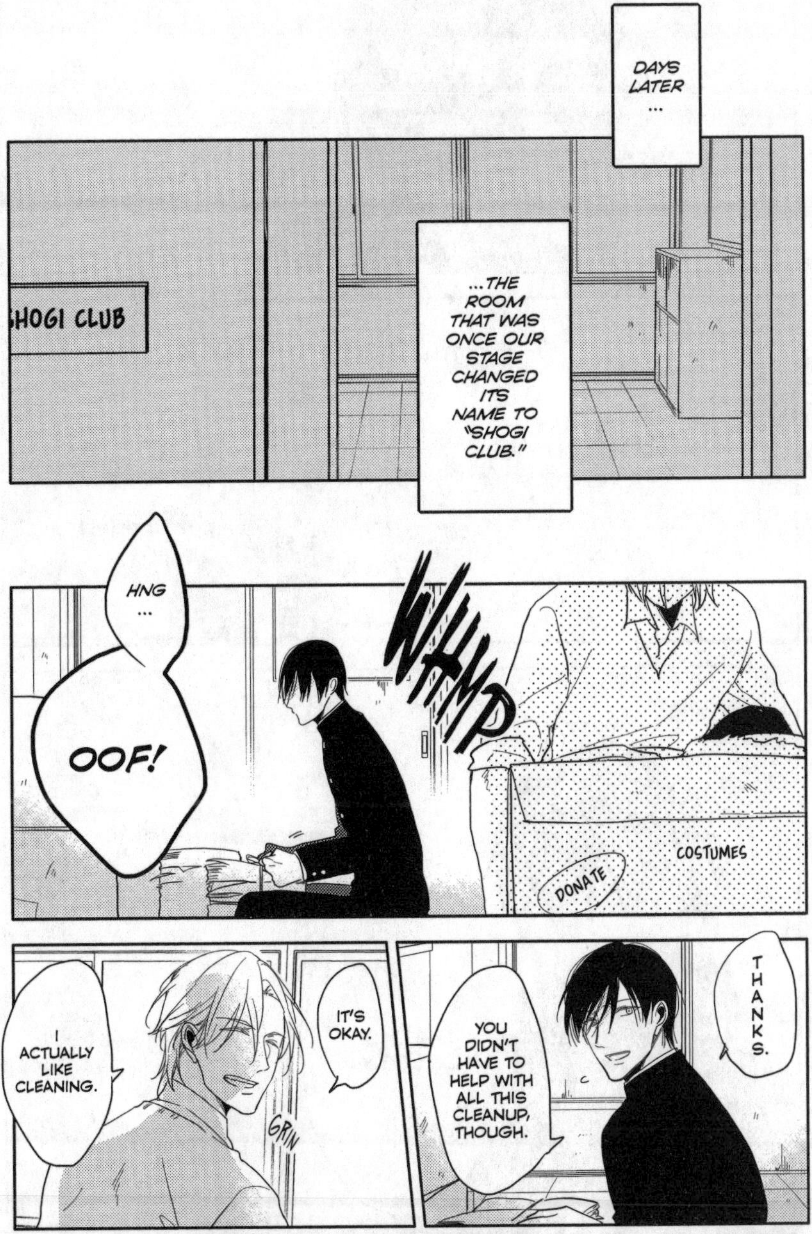
DAYS LATER...
SHOGI CLUB
...THE ROOM THAT WAS ONCE OUR STAGE CHANGED ITS NAME TO "SHOGI CLUB."
WHMP
COSTUMES
DONATE
HNG...
OOF!
THANKS.
YOU DIDN'T HAVE TO HELP WITH ALL THIS CLEANUP, THOUGH.
IT'S OKAY.
GRIN
I ACTUALLY LIKE CLEANING.

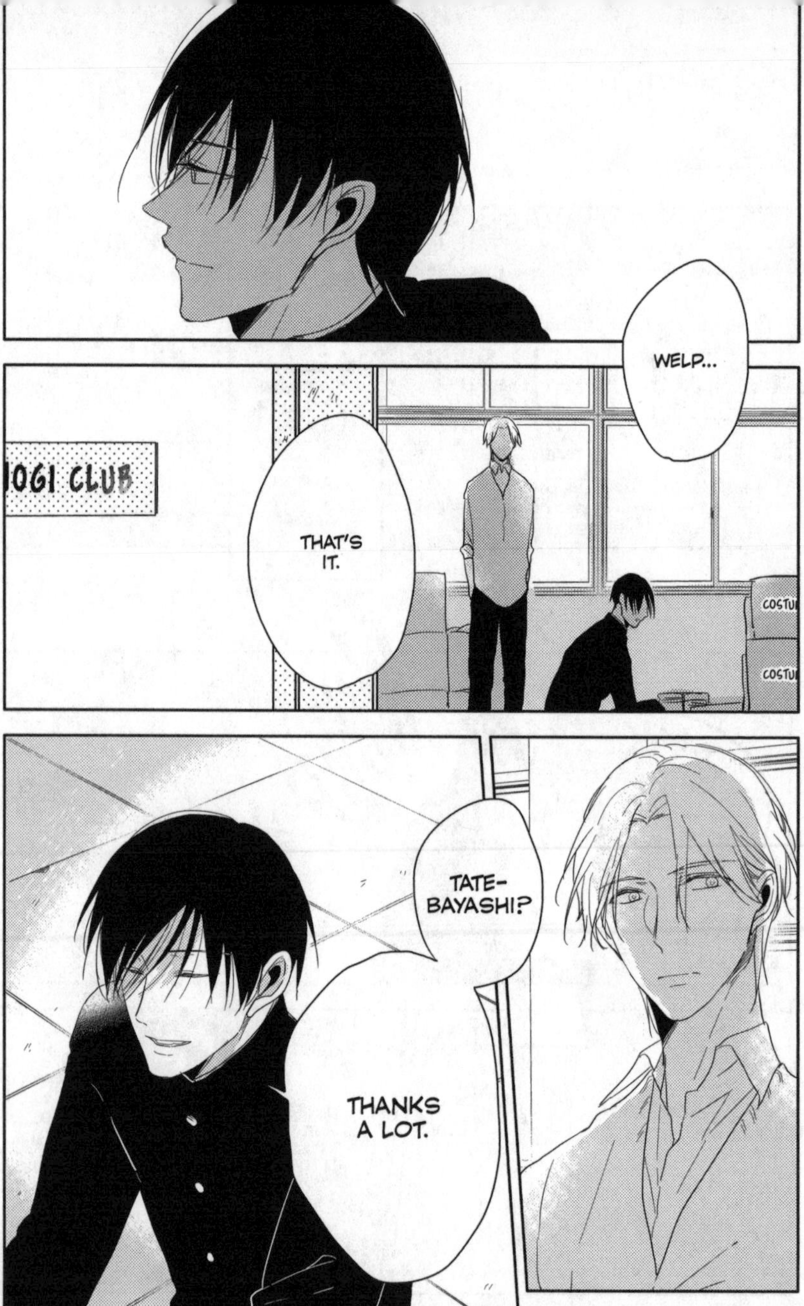
WELP...
THAT'S IT.
OGI CLUB
COSTU
COSTU
TATE-BAYASHI?
THANKS A LOT.

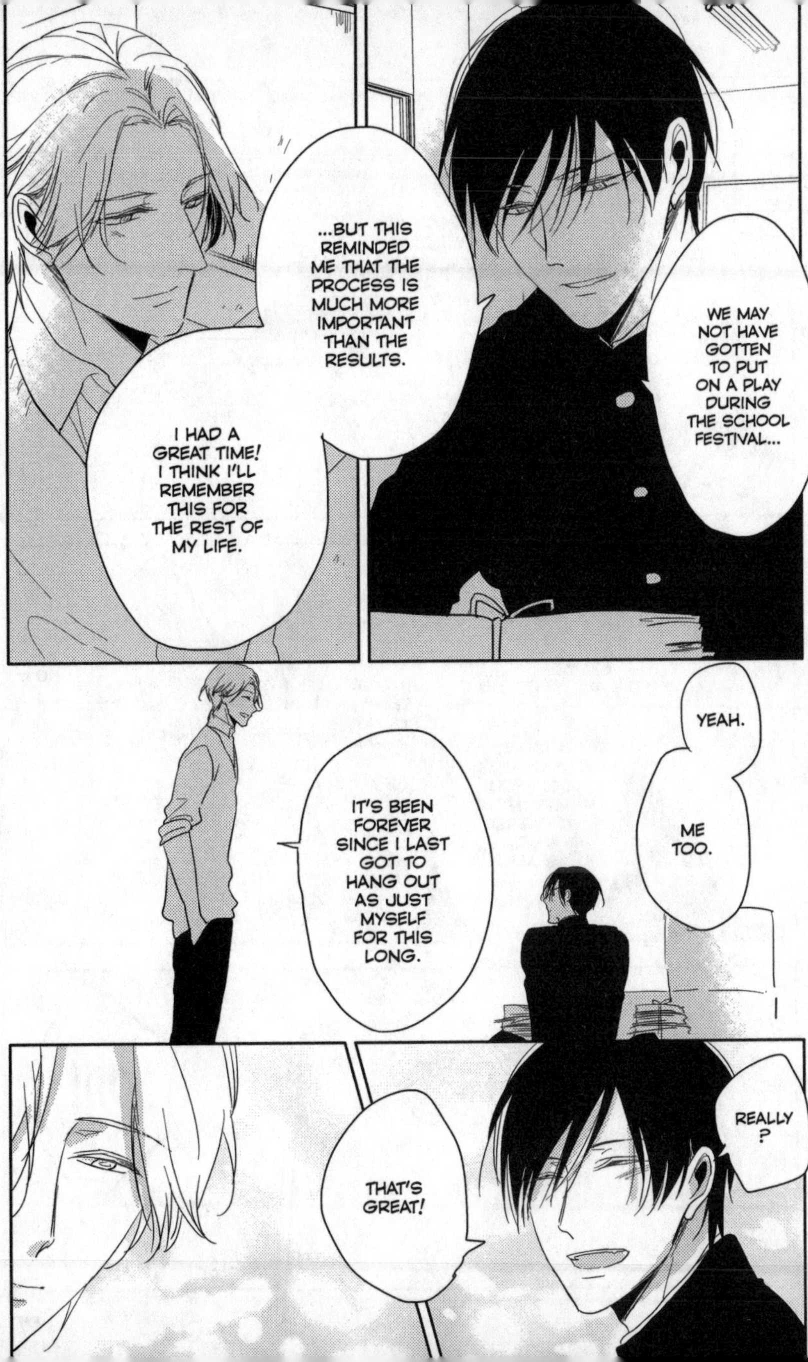
WE MAY NOT HAVE GOTTEN TO PUT ON A PLAY DURING THE SCHOOL FESTIVAL...
...BUT THIS REMINDED ME THAT THE PROCESS IS MUCH MORE IMPORTANT THAN THE RESULTS.
I HAD A GREAT TIME! I THINK I'LL REMEMBER THIS FOR THE REST OF MY LIFE.
YEAH.
ME TOO.
IT'S BEEN FOREVER SINCE I LAST GOT TO HANG OUT AS JUST MYSELF FOR THIS LONG.
REALLY ?
THAT'S GREAT!

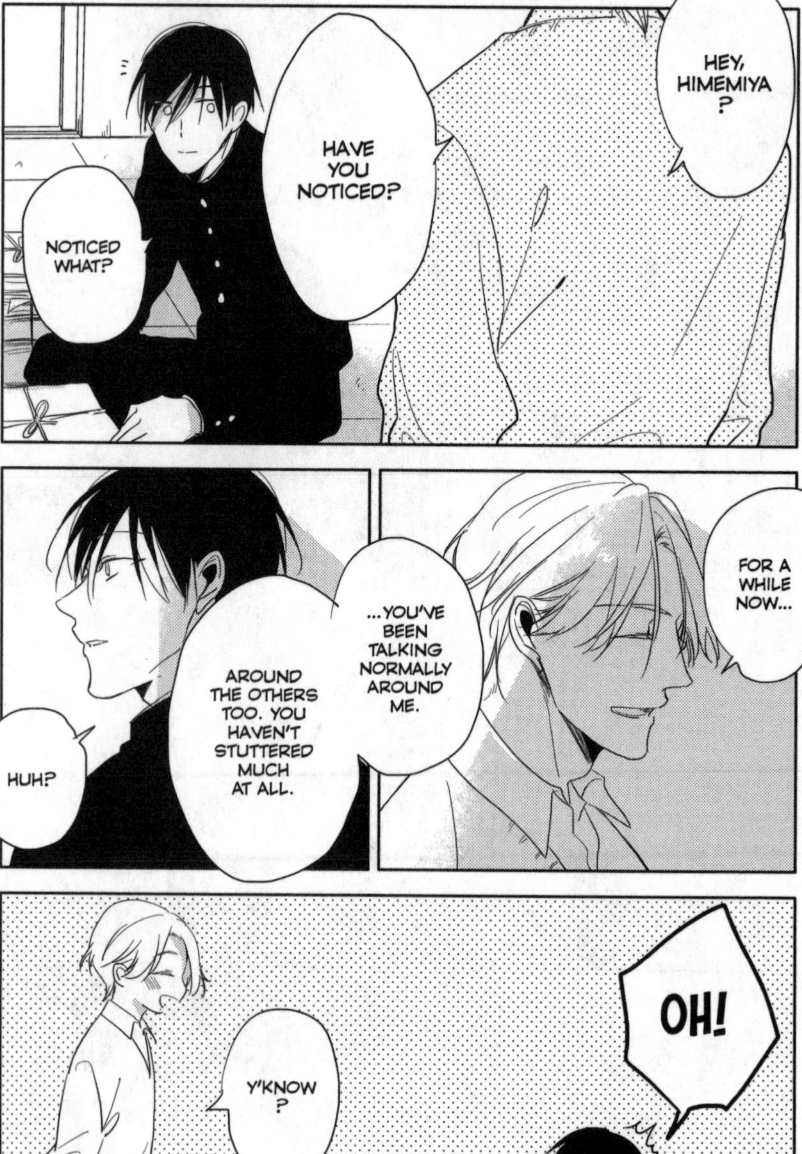
HEY, HIMEMIYA?
HAVE YOU NOTICED?
NOTICED WHAT?
FOR A WHILE NOW...
...YOU'VE BEEN TALKING NORMALLY AROUND ME.
AROUND THE OTHERS TOO. YOU HAVEN'T STUTTERED MUCH AT ALL.
HUH?
OH!
Y'KNOW?

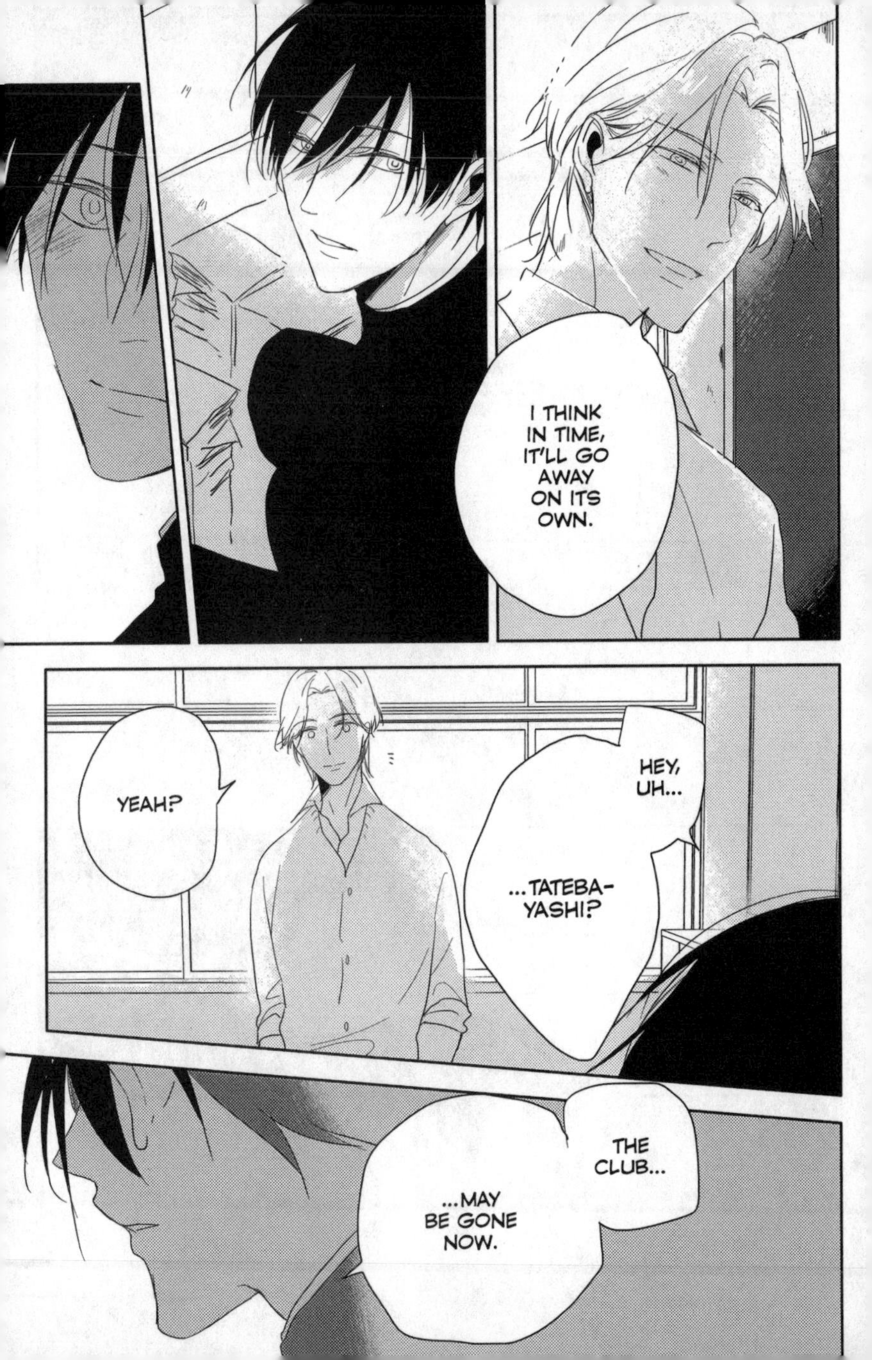
I THINK IN TIME, IT'LL GO AWAY ON ITS OWN.
HEY, UH...
...TATEBA-YASHI?
YEAH?
THE CLUB...
...MAY BE GONE NOW.

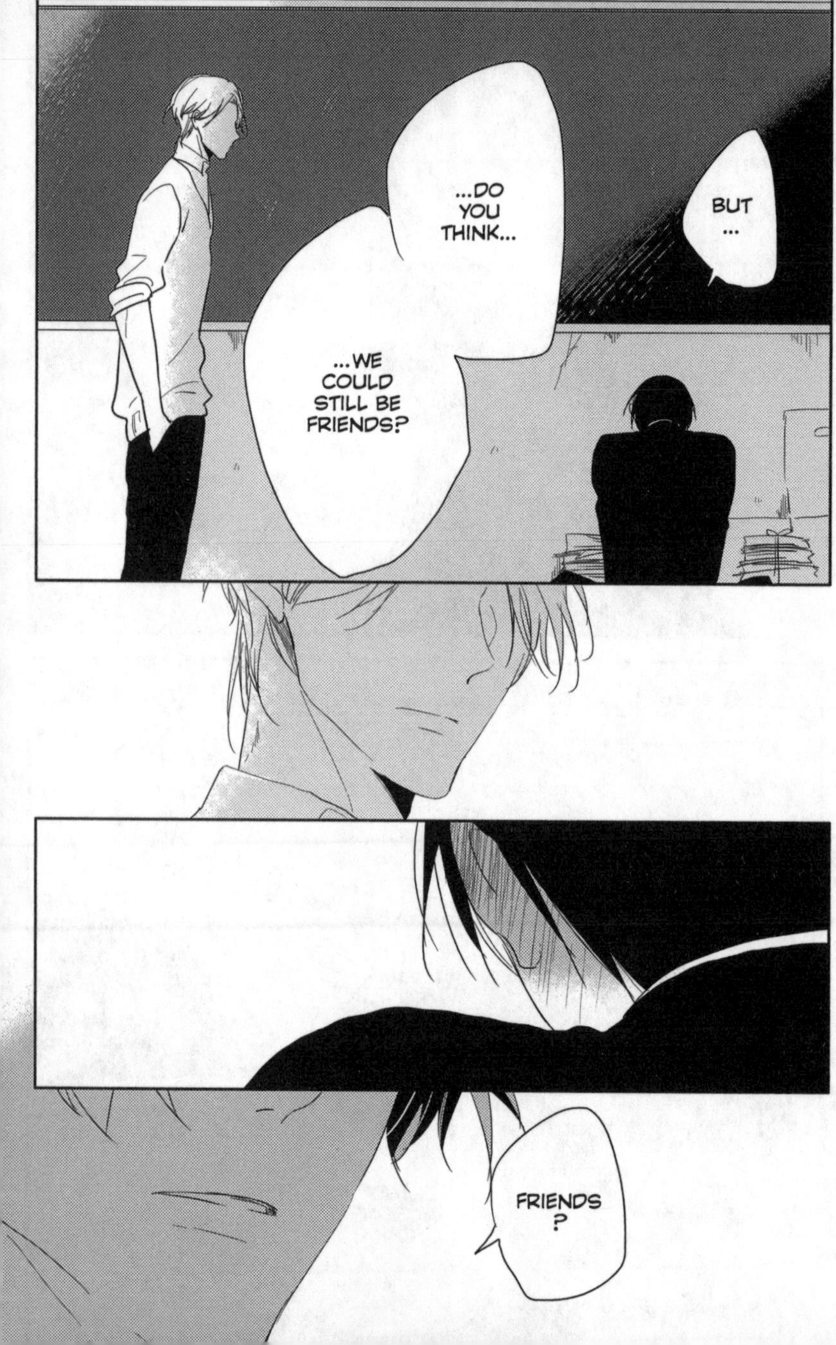
BUT ...
...DO YOU THINK...
...WE COULD STILL BE FRIENDS?
FRIENDS ?

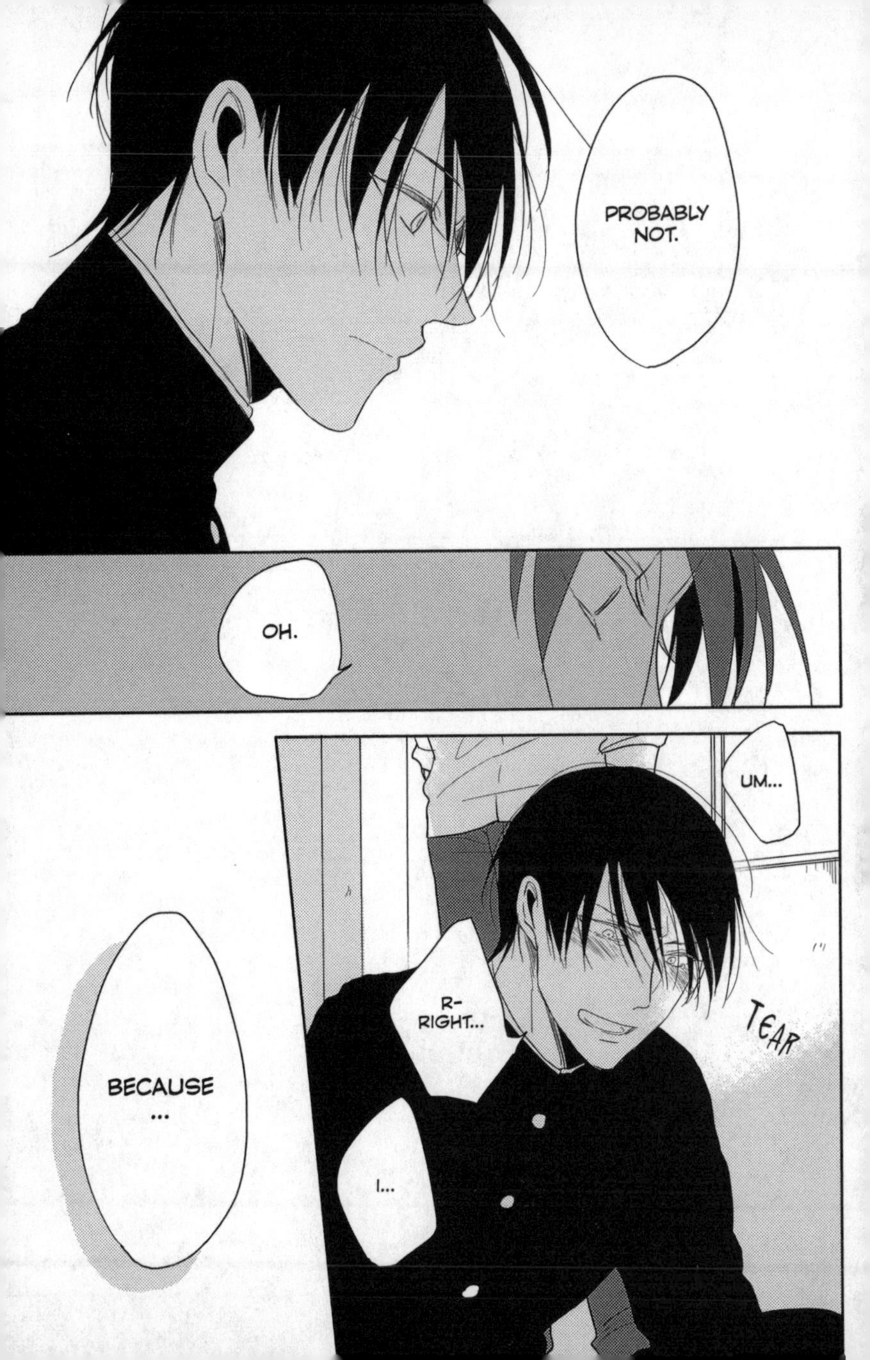
PROBABLY NOT.
OH.
UM...
TEAR
R-RIGHT...
BECAUSE ...
I...

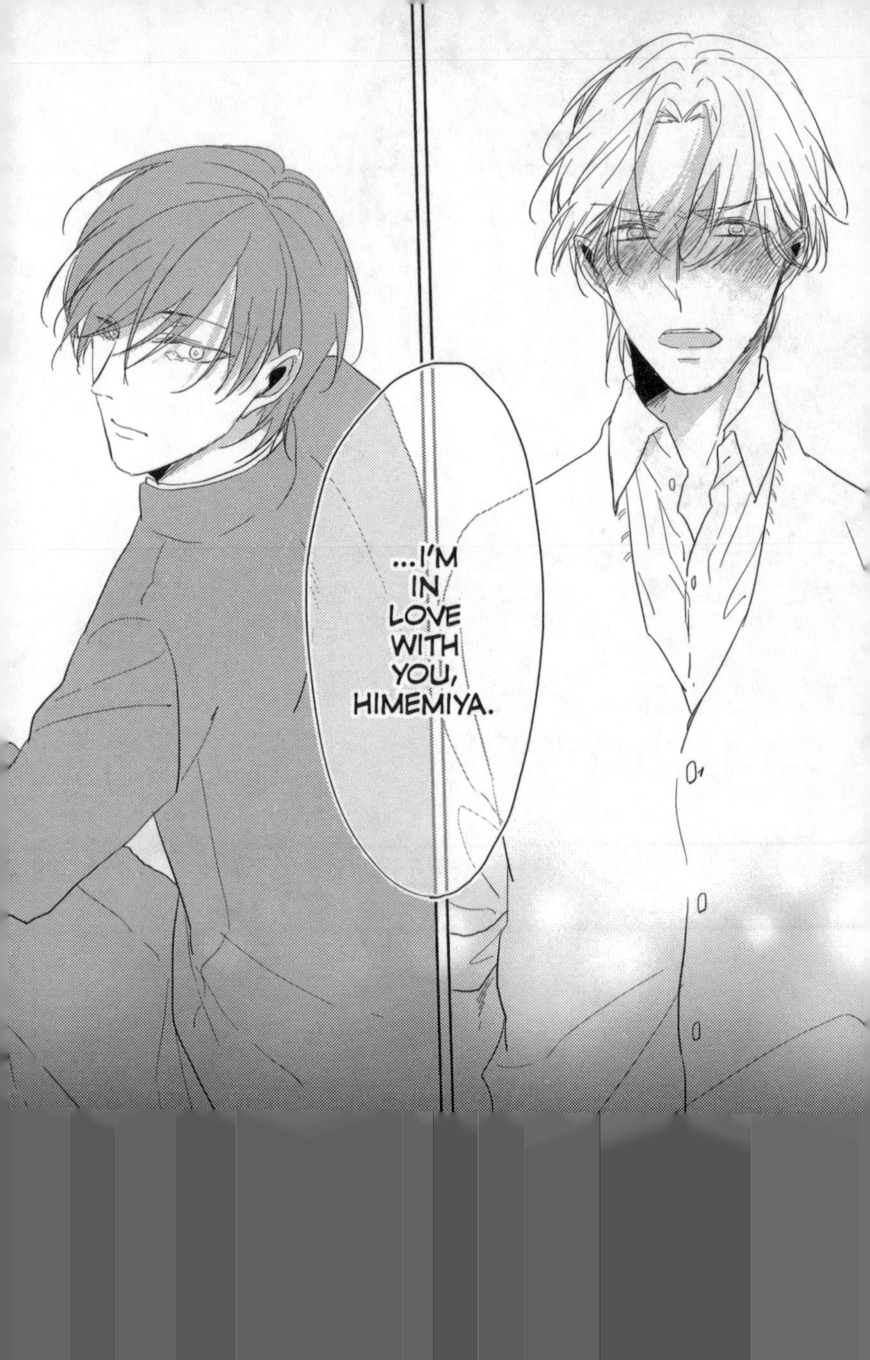
...I'M IN LOVE WITH YOU, HIMEMIYA.

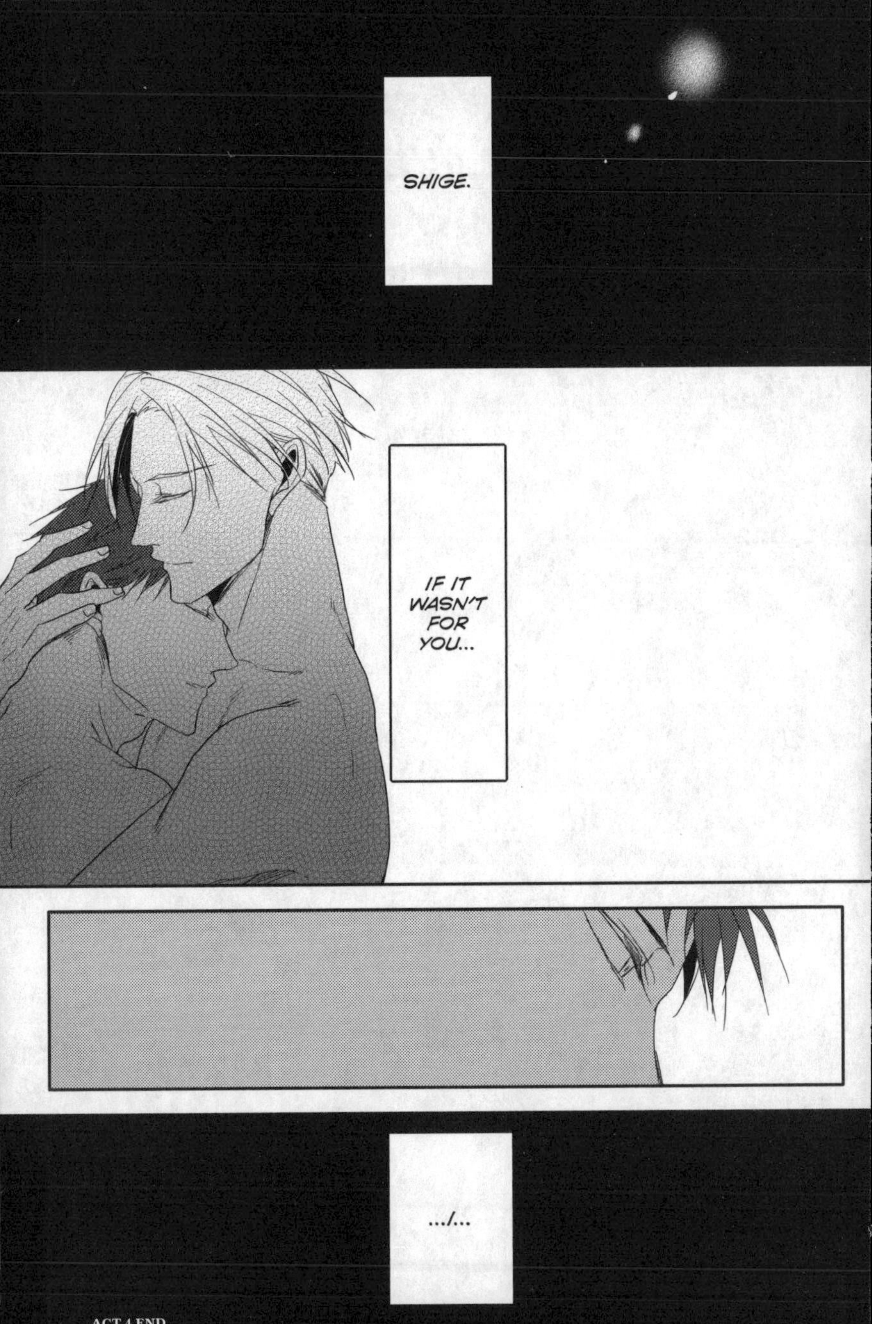
SHIGE.
IF IT WASN'T FOR YOU...
.../...

ACT 4 END

Black
or White

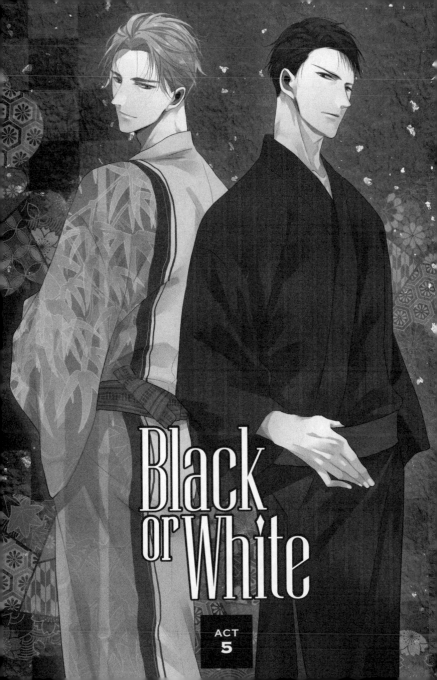

Black
or White

ACT
5

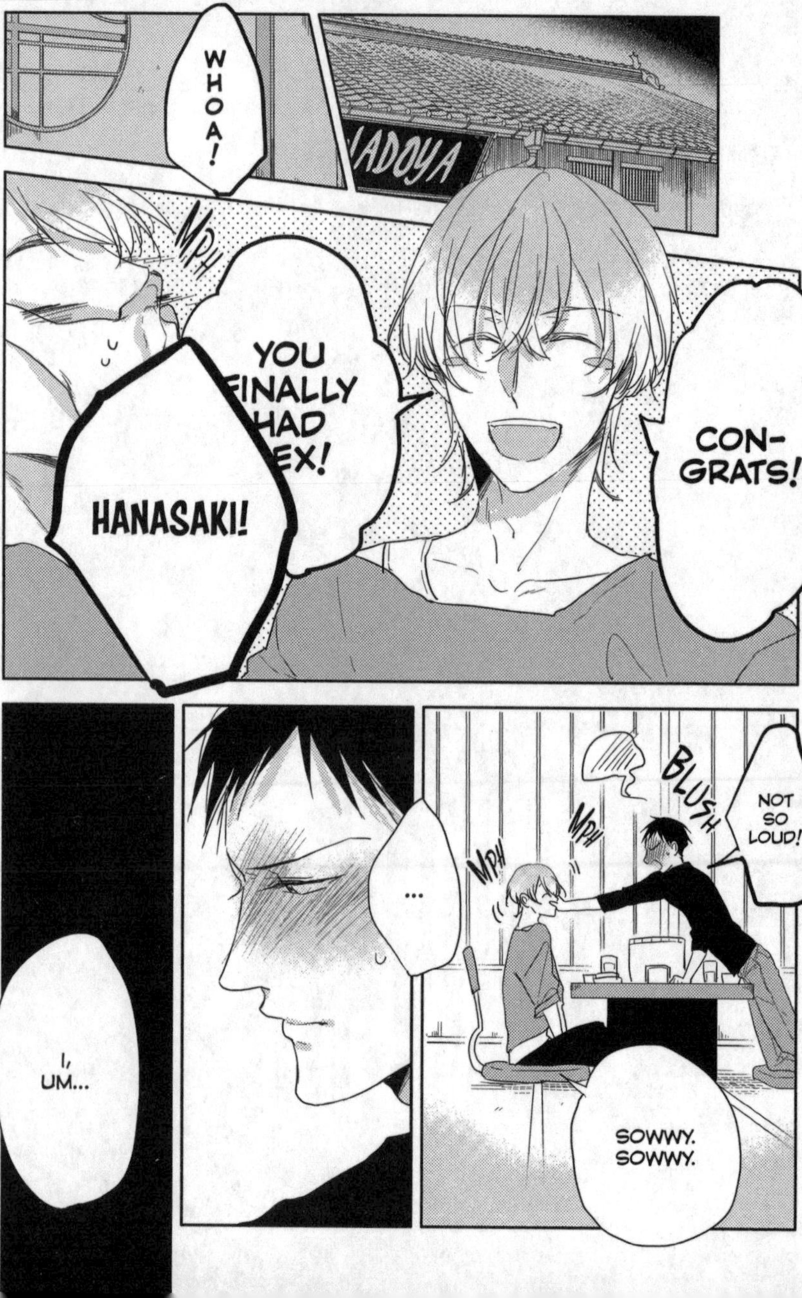
ADOYA
WHOA!
CON-GRATS!
YOU FINALLY HAD EX!
MPH
HANASAKI!
NOT SO LOUD!
BLUSH
MPH
MPH
SOWWY. SOWWY.
...
I, UM...

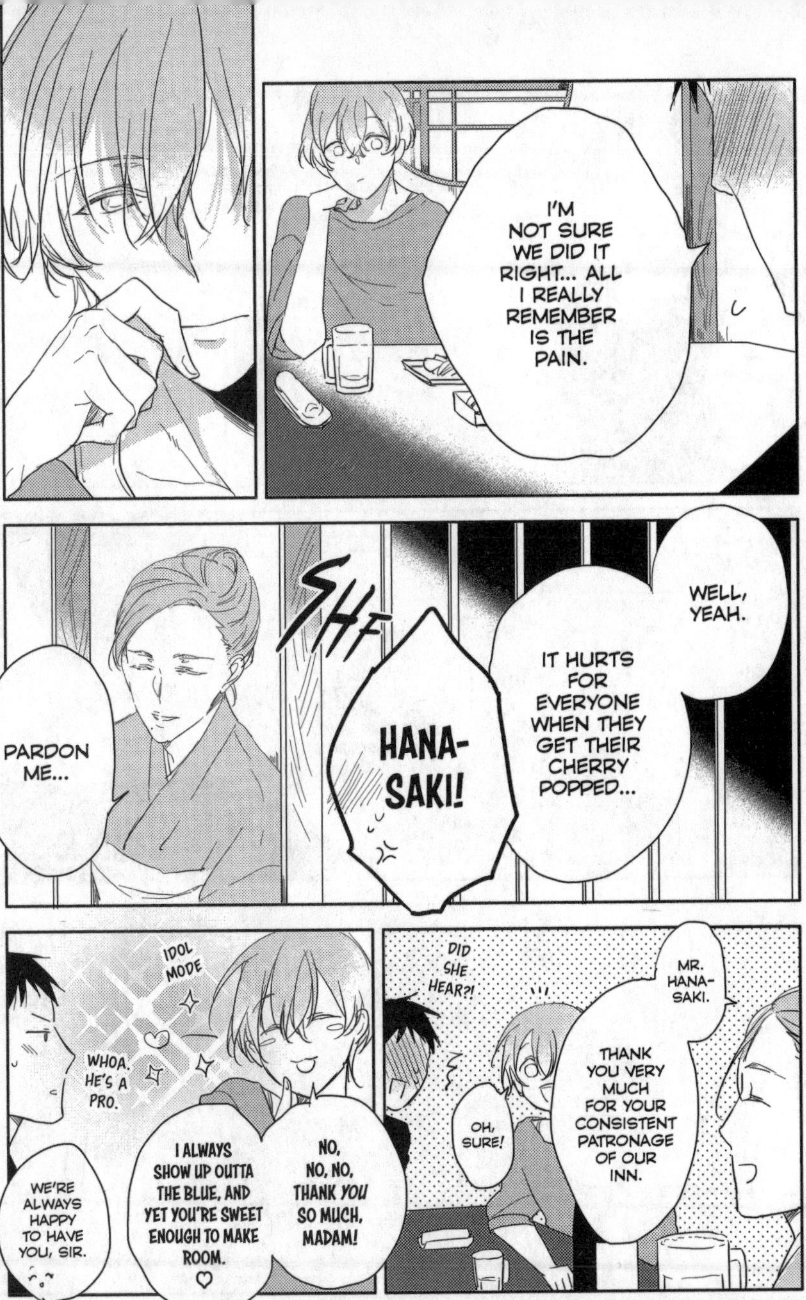
I'M NOT SURE WE DID IT RIGHT... ALL I REALLY REMEMBER IS THE PAIN.
WELL, YEAH.
IT HURTS FOR EVERYONE WHEN THEY GET THEIR CHERRY POPPED...
SHF
HANA-SAKI!
PARDON ME...
MR. HANA-SAKI.
THANK YOU VERY MUCH FOR YOUR CONSISTENT PATRONAGE OF OUR INN.
DID SHE HEAR?!
OH, SURE!
IDOL MODE
NO, NO, NO, THANK YOU SO MUCH, MADAM!
I ALWAYS SHOW UP OUTTA THE BLUE, AND YET YOU'RE SWEET ENOUGH TO MAKE ROOM. ♡
WHOA. HE'S A PRO.
WE'RE ALWAYS HAPPY TO HAVE YOU, SIR.

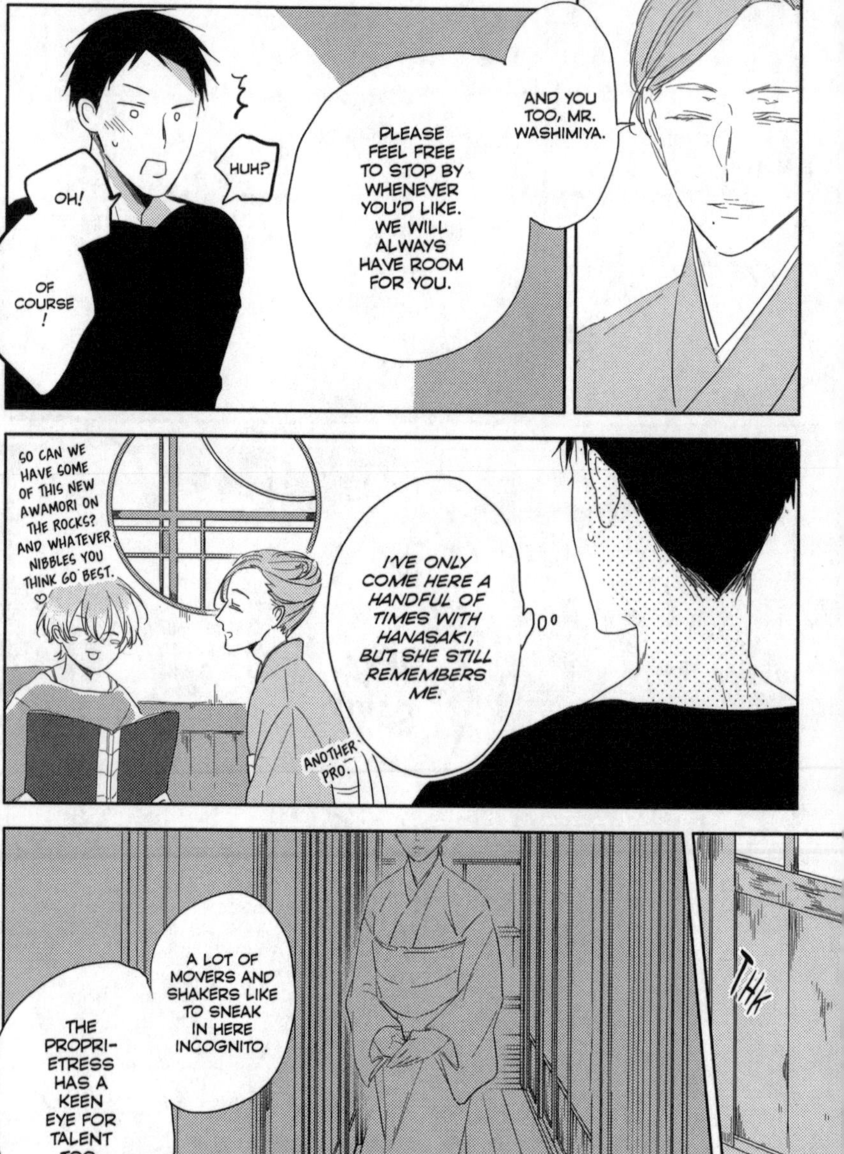

PLEASE FEEL FREE TO STOP BY WHENEVER YOU'D LIKE. WE WILL ALWAYS HAVE ROOM FOR YOU.
AND YOU TOO, MR. WASHIMIYA.
HUH?
OH!
OF COURSE!
I'VE ONLY COME HERE A HANDFUL OF TIMES WITH HANASAKI, BUT SHE STILL REMEMBERS ME.
ANOTHER PRO.
SO CAN WE HAVE SOME OF THIS NEW AWAMORI ON THE ROCKS? AND WHATEVER NIBBLES YOU THINK GO BEST.
THK
A LOT OF MOVERS AND SHAKERS LIKE TO SNEAK IN HERE INCOGNITO.
THE PROPRIETRESS HAS A KEEN EYE FOR TALENT TOO.

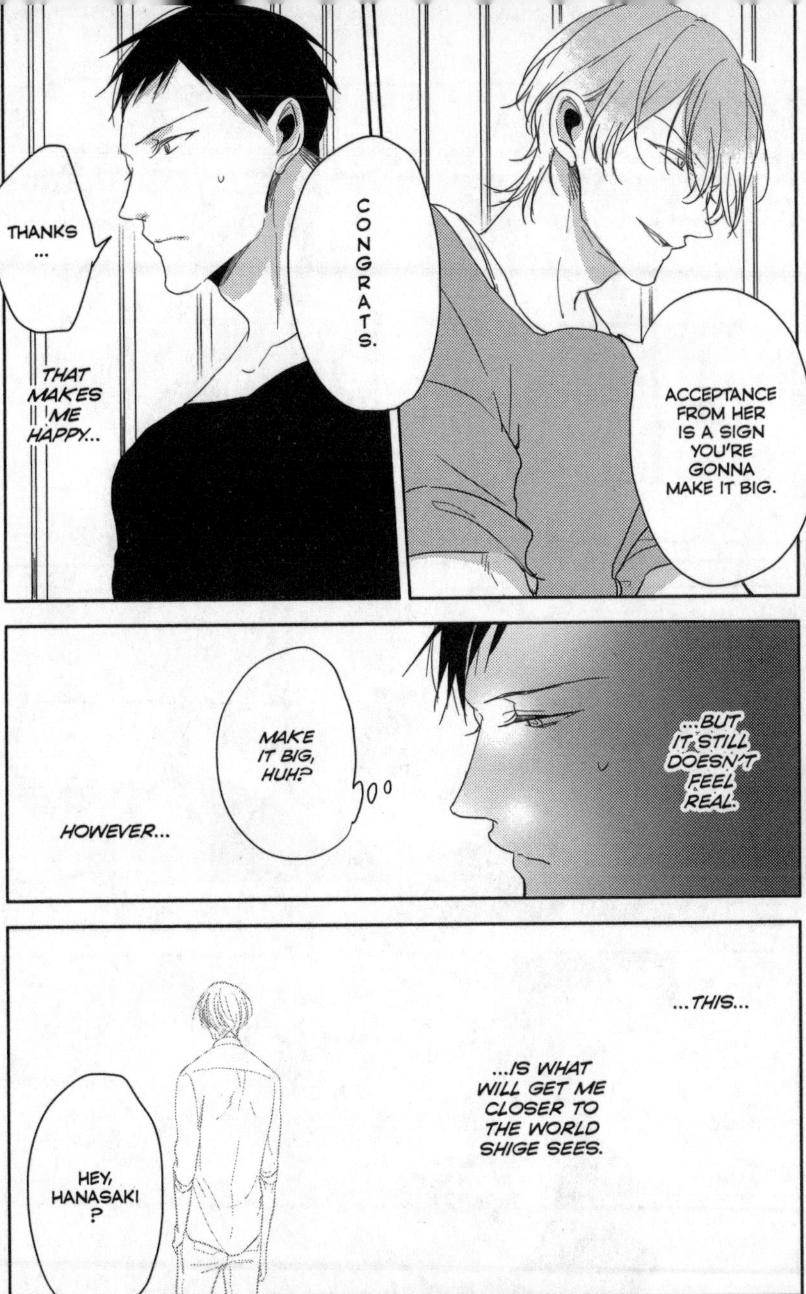
CONGRATS.
ACCEPTANCE FROM HER IS A SIGN YOU'RE GONNA MAKE IT BIG.
THANKS...
THAT MAKES ME HAPPY...
...BUT IT STILL DOESN'T FEEL REAL.
MAKE IT BIG, HUH?
HOWEVER...
...THIS...
...IS WHAT WILL GET ME CLOSER TO THE WORLD SHIGE SEES.
HEY, HANASAKI?

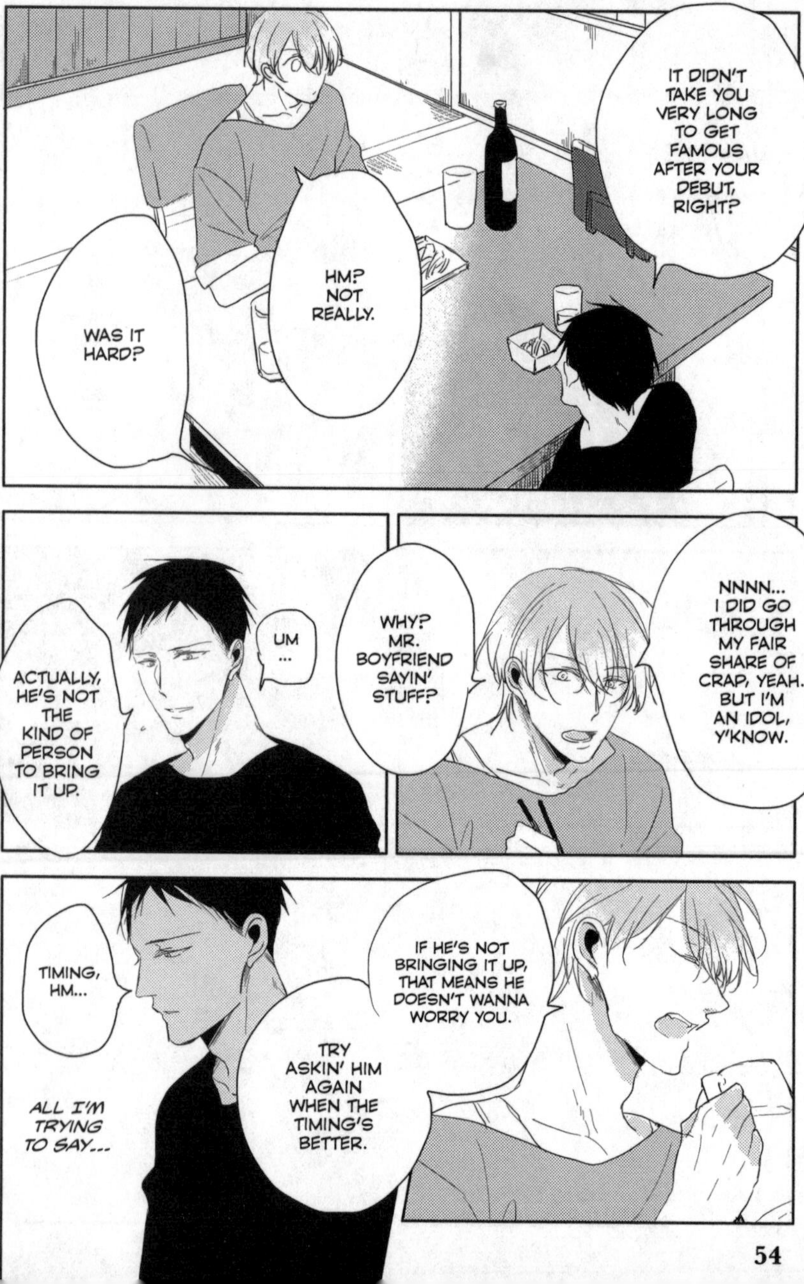
IT DIDN'T TAKE YOU VERY LONG TO GET FAMOUS AFTER YOUR DEBUT, RIGHT?
HM? NOT REALLY.
WAS IT HARD?
NNNN... I DID GO THROUGH MY FAIR SHARE OF CRAP, YEAH. BUT I'M AN IDOL, Y'KNOW.
WHY? MR. BOYFRIEND SAYIN' STUFF?
UM ...
ACTUALLY, HE'S NOT THE KIND OF PERSON TO BRING IT UP.
IF HE'S NOT BRINGING IT UP, THAT MEANS HE DOESN'T WANNA WORRY YOU.
TRY ASKIN' HIM AGAIN WHEN THE TIMING'S BETTER.
TIMING, HM...
ALL I'M TRYING TO SAY...

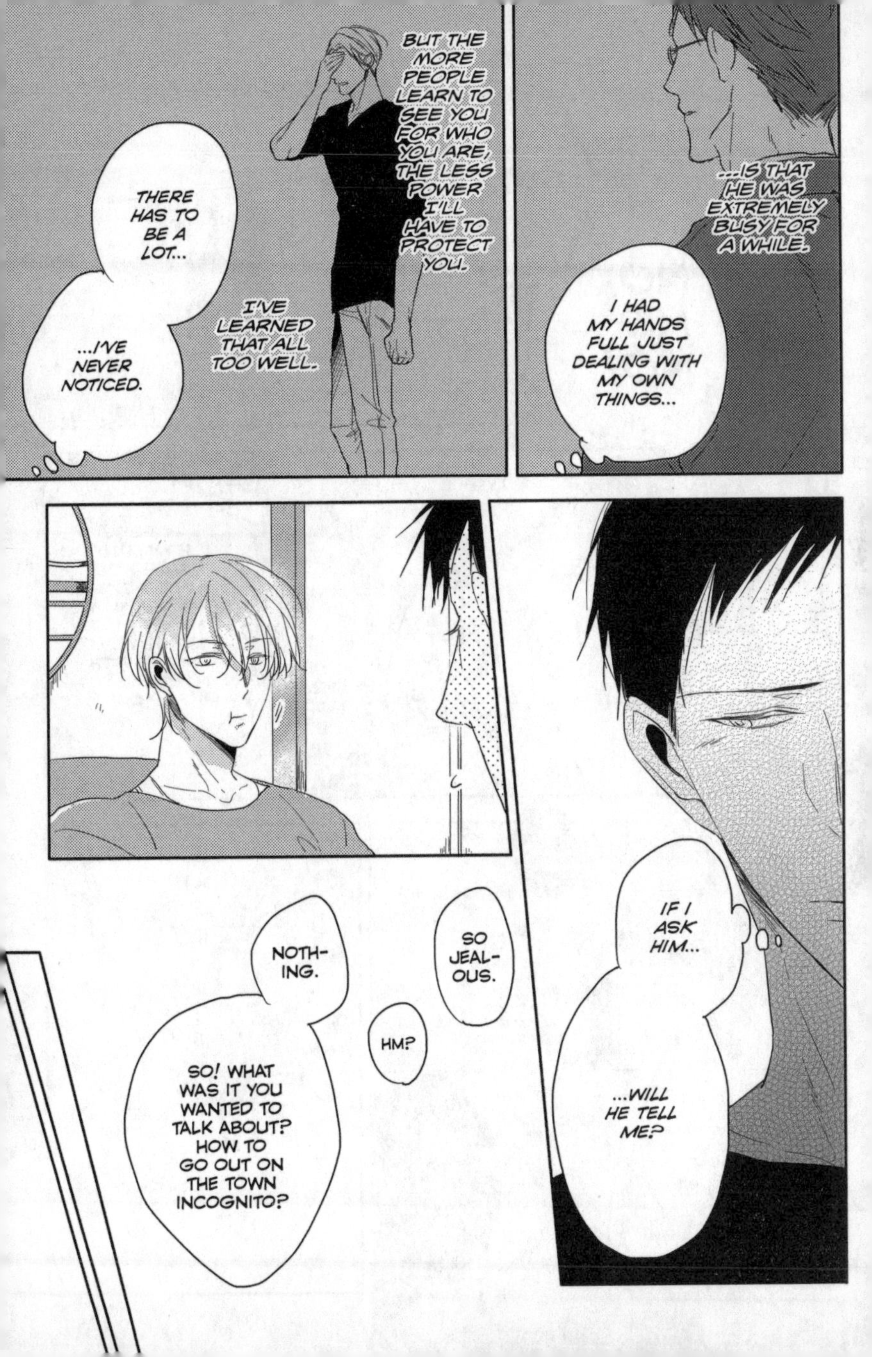
...IS THAT HE WAS EXTREMELY BUSY FOR A WHILE.
I HAD MY HANDS FULL JUST DEALING WITH MY OWN THINGS...
BUT THE MORE PEOPLE LEARN TO SEE YOU FOR WHO YOU ARE, THE LESS POWER I'LL HAVE TO PROTECT YOU.
I'VE LEARNED THAT ALL TOO WELL.
THERE HAS TO BE A LOT...
...I'VE NEVER NOTICED.
IF I ASK HIM...
...WILL HE TELL ME?
SO JEAL-OUS.
NOTH-ING.
HM?
SO! WHAT WAS IT YOU WANTED TO TALK ABOUT? HOW TO GO OUT ON THE TOWN INCOGNITO?

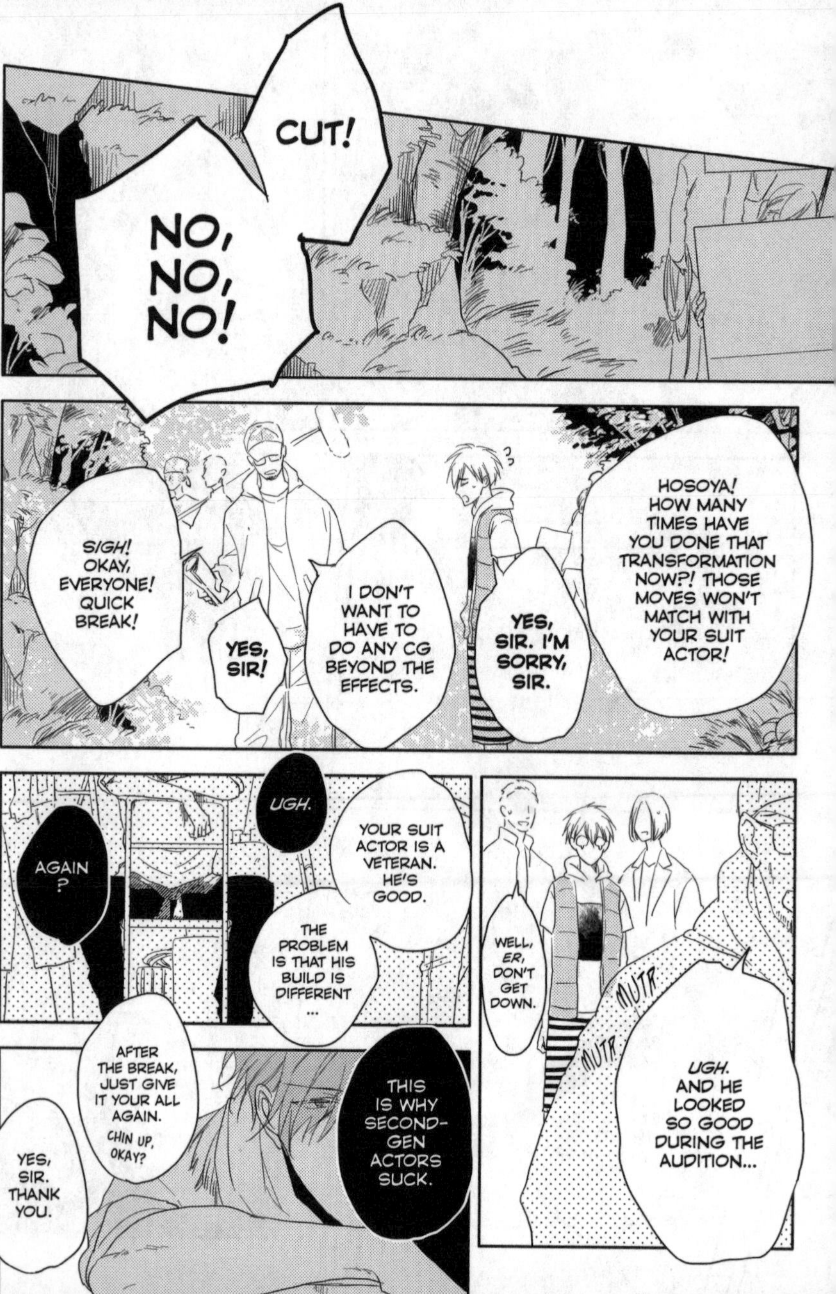
CUT!
NO, NO, NO!
HOSOYA! HOW MANY TIMES HAVE YOU DONE THAT TRANSFORMATION NOW?! THOSE MOVES WON'T MATCH WITH YOUR SUIT ACTOR!
YES, SIR. I'M SORRY, SIR.
I DON'T WANT TO HAVE TO DO ANY CG BEYOND THE EFFECTS.
YES, SIR!
SIGH! OKAY, EVERYONE! QUICK BREAK!
MUTR
MUTR
UGH. AND HE LOOKED SO GOOD DURING THE AUDITION...
WELL, ER, DON'T GET DOWN.
UGH.
YOUR SUIT ACTOR IS A VETERAN. HE'S GOOD.
THE PROBLEM IS THAT HIS BUILD IS DIFFERENT...
AGAIN?
THIS IS WHY SECOND-GEN ACTORS SUCK.
AFTER THE BREAK, JUST GIVE IT YOUR ALL AGAIN.
CHIN UP, OKAY?
YES, SIR. THANK YOU.

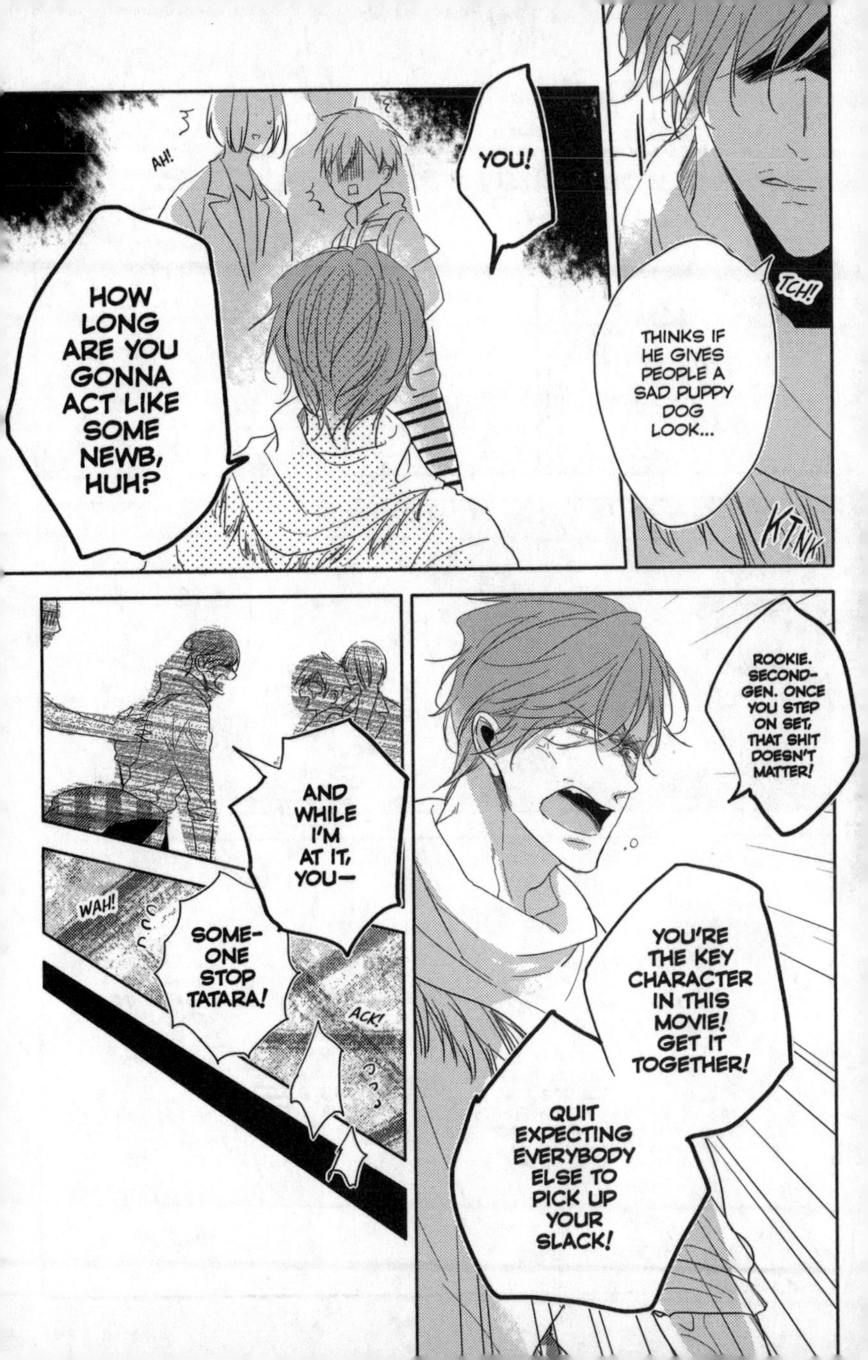
TCH!
THINKS IF HE GIVES PEOPLE A SAD PUPPY DOG LOOK...
KTNK
YOU!
AH!
HOW LONG ARE YOU GONNA ACT LIKE SOME NEWB, HUH?
ROOKIE. SECOND-GEN. ONCE YOU STEP ON SET, THAT SHIT DOESN'T MATTER!
YOU'RE THE KEY CHARACTER IN THIS MOVIE! GET IT TOGETHER!
QUIT EXPECTING EVERYBODY ELSE TO PICK UP YOUR SLACK!
AND WHILE I'M AT IT, YOU—
WAH!
SOME-ONE STOP TATARA!
ACK!

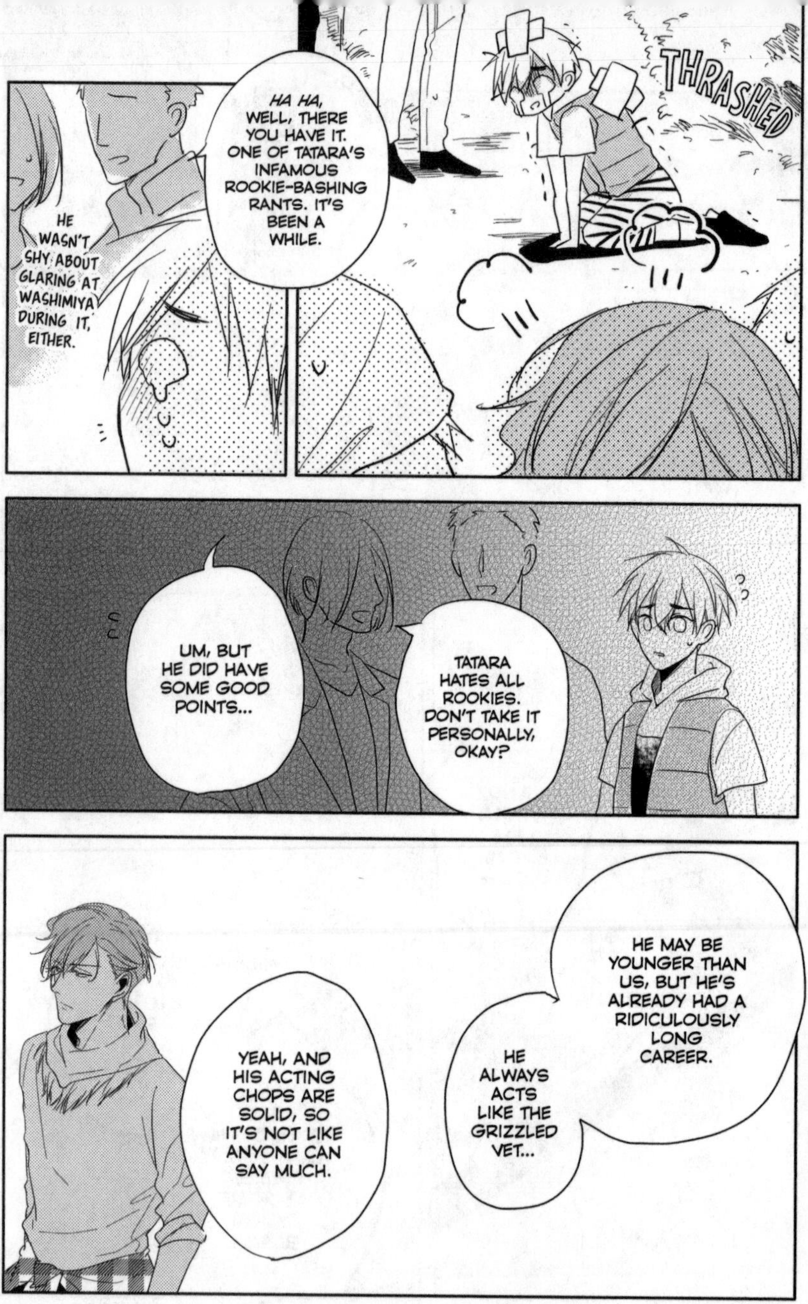
THRASHED
HA HA, WELL, THERE YOU HAVE IT. ONE OF TATARA'S INFAMOUS ROOKIE-BASHING RANTS. IT'S BEEN A WHILE.
HE WASN'T SHY ABOUT GLARING AT WASHIMIYA DURING IT, EITHER.
TATARA HATES ALL ROOKIES. DON'T TAKE IT PERSONALLY, OKAY?
UM, BUT HE DID HAVE SOME GOOD POINTS...
HE MAY BE YOUNGER THAN US, BUT HE'S ALREADY HAD A RIDICULOUSLY LONG CAREER.
HE ALWAYS ACTS LIKE THE GRIZZLED VET...
YEAH, AND HIS ACTING CHOPS ARE SOLID, SO IT'S NOT LIKE ANYONE CAN SAY MUCH.

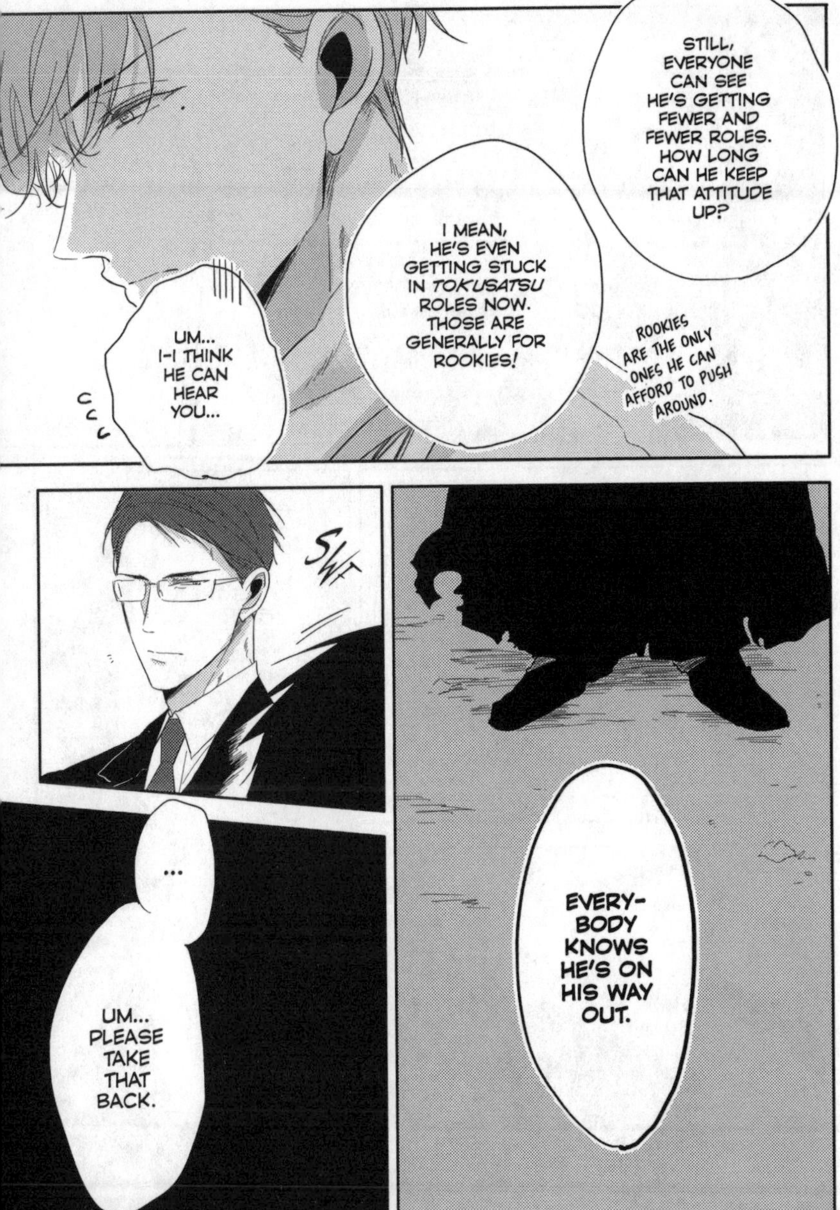
STILL, EVERYONE CAN SEE HE'S GETTING FEWER AND FEWER ROLES. HOW LONG CAN HE KEEP THAT ATTITUDE UP?
I MEAN, HE'S EVEN GETTING STUCK IN *TOKUSATSU* ROLES NOW. THOSE ARE GENERALLY FOR ROOKIES!
ROOKIES ARE THE ONLY ONES HE CAN AFFORD TO PUSH AROUND.
UM... I-I THINK HE CAN HEAR YOU...
EVERY-BODY KNOWS HE'S ON HIS WAY OUT.
SWF
...
UM... PLEASE TAKE THAT BACK.

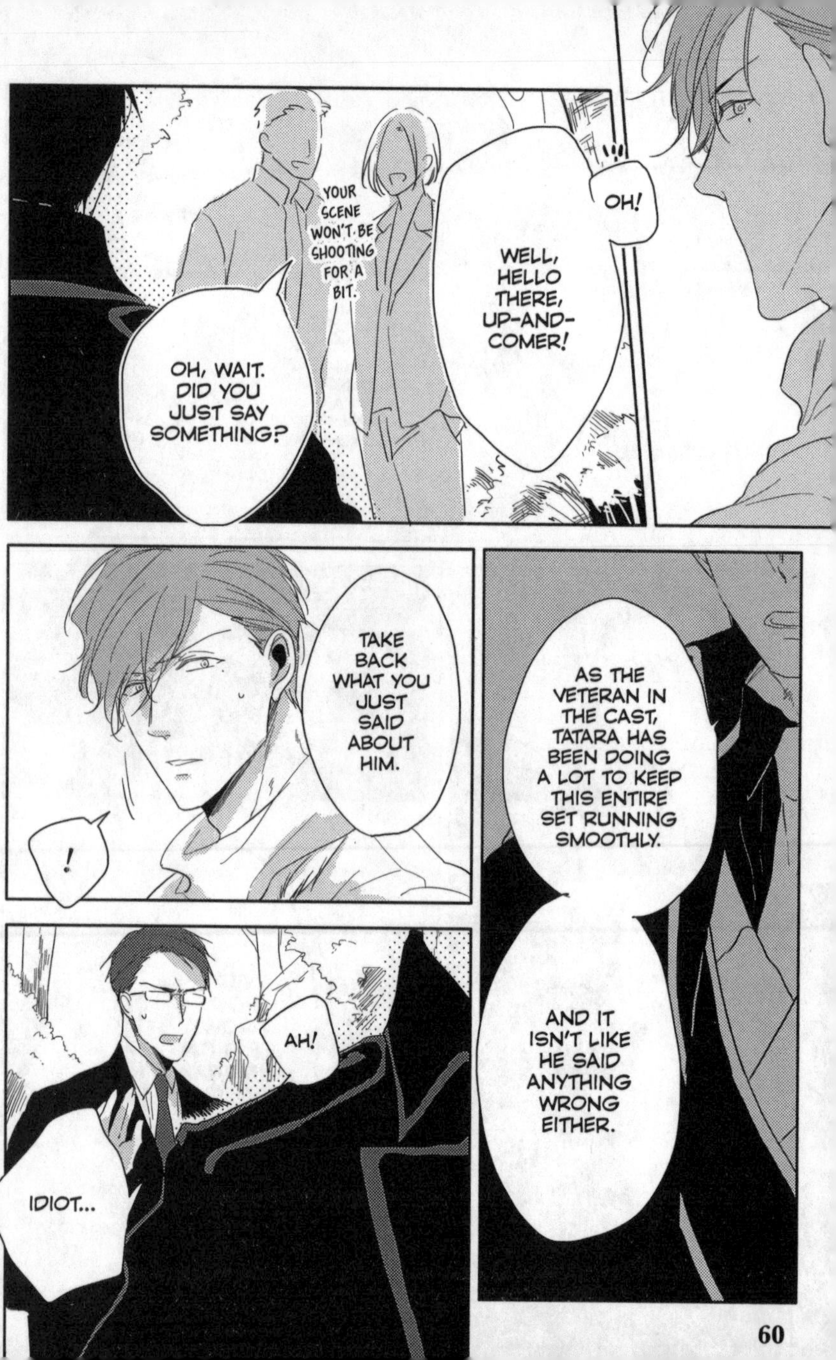
OH!
WELL, HELLO THERE, UP-AND-COMER!
YOUR SCENE WON'T BE SHOOTING FOR A BIT.
OH, WAIT. DID YOU JUST SAY SOMETHING?
AS THE VETERAN IN THE CAST, TATARA HAS BEEN DOING A LOT TO KEEP THIS ENTIRE SET RUNNING SMOOTHLY.
AND IT ISN'T LIKE HE SAID ANYTHING WRONG EITHER.
TAKE BACK WHAT YOU JUST SAID ABOUT HIM.
!
AH!
IDIOT...

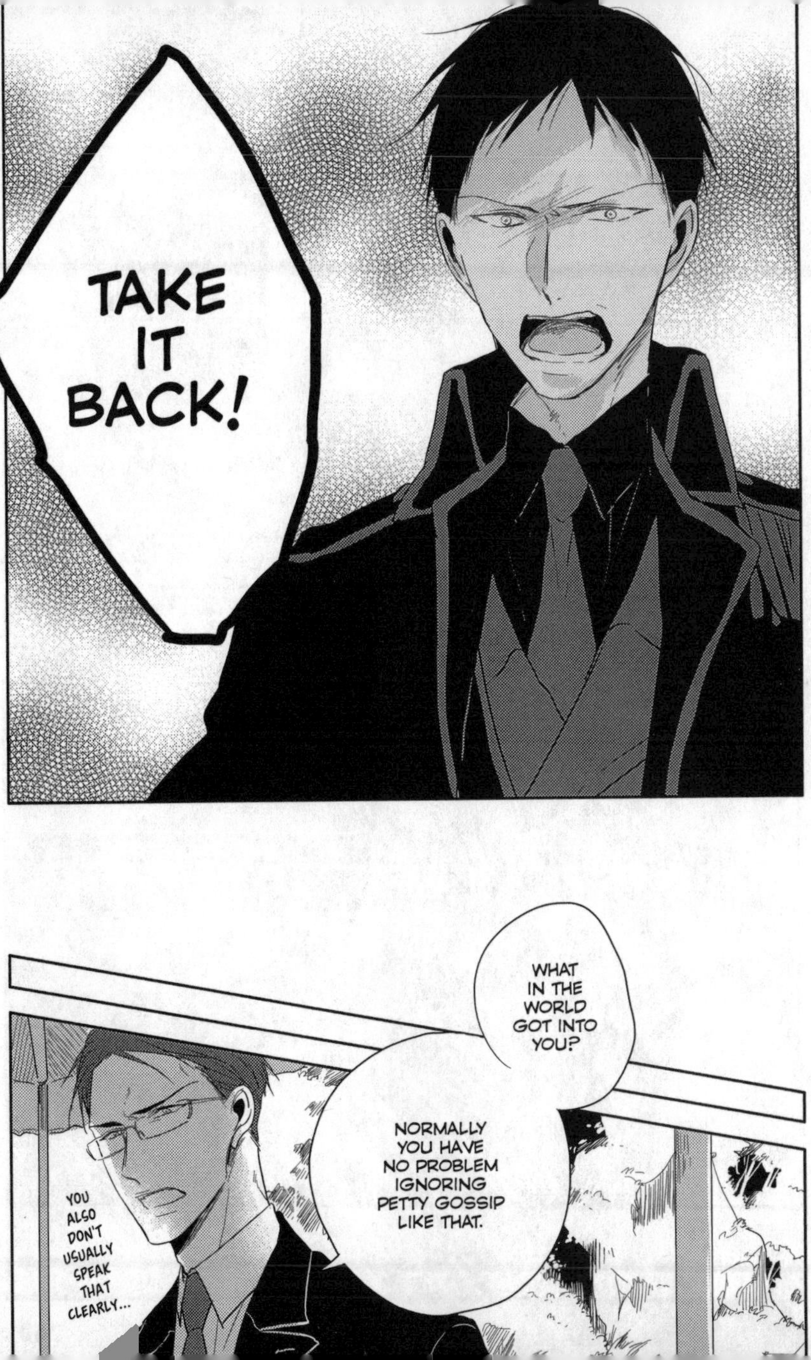
TAKE IT BACK!
WHAT IN THE WORLD GOT INTO YOU?
NORMALLY YOU HAVE NO PROBLEM IGNORING PETTY GOSSIP LIKE THAT.
YOU ALSO DON'T USUALLY SPEAK THAT CLEARLY...

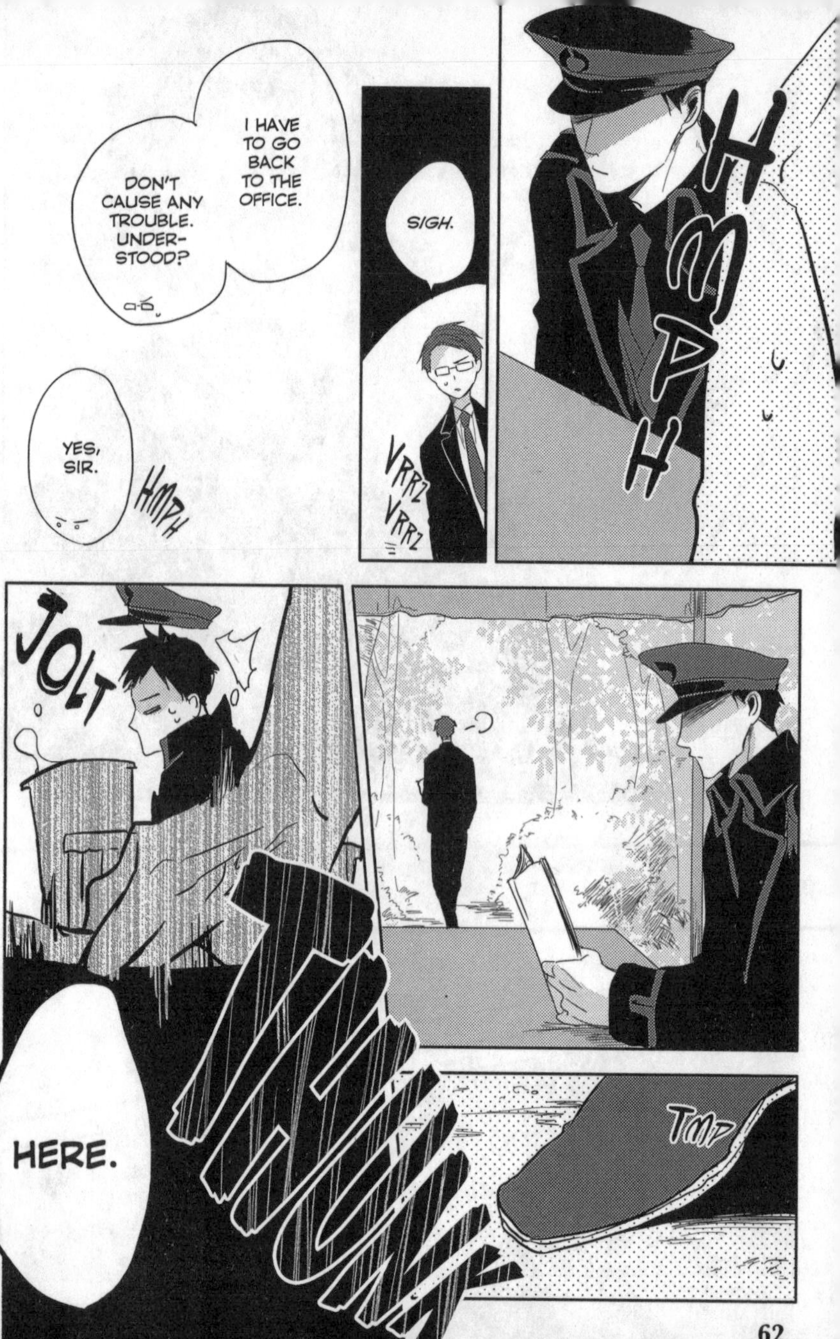
HMPH
SIGH.
VRRZ VRRZ
I HAVE TO GO BACK TO THE OFFICE.
DON'T CAUSE ANY TROUBLE. UNDER-STOOD?
YES, SIR.
HMPH
JOLT
TMP
HERE.

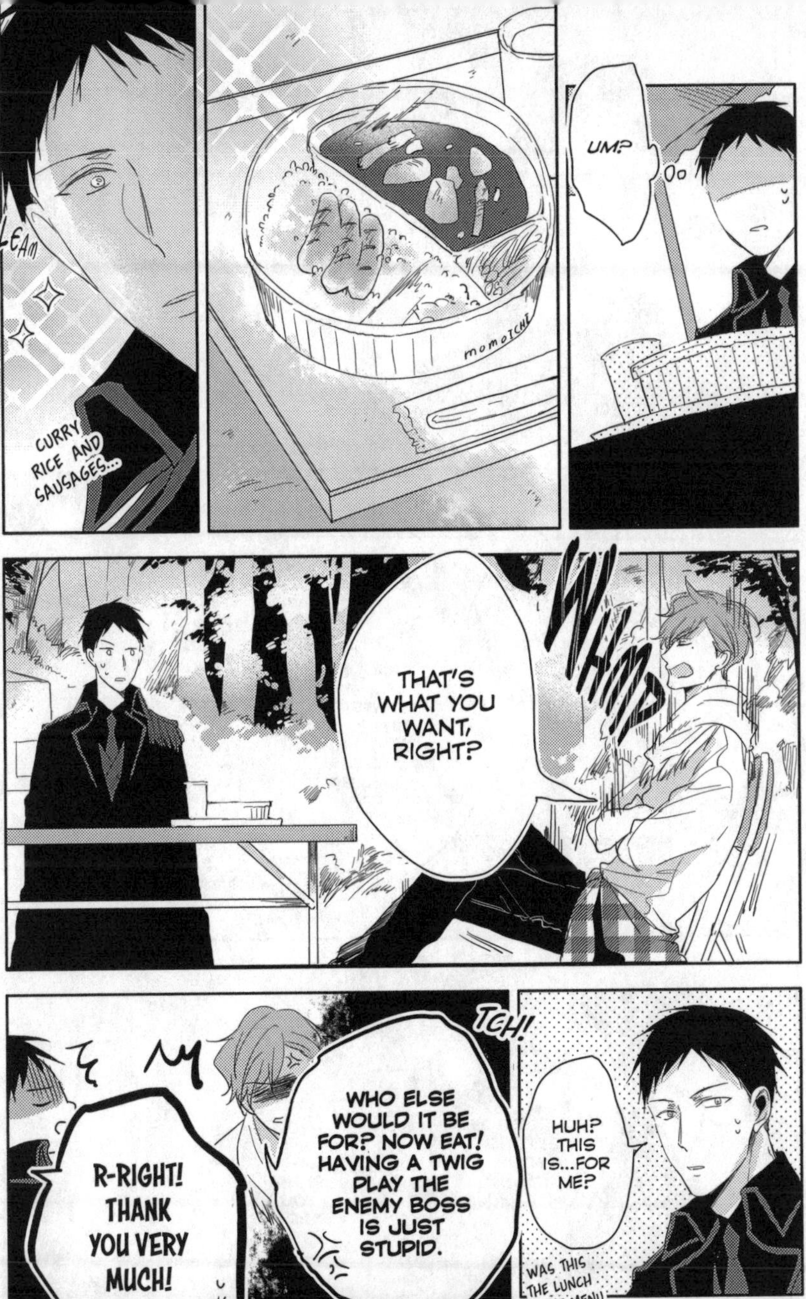
UM?
momotchi
GLEAM
CURRY RICE AND SAUSAGES...
THAT'S WHAT YOU WANT, RIGHT?
HUH? THIS IS...FOR ME?
WAS THIS THE LUNCH ON THE MENU FOR TODAY?
TCH!
WHO ELSE WOULD IT BE FOR? NOW EAT! HAVING A TWIG PLAY THE ENEMY BOSS IS JUST STUPID.
R-RIGHT! THANK YOU VERY MUCH!

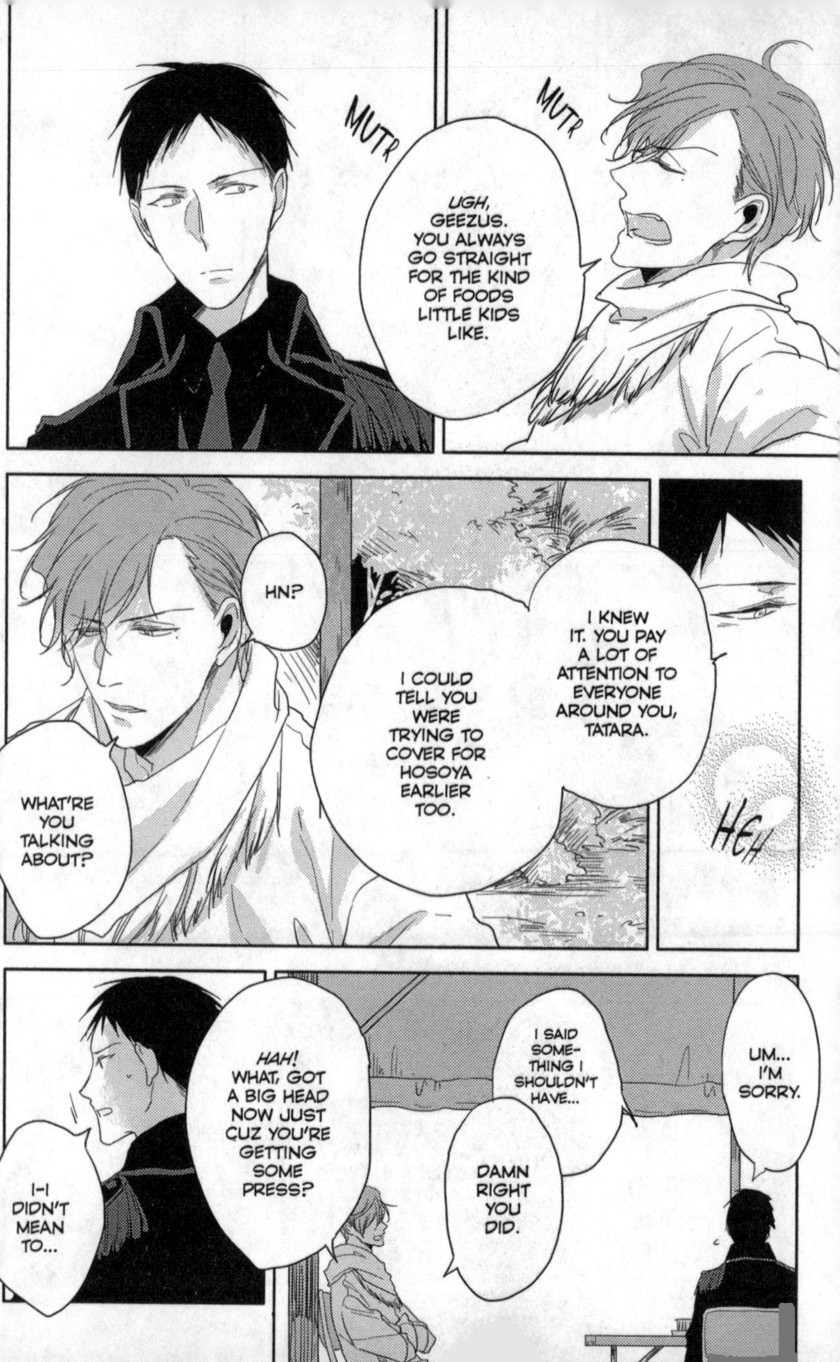
MUTR
UGH, GEEZUS. YOU ALWAYS GO STRAIGHT FOR THE KIND OF FOODS LITTLE KIDS LIKE.
MUTR
I KNEW IT. YOU PAY A LOT OF ATTENTION TO EVERYONE AROUND YOU, TATARA.
HEH
I COULD TELL YOU WERE TRYING TO COVER FOR HOSOYA EARLIER TOO.
HN?
WHAT'RE YOU TALKING ABOUT?
UM... I'M SORRY.
I SAID SOME-THING I SHOULDN'T HAVE...
DAMN RIGHT YOU DID.
HAH! WHAT, GOT A BIG HEAD NOW JUST CUZ YOU'RE GETTING SOME PRESS?
I-I DIDN'T MEAN TO...

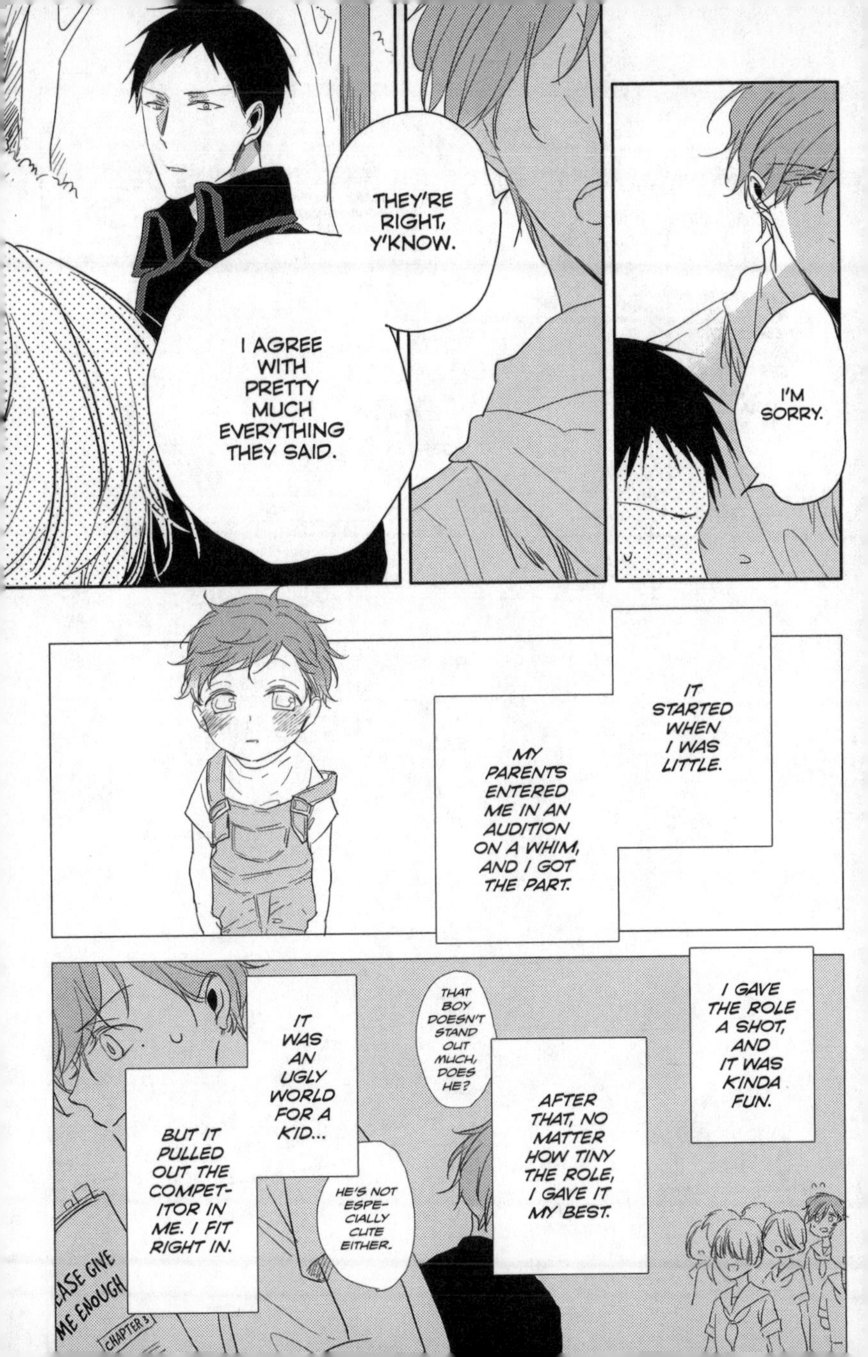
I'M SORRY.
THEY'RE RIGHT, Y'KNOW.
I AGREE WITH PRETTY MUCH EVERYTHING THEY SAID.
IT STARTED WHEN I WAS LITTLE.
MY PARENTS ENTERED ME IN AN AUDITION ON A WHIM, AND I GOT THE PART.
I GAVE THE ROLE A SHOT, AND IT WAS KINDA FUN.
THAT BOY DOESN'T STAND OUT MUCH, DOES HE?
AFTER THAT, NO MATTER HOW TINY THE ROLE, I GAVE IT MY BEST.
HE'S NOT ESPE-CIALLY CUTE EITHER.
IT WAS AN UGLY WORLD FOR A KID...
BUT IT PULLED OUT THE COMPET-ITOR IN ME. I FIT RIGHT IN.
EASE GIVE ME ENOUGH
CHAPTER 3

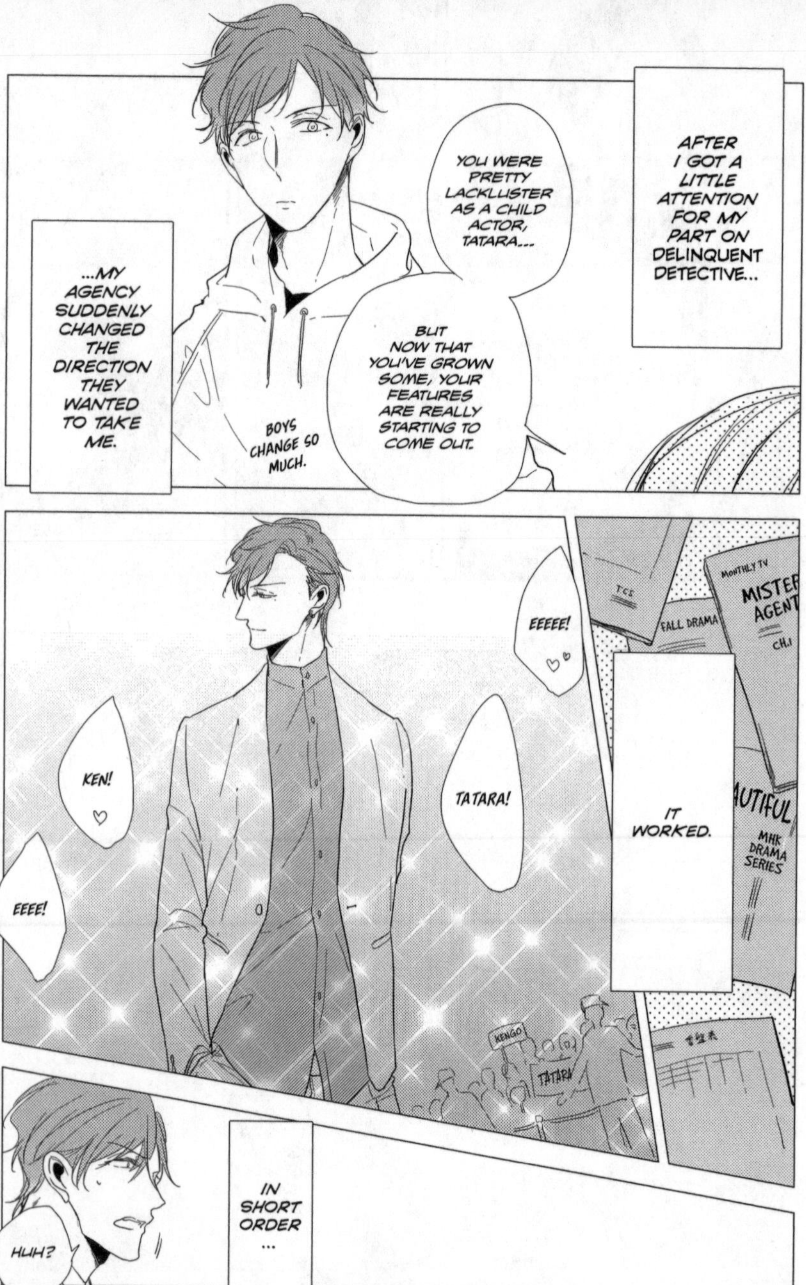
AFTER I GOT A LITTLE ATTENTION FOR MY PART ON DELINQUENT DETECTIVE...
YOU WERE PRETTY LACKLUSTER AS A CHILD ACTOR, TATARA...
BUT NOW THAT YOU'VE GROWN SOME, YOUR FEATURES ARE REALLY STARTING TO COME OUT.
BOYS CHANGE SO MUCH.
...MY AGENCY SUDDENLY CHANGED THE DIRECTION THEY WANTED TO TAKE ME.
MONTHLY TV
FALL DRAMA
CH.1
IT WORKED.
MHK DRAMA SERIES
EEEEE!
TATARA!
KEN!
EEEE!
KENGO
TATARA
IN SHORT ORDER...
HUH?

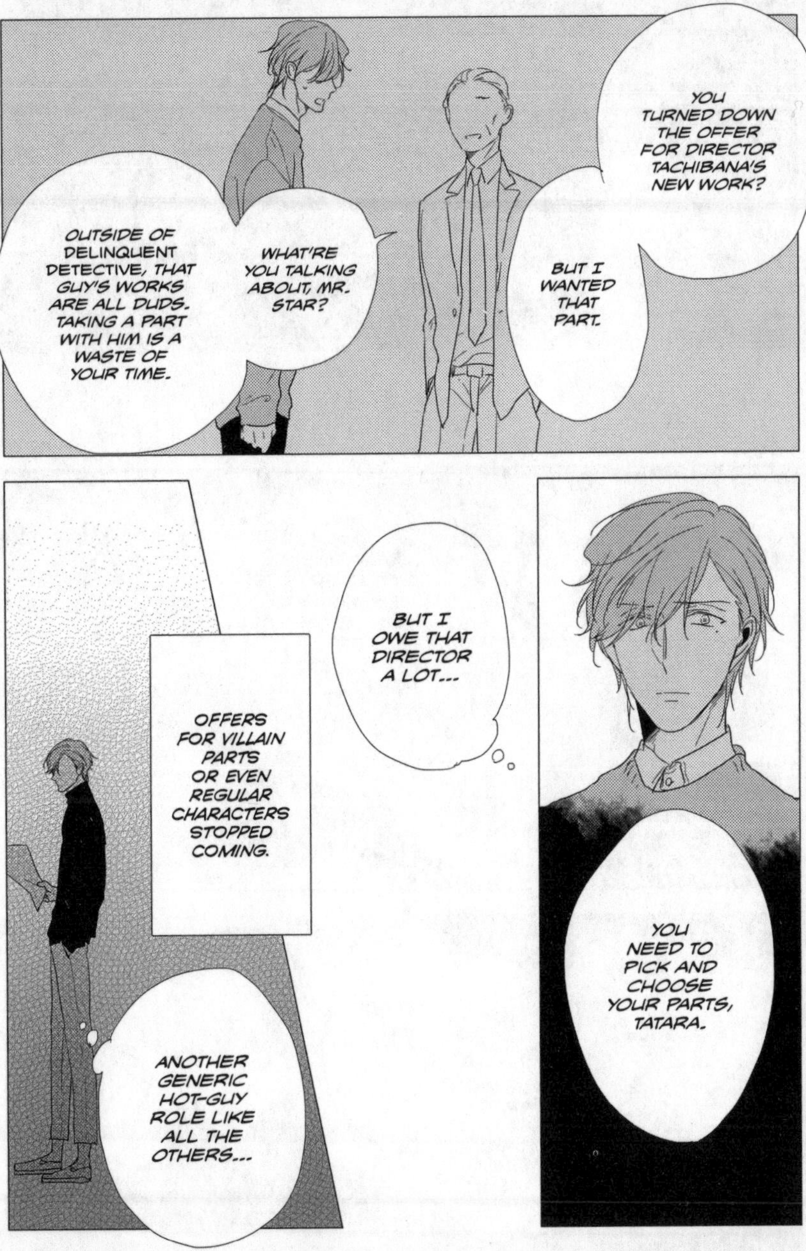
YOU TURNED DOWN THE OFFER FOR DIRECTOR TACHIBANA'S NEW WORK?
BUT I WANTED THAT PART.
WHAT'RE YOU TALKING ABOUT, MR. STAR?
OUTSIDE OF DELINQUENT DETECTIVE, THAT GUY'S WORKS ARE ALL DUDS. TAKING A PART WITH HIM IS A WASTE OF YOUR TIME.
YOU NEED TO PICK AND CHOOSE YOUR PARTS, TATARA.
BUT I OWE THAT DIRECTOR A LOT...
OFFERS FOR VILLAIN PARTS OR EVEN REGULAR CHARACTERS STOPPED COMING.
ANOTHER GENERIC HOT-GUY ROLE LIKE ALL THE OTHERS...

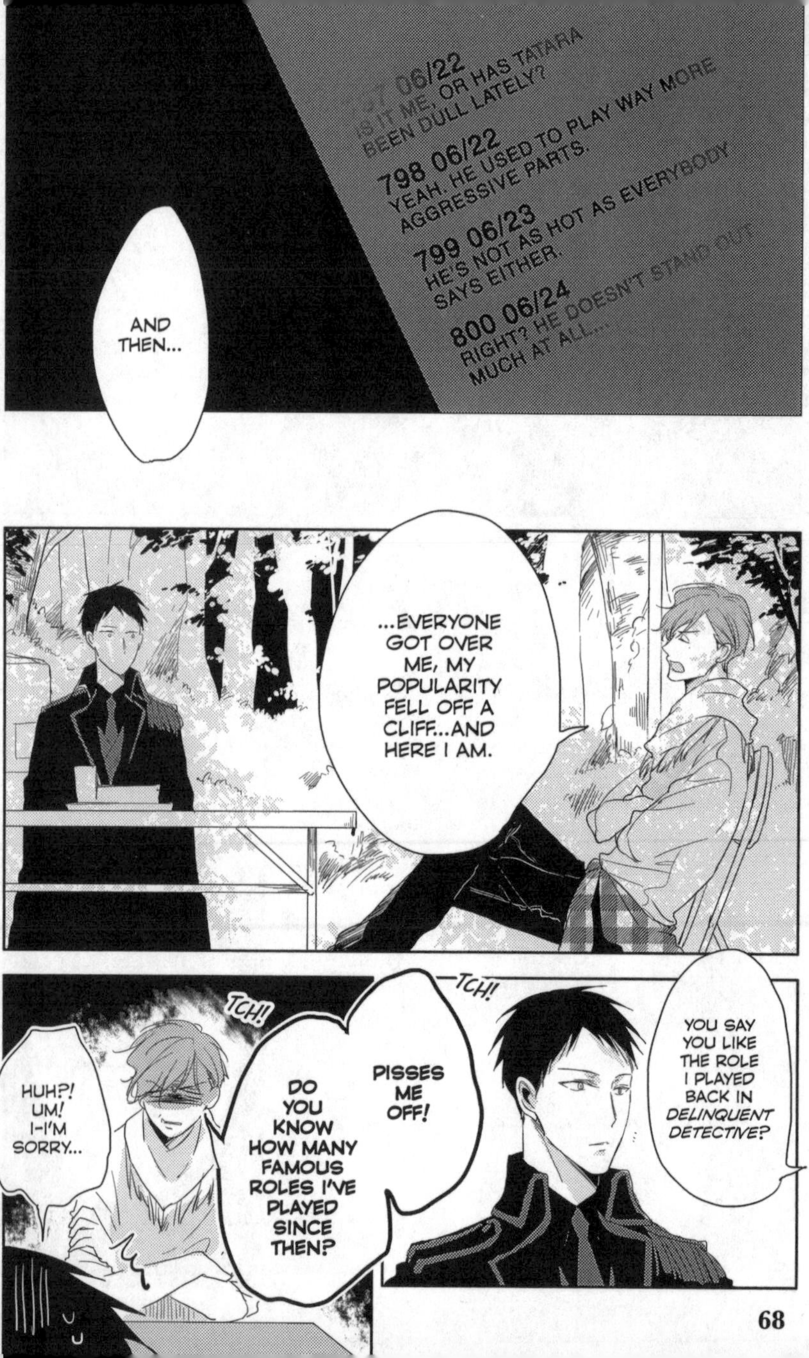
06/22
IS IT ME, OR HAS TATARA BEEN DULL LATELY?
798 06/22
YEAH. HE USED TO PLAY WAY MORE AGGRESSIVE PARTS.
799 06/23
HE'S NOT AS HOT AS EVERYBODY SAYS EITHER.
800 06/24
RIGHT? HE DOESN'T STAND OUT MUCH AT ALL...
AND THEN...
...EVERYONE GOT OVER ME, MY POPULARITY FELL OFF A CLIFF...AND HERE I AM.
YOU SAY YOU LIKE THE ROLE I PLAYED BACK IN *DELINQUENT DETECTIVE*?
—TCH!
PISSES ME OFF!
DO YOU KNOW HOW MANY FAMOUS ROLES I'VE PLAYED SINCE THEN?
TCH!
HUH?! UM! I-I'M SORRY...

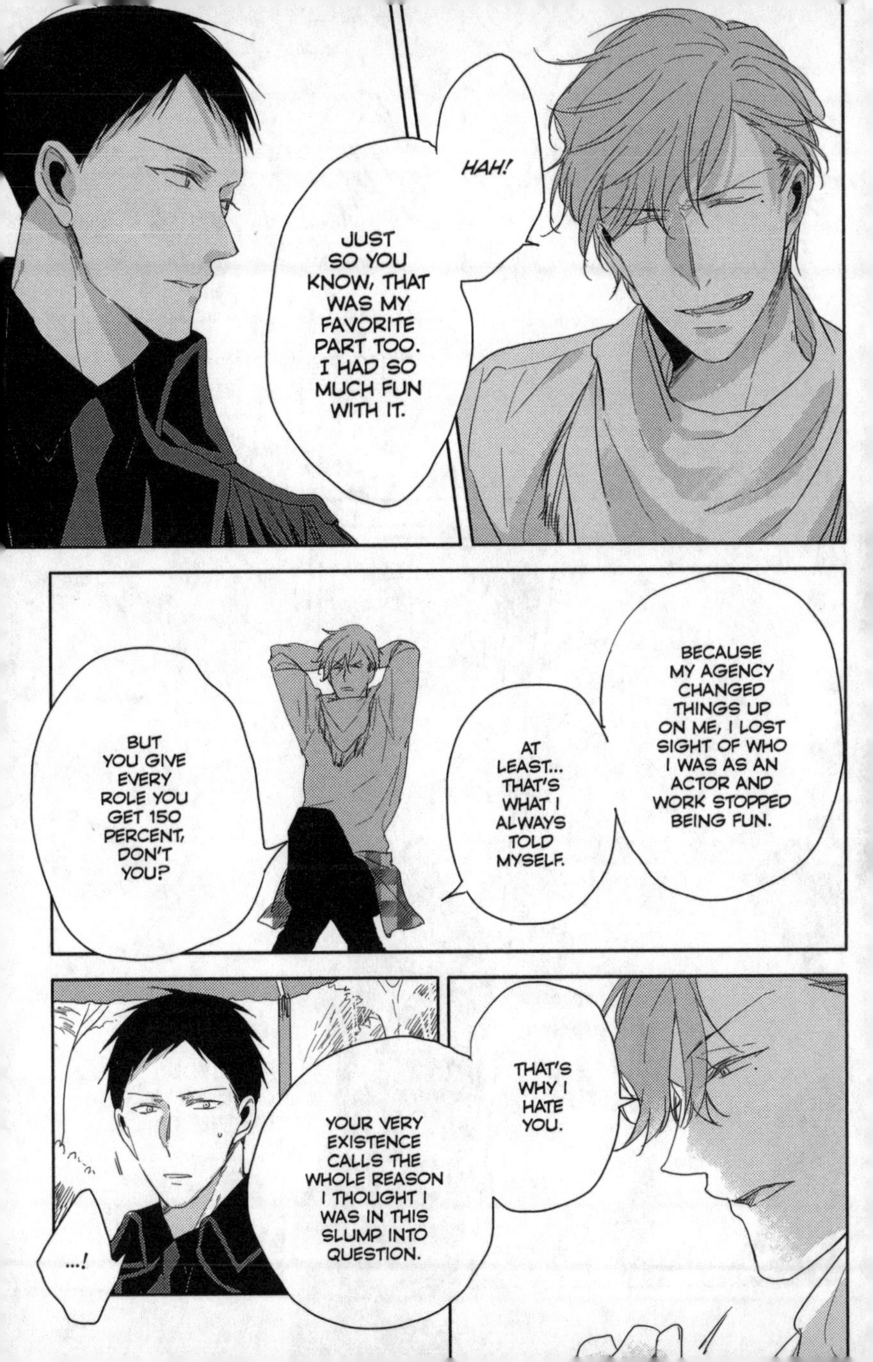
HAH!
JUST SO YOU KNOW, THAT WAS MY FAVORITE PART TOO. I HAD SO MUCH FUN WITH IT.
BECAUSE MY AGENCY CHANGED THINGS UP ON ME, I LOST SIGHT OF WHO I WAS AS AN ACTOR AND WORK STOPPED BEING FUN.
AT LEAST... THAT'S WHAT I ALWAYS TOLD MYSELF.
BUT YOU GIVE EVERY ROLE YOU GET 150 PERCENT, DON'T YOU?
THAT'S WHY I HATE YOU.
YOUR VERY EXISTENCE CALLS THE WHOLE REASON I THOUGHT I WAS IN THIS SLUMP INTO QUESTION.
...!

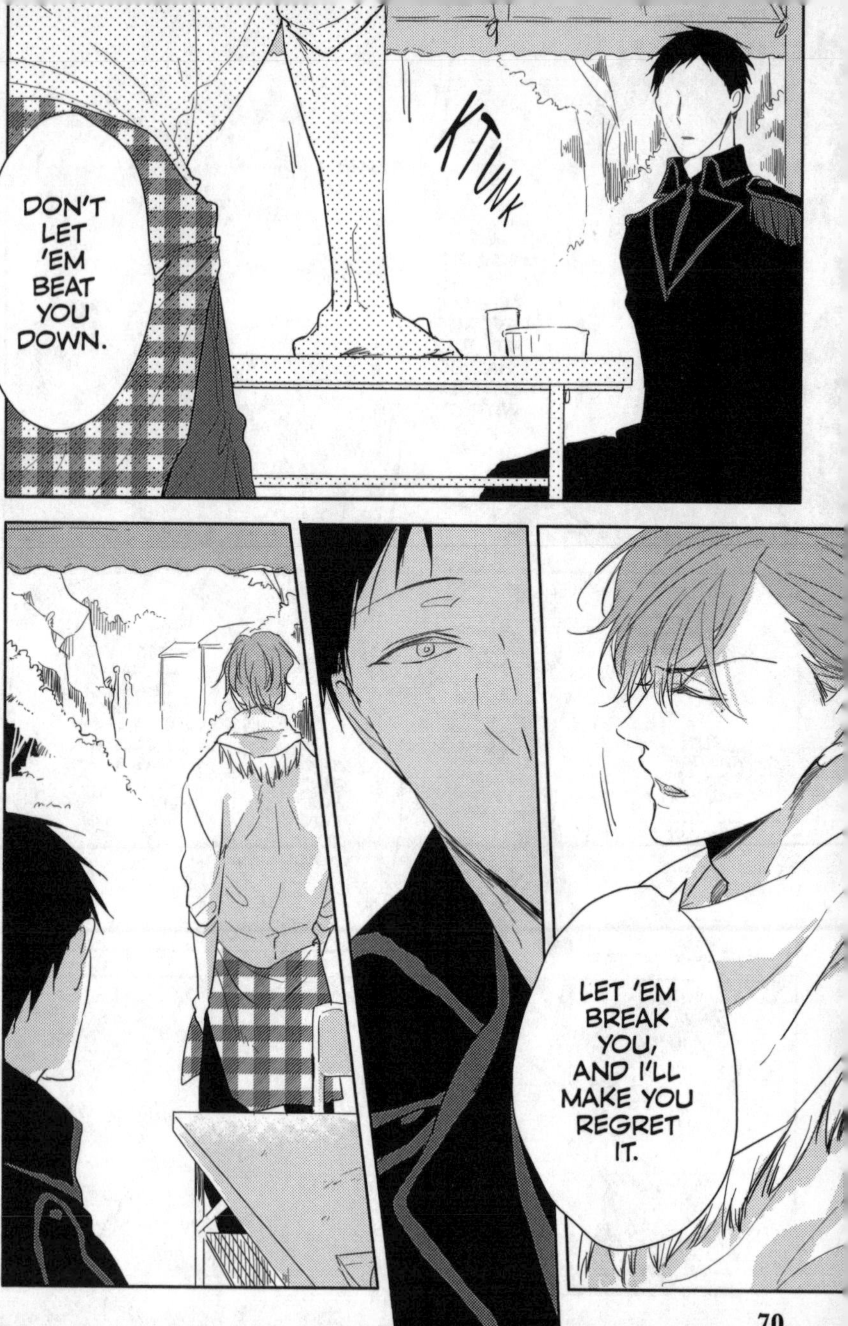
KTUNK
DON'T LET 'EM BEAT YOU DOWN.
LET 'EM BREAK YOU, AND I'LL MAKE YOU REGRET IT.

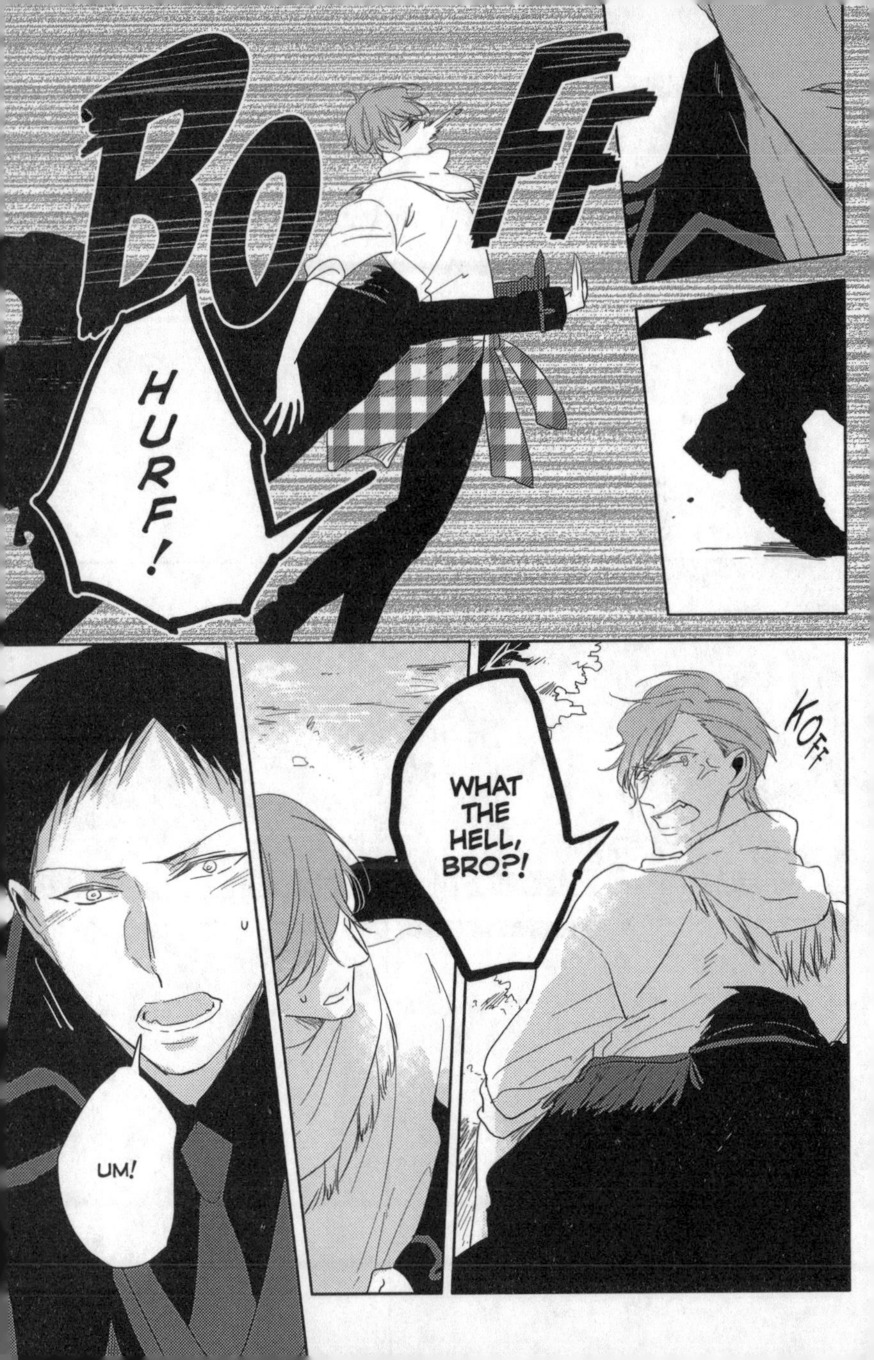
BOFF
HURF!
KOFF
WHAT THE HELL, BRO?!
UM!

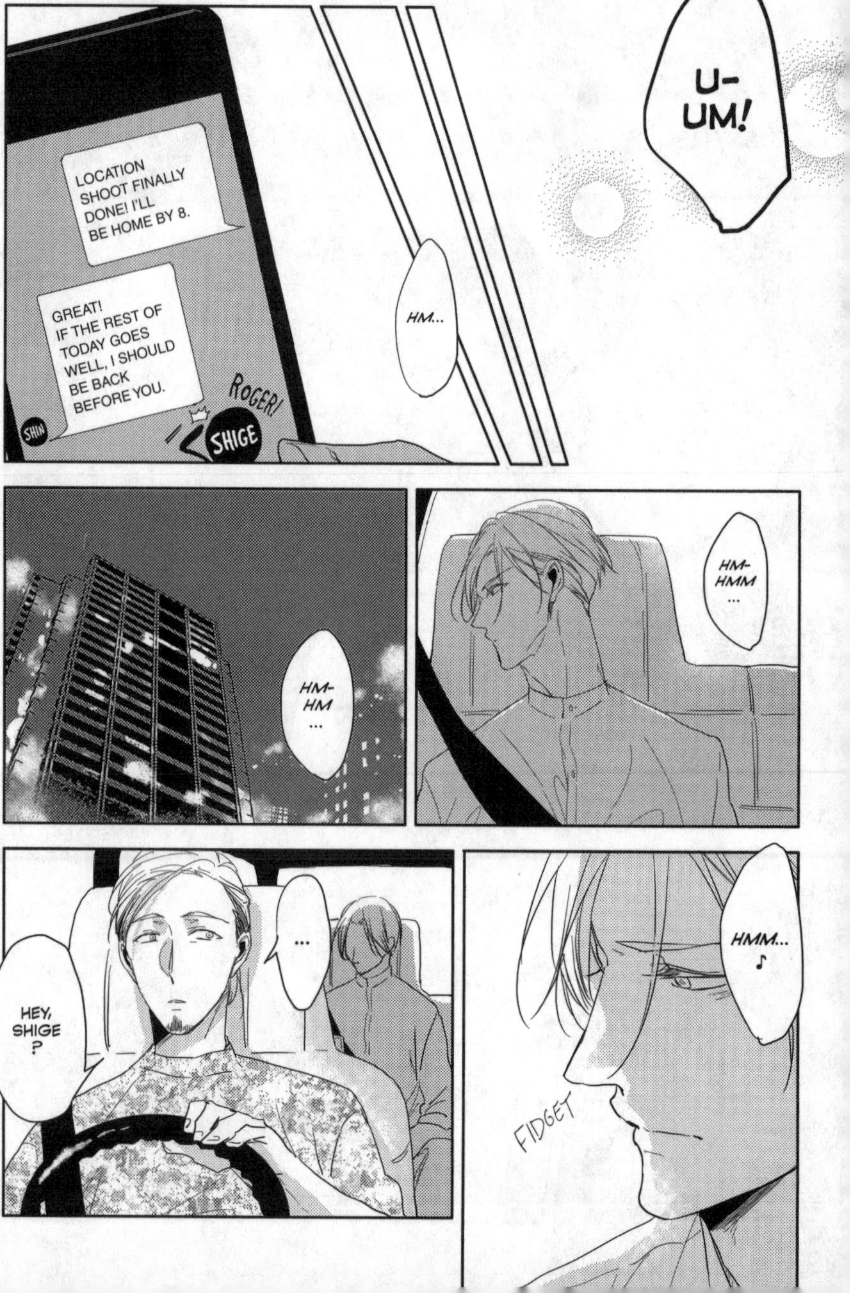
U-UM!
HM...
LOCATION SHOOT FINALLY DONE! I'LL BE HOME BY 8.
GREAT! IF THE REST OF TODAY GOES WELL, I SHOULD BE BACK BEFORE YOU.
ROGER!
SHIN
SHIGE
HM-HMM...
HM-HM...
HMM... ♪
FIDGET
...
HEY, SHIGE?

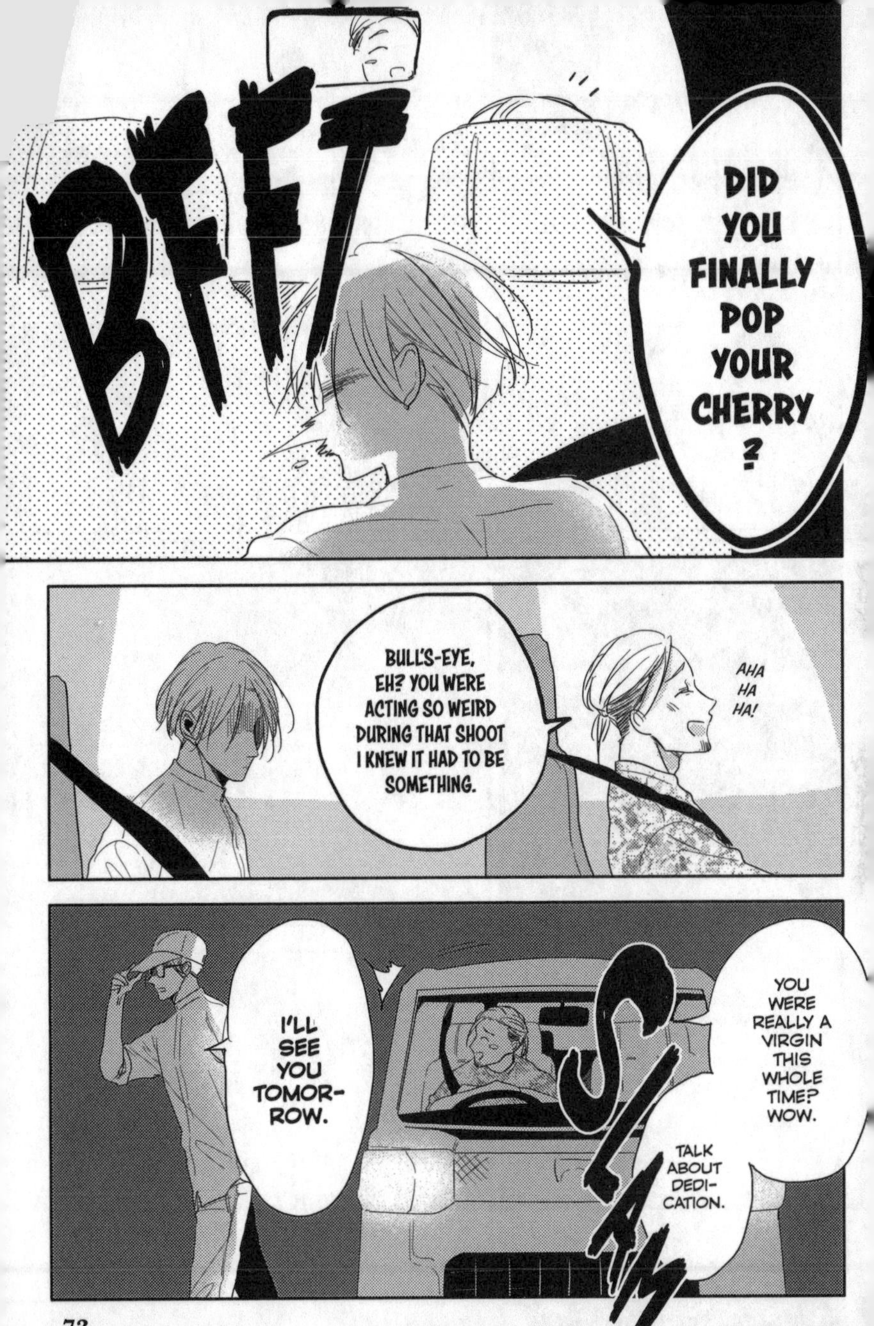
DID YOU FINALLY POP YOUR CHERRY?
BFFT
AHA HA HA!
BULL'S-EYE, EH? YOU WERE ACTING SO WEIRD DURING THAT SHOOT I KNEW IT HAD TO BE SOMETHING.
YOU WERE REALLY A VIRGIN THIS WHOLE TIME? WOW.
TALK ABOUT DEDICATION.
SLAM
I'LL SEE YOU TOMORROW.

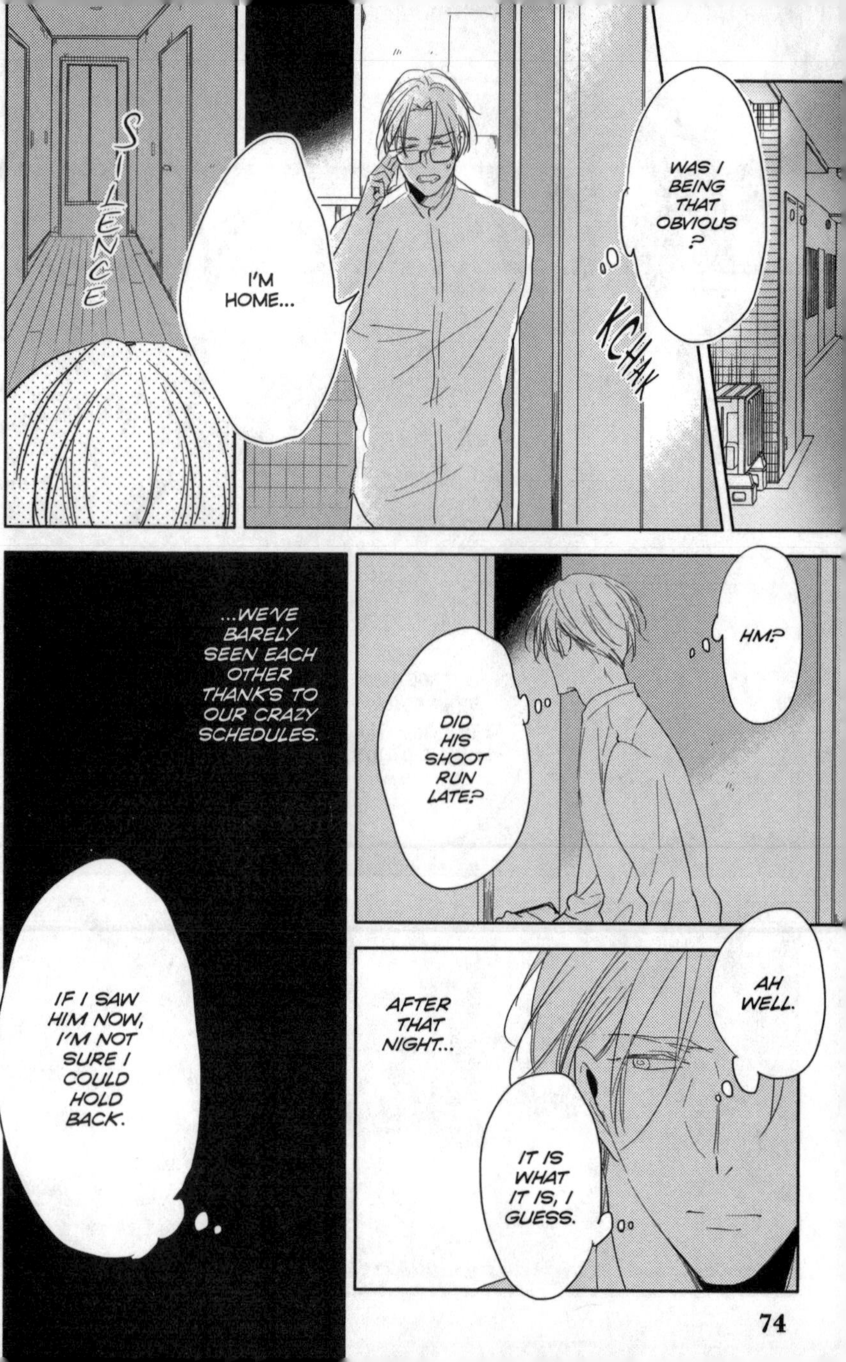
WAS I BEING THAT OBVIOUS?
KCHAK
I'M HOME...
SILENCE
HM?
DID HIS SHOOT RUN LATE?
AH WELL.
AFTER THAT NIGHT...
IT IS WHAT IT IS, I GUESS.
...WE'VE BARELY SEEN EACH OTHER THANKS TO OUR CRAZY SCHEDULES.
IF I SAW HIM NOW, I'M NOT SURE I COULD HOLD BACK.

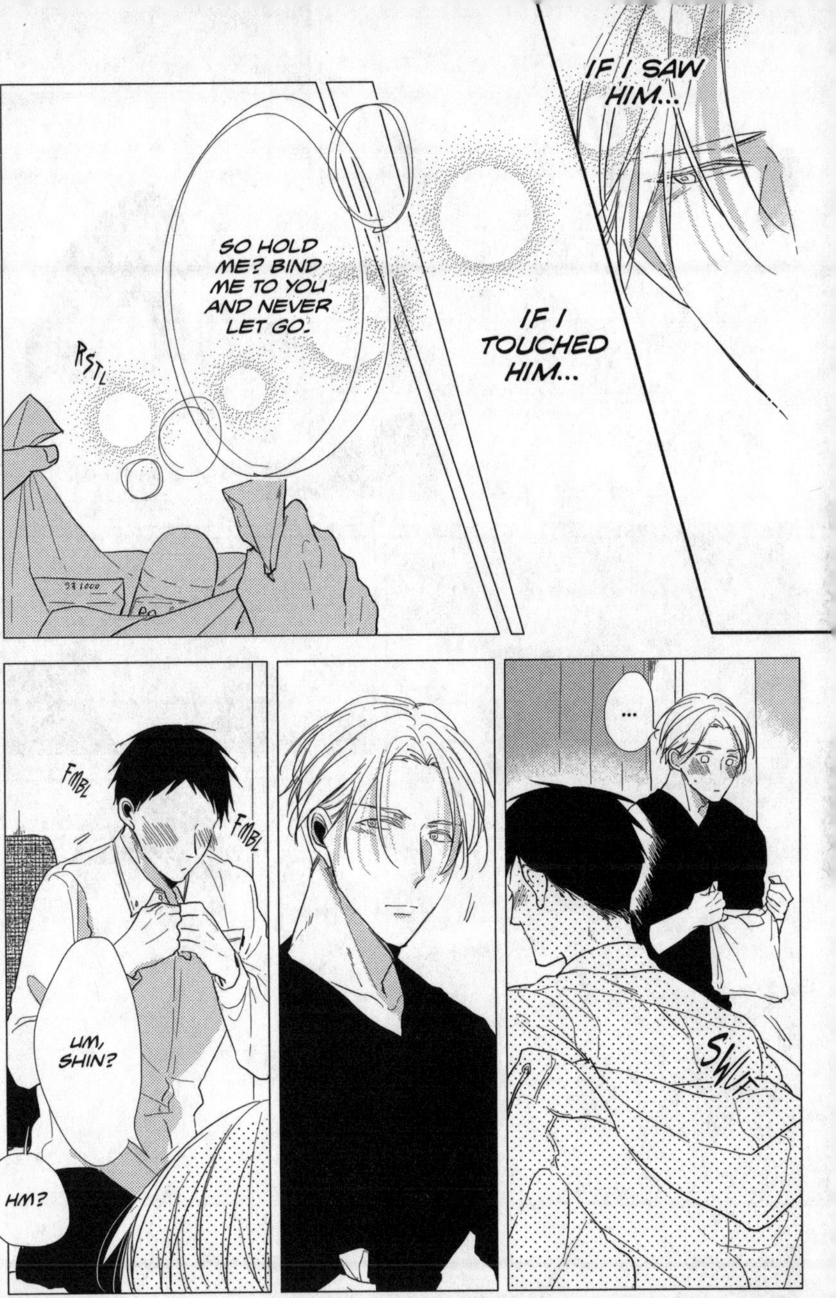
IF I SAW HIM...
IF I TOUCHED HIM...
SO HOLD ME? BIND ME TO YOU AND NEVER LET GO.
RSTL
...
SWUF
FMBL
FMBL
UM, SHIN?
HM?

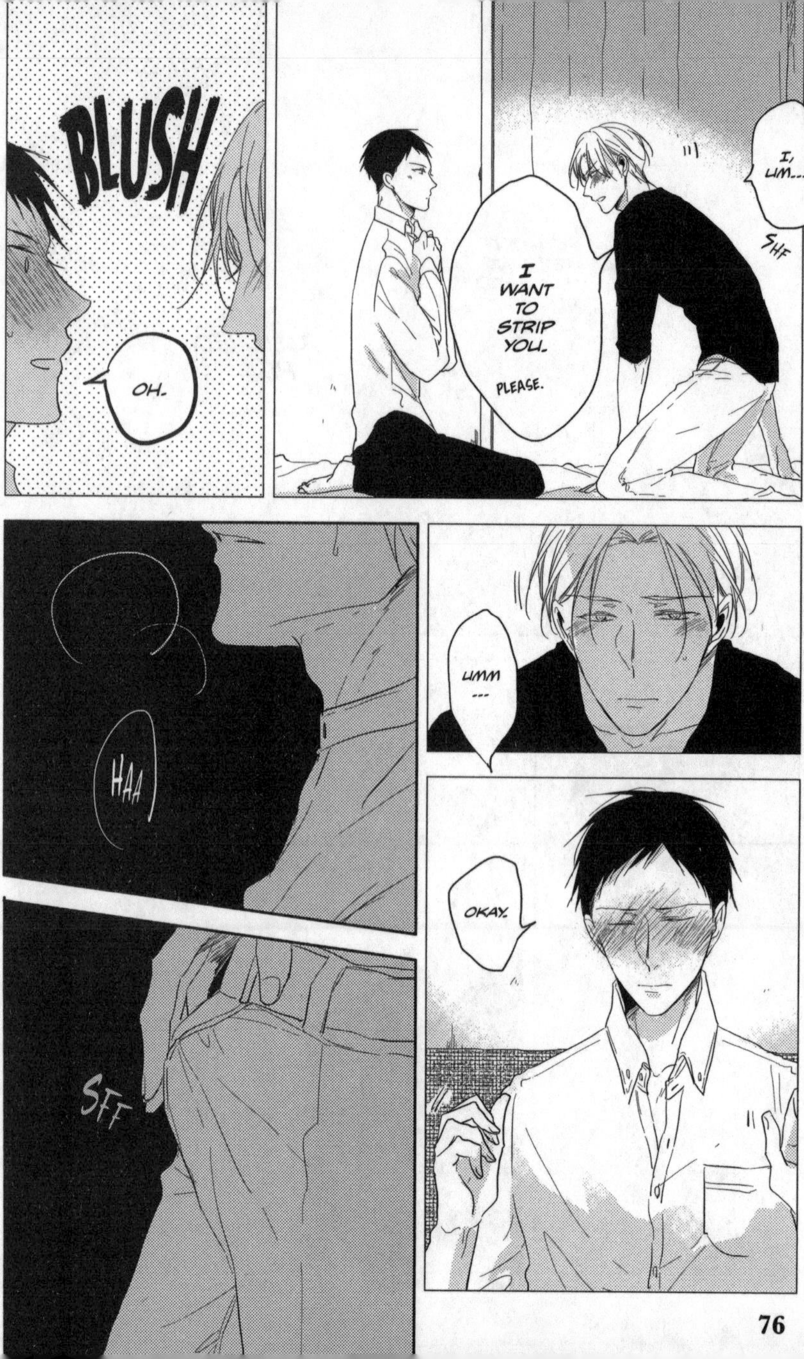
I, UM...
SHF
I WANT TO STRIP YOU.
PLEASE.
BLUSH
OH.
UMM ...
OKAY.
HAA
SFF

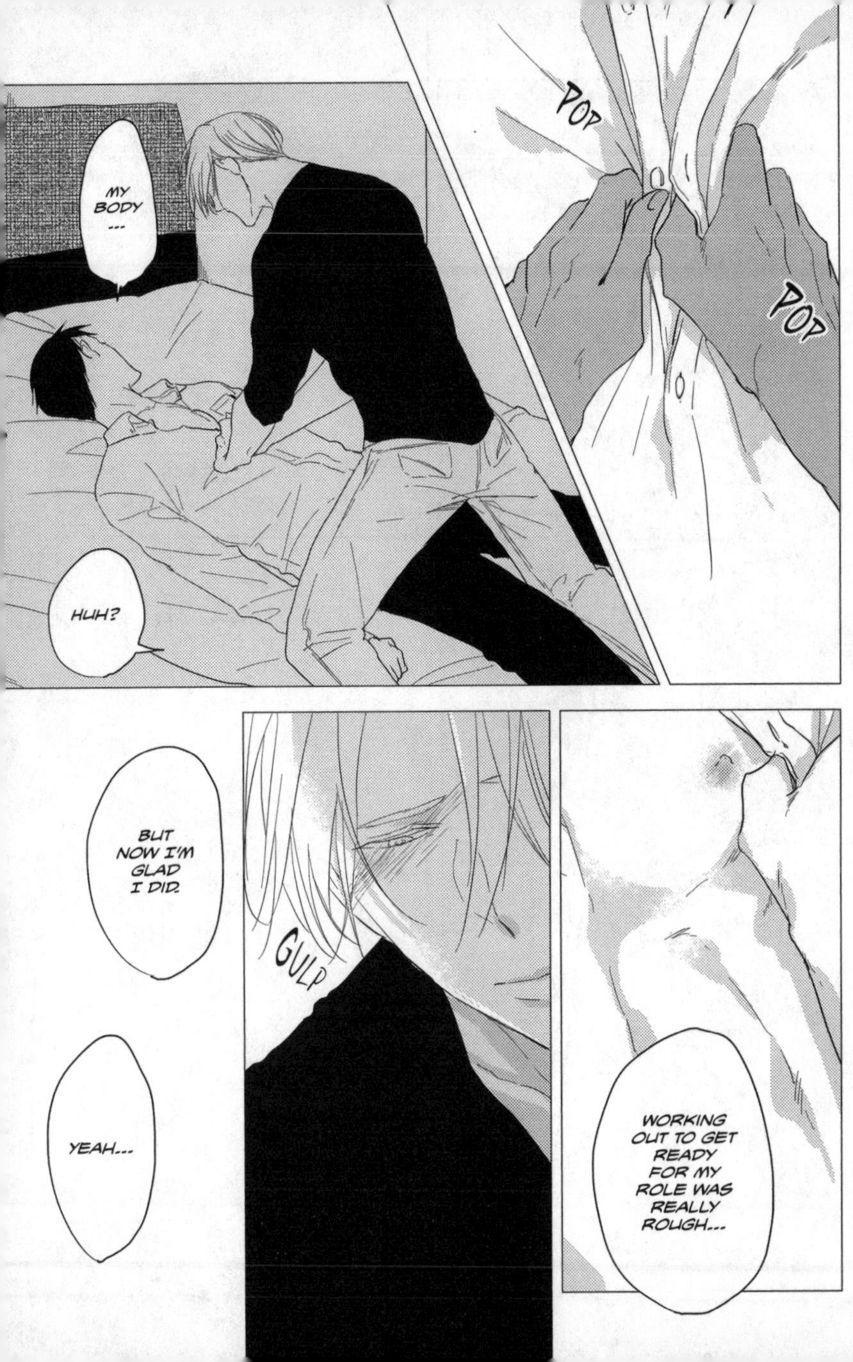
POP
POP
MY BODY ---
HUH?
WORKING OUT TO GET READY FOR MY ROLE WAS REALLY ROUGH...
GULP
BUT NOW I'M GLAD I DID.
YEAH...

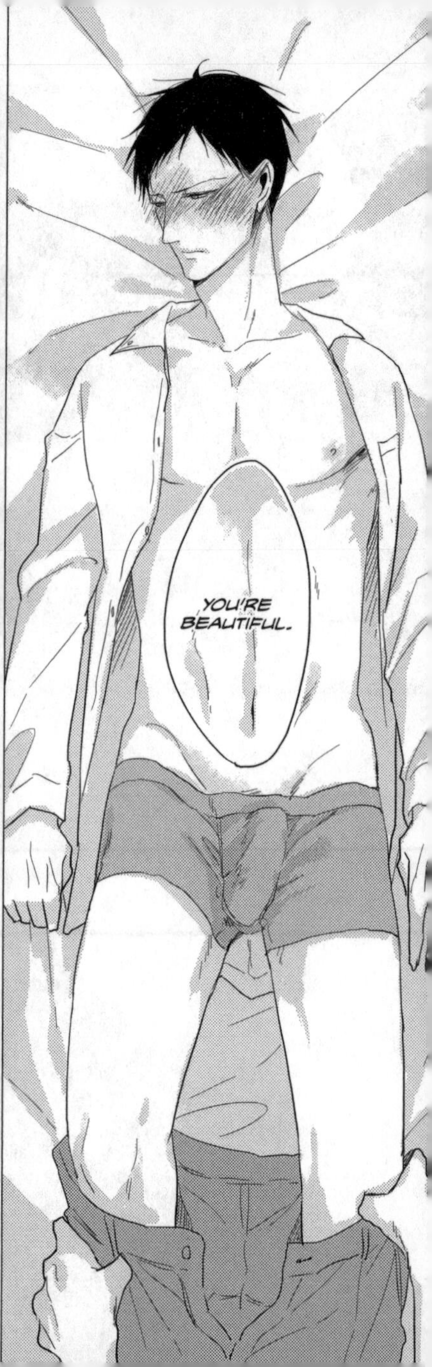
YOU'RE BEAUTIFUL.
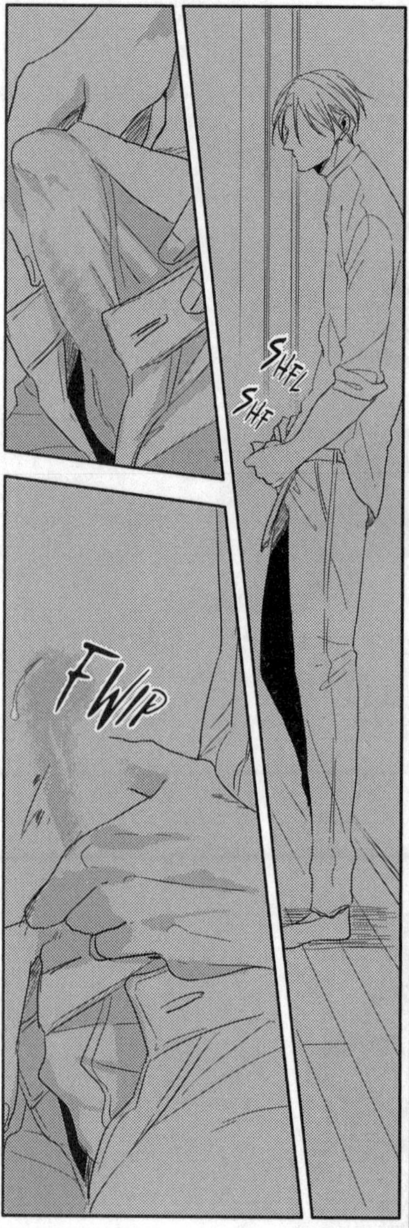
SHFL
SHF
FWIP

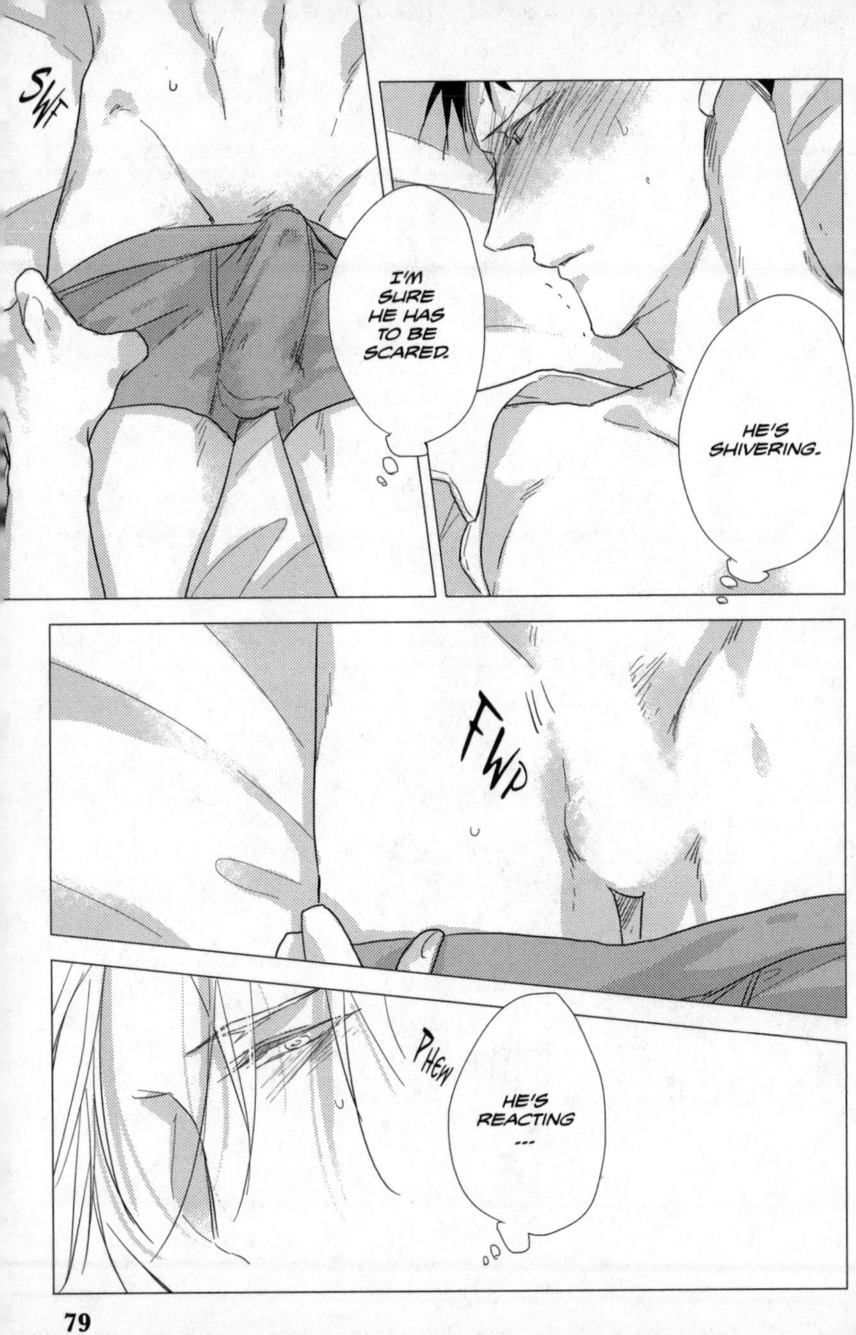
HE'S SHIVERING.
I'M SURE HE HAS TO BE SCARED.
SWF
FWP
PHEW
HE'S REACTING ...

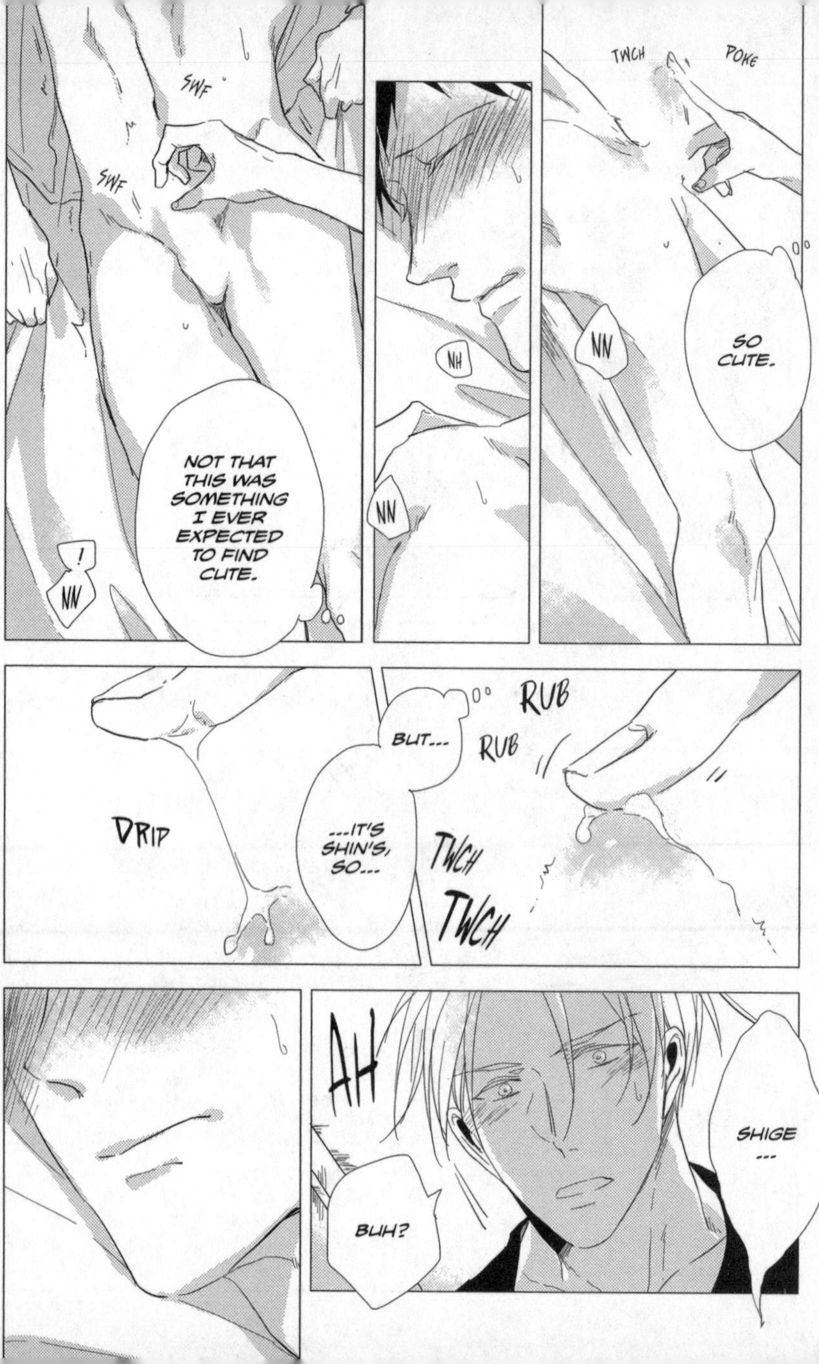
TWCH
POKE
SO CUTE.
NN
NH
NN
SWF
SWF
NOT THAT THIS WAS SOMETHING I EVER EXPECTED TO FIND CUTE.
!
NN
RUB
RUB
BUT...
...IT'S SHIN'S, SO...
TWCH
TWCH
DRIP
SHIGE...
AH
BUH?

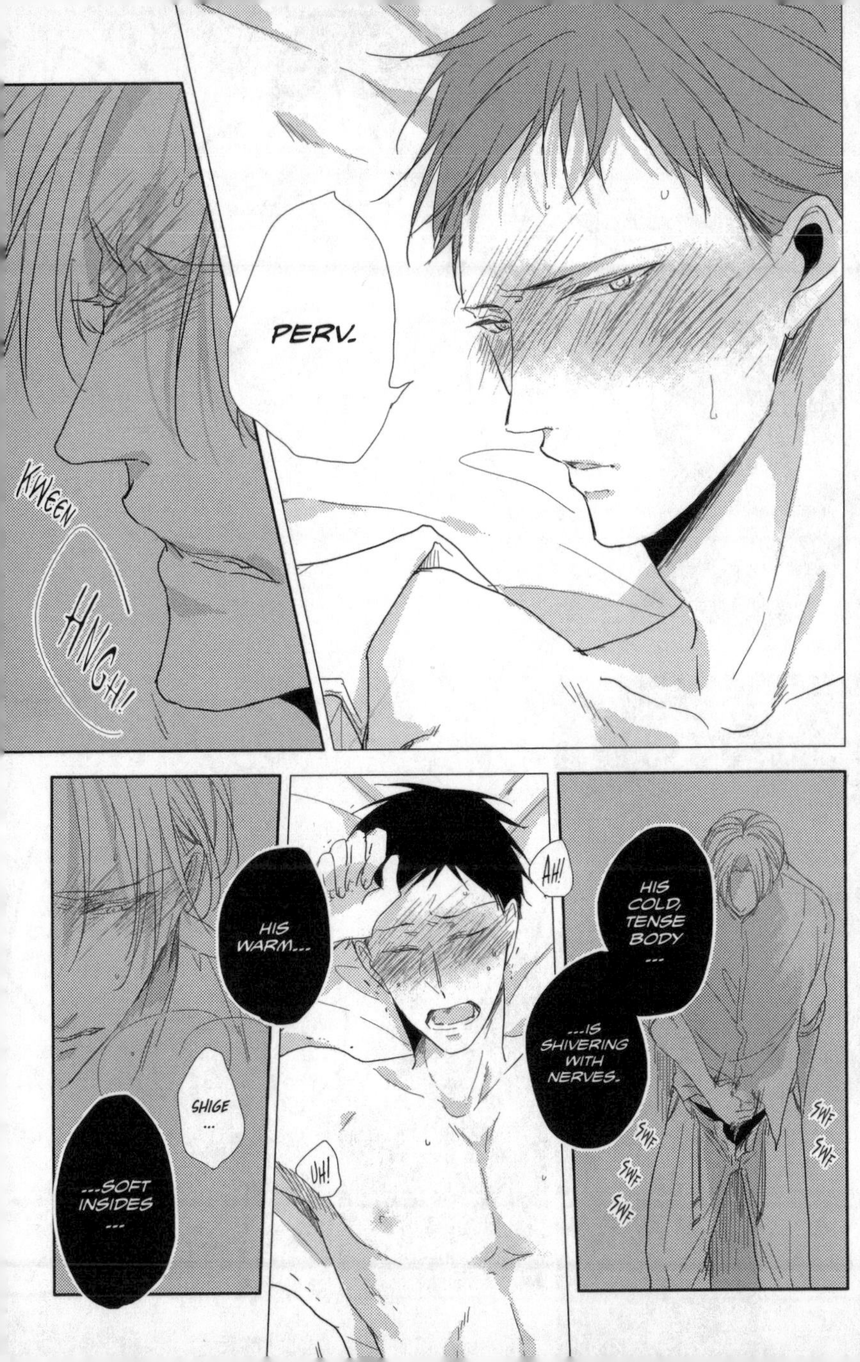
PERV.
KWEEN
HNGH!
HIS COLD, TENSE BODY...
...IS SHIVERING WITH NERVES.
SWF
SWF
SWF
SWF
SWF
AH!
HIS WARM...
UH!
SHIGE...
...SOFT INSIDES...

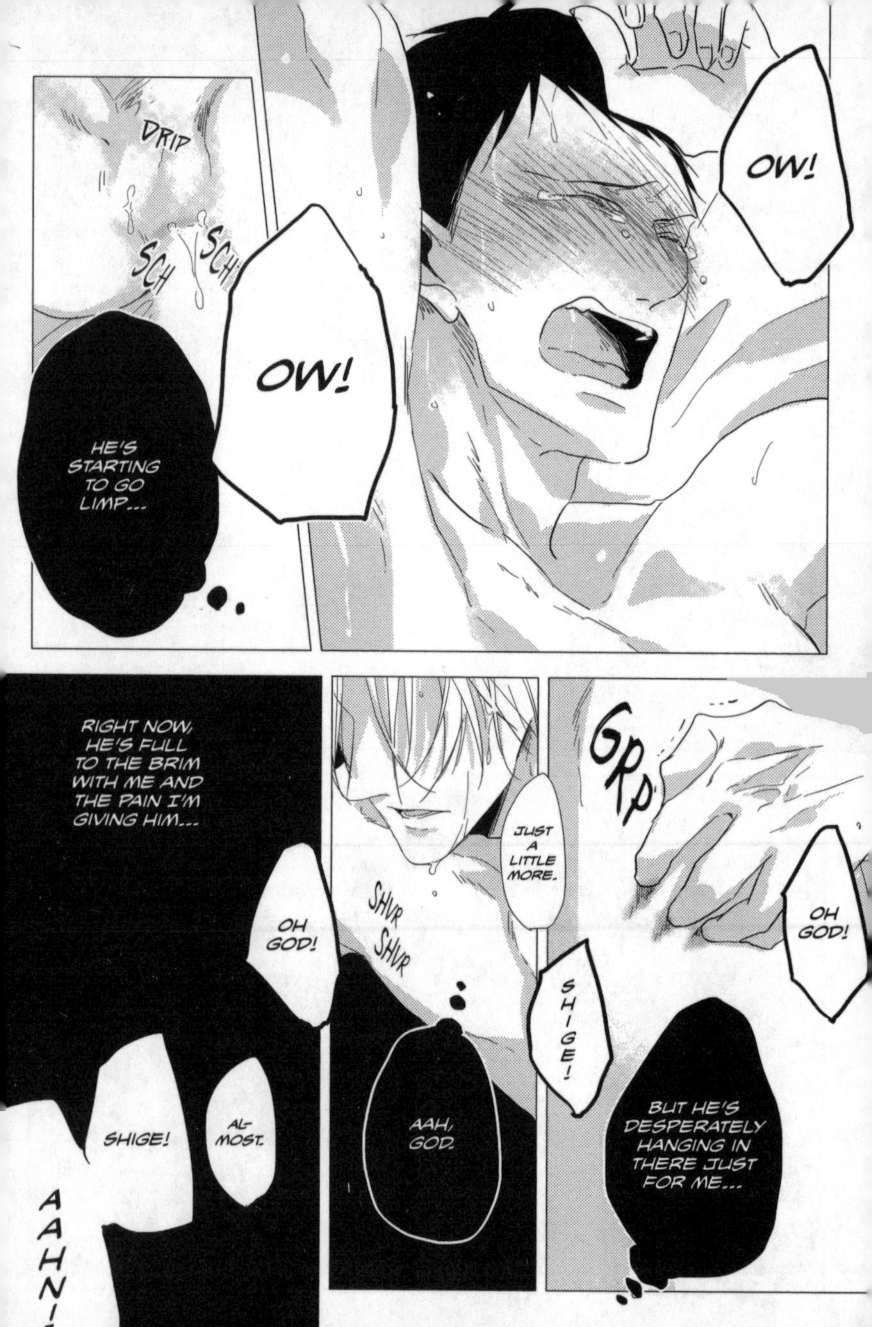

OW!
OW!
DRIP
SCH SCH
HE'S STARTING TO GO LIMP...
GRP
OH GOD!
SHIGE!
BUT HE'S DESPERATELY HANGING IN THERE JUST FOR ME...
JUST A LITTLE MORE.
SHVR SHVR
AAH, GOD.
RIGHT NOW, HE'S FULL TO THE BRIM WITH ME AND THE PAIN I'M GIVING HIM...
OH GOD!
AL-MOST.
SHIGE!
AAHN!

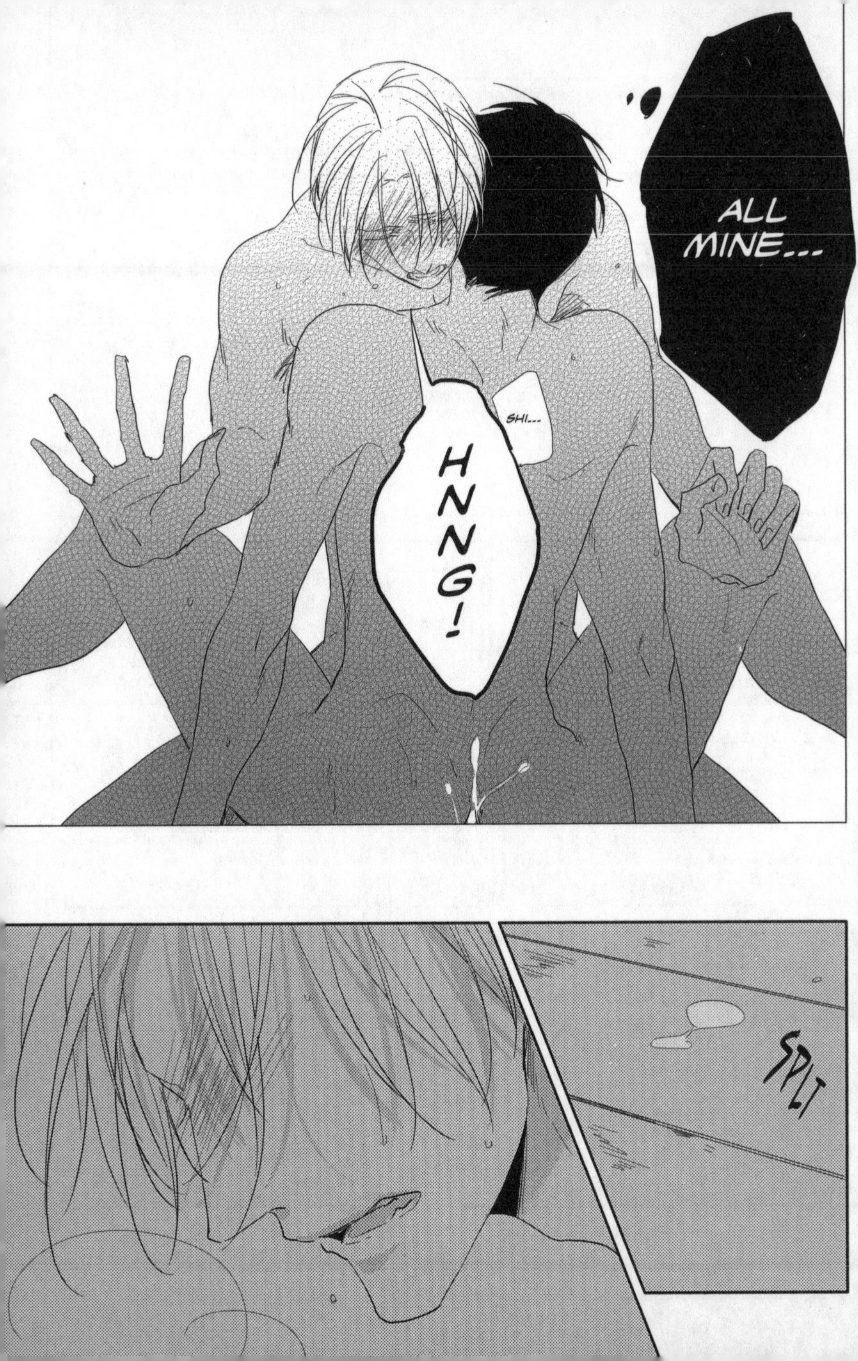
ALL MINE...
SHI...
HNNG!
SPLT

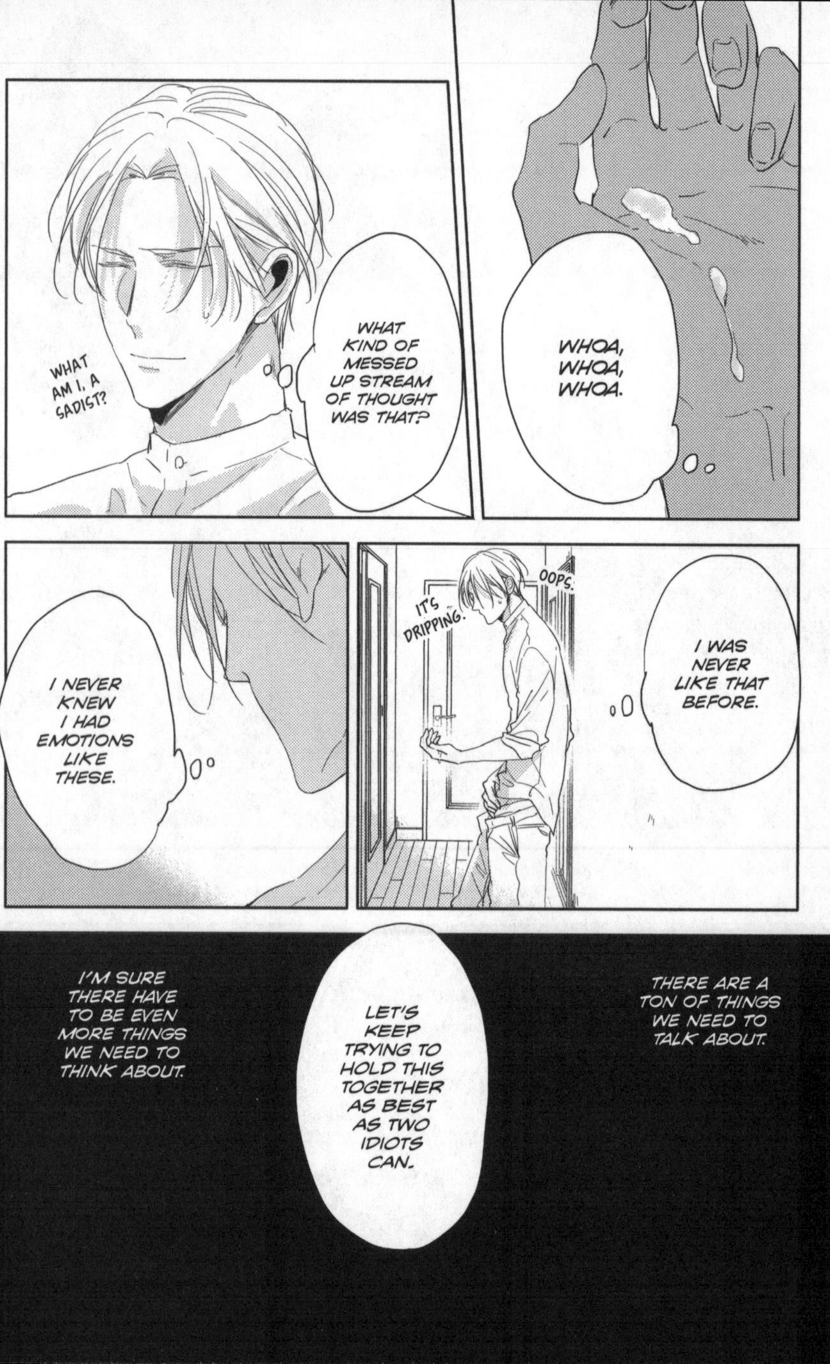
WHOA, WHOA, WHOA.
WHAT KIND OF MESSED UP STREAM OF THOUGHT WAS THAT?
WHAT AM I, A SADIST?
I WAS NEVER LIKE THAT BEFORE.
OOPS.
IT'S DRIPPING.
I NEVER KNEW I HAD EMOTIONS LIKE THESE.
THERE ARE A TON OF THINGS WE NEED TO TALK ABOUT.
LET'S KEEP TRYING TO HOLD THIS TOGETHER AS BEST AS TWO IDIOTS CAN.
I'M SURE THERE HAVE TO BE EVEN MORE THINGS WE NEED TO THINK ABOUT.

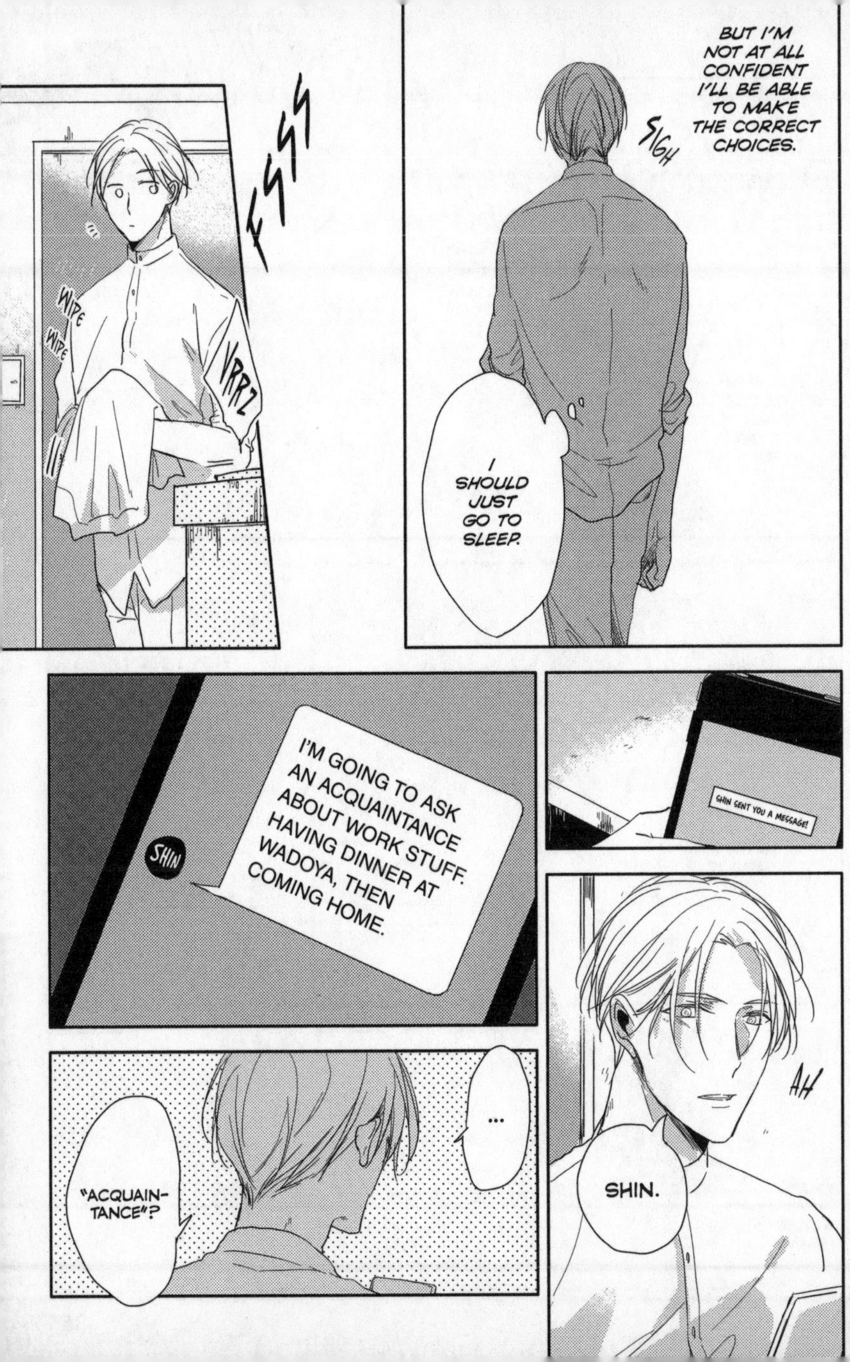
BUT I'M NOT AT ALL CONFIDENT I'LL BE ABLE TO MAKE THE CORRECT CHOICES.
SIGH
I SHOULD JUST GO TO SLEEP.
FSSS
WIPE WIPE
VRRZ
SHIN SENT YOU A MESSAGE!
AH
SHIN.
SHIN
I'M GOING TO ASK AN ACQUAINTANCE ABOUT WORK STUFF. HAVING DINNER AT WADOYA, THEN COMING HOME.
...
"ACQUAIN-TANCE"?

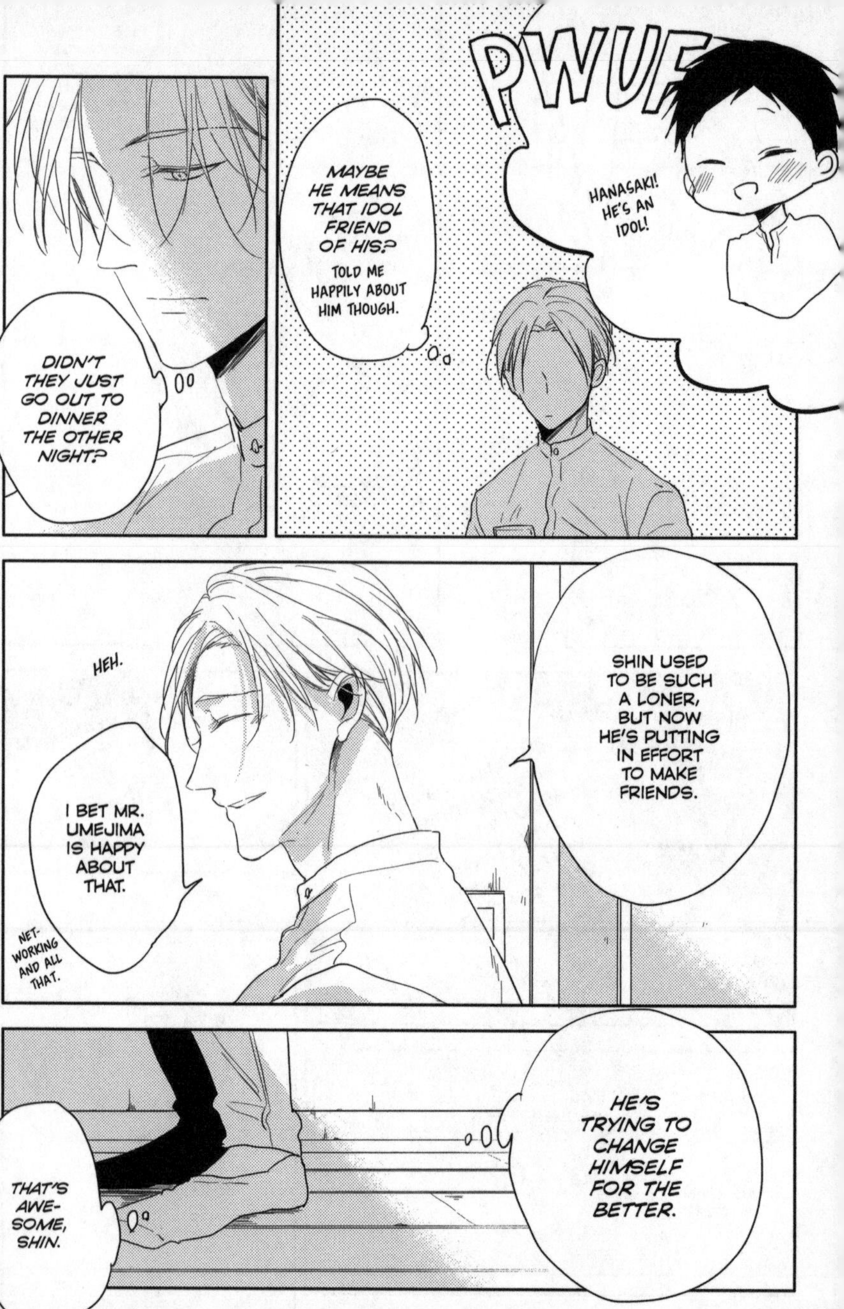
PWUF
HANASAKI! HE'S AN IDOL!
MAYBE HE MEANS THAT IDOL FRIEND OF HIS?
TOLD ME HAPPILY ABOUT HIM THOUGH.
DIDN'T THEY JUST GO OUT TO DINNER THE OTHER NIGHT?
SHIN USED TO BE SUCH A LONER, BUT NOW HE'S PUTTING IN EFFORT TO MAKE FRIENDS.
HEH.
I BET MR. UMEJIMA IS HAPPY ABOUT THAT.
NET-WORKING AND ALL THAT.
HE'S TRYING TO CHANGE HIMSELF FOR THE BETTER.
THAT'S AWE-SOME, SHIN.

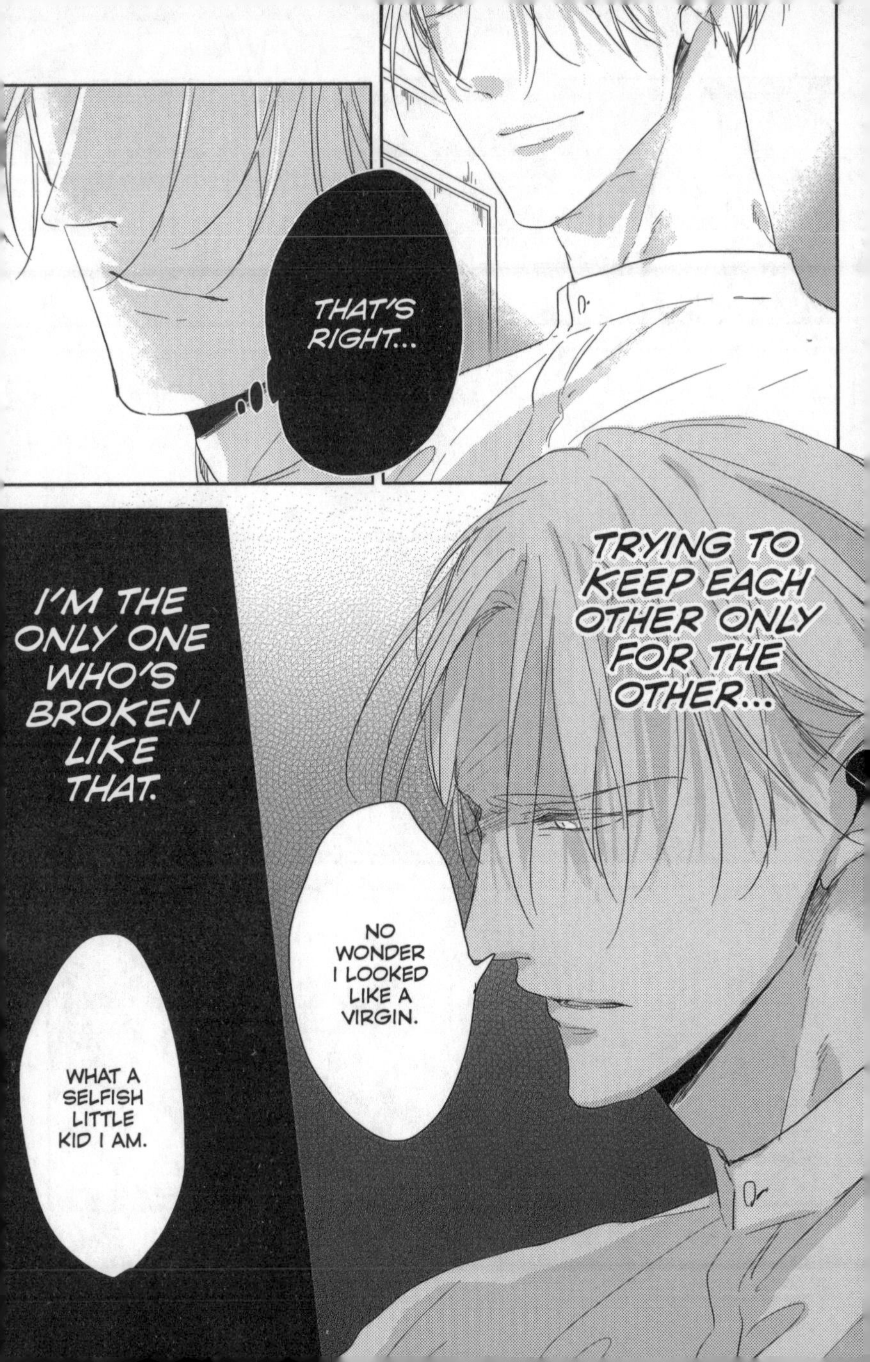
THAT'S RIGHT...
TRYING TO KEEP EACH OTHER ONLY FOR THE OTHER...
I'M THE ONLY ONE WHO'S BROKEN LIKE THAT.
NO WONDER I LOOKED LIKE A VIRGIN.
WHAT A SELFISH LITTLE KID I AM.

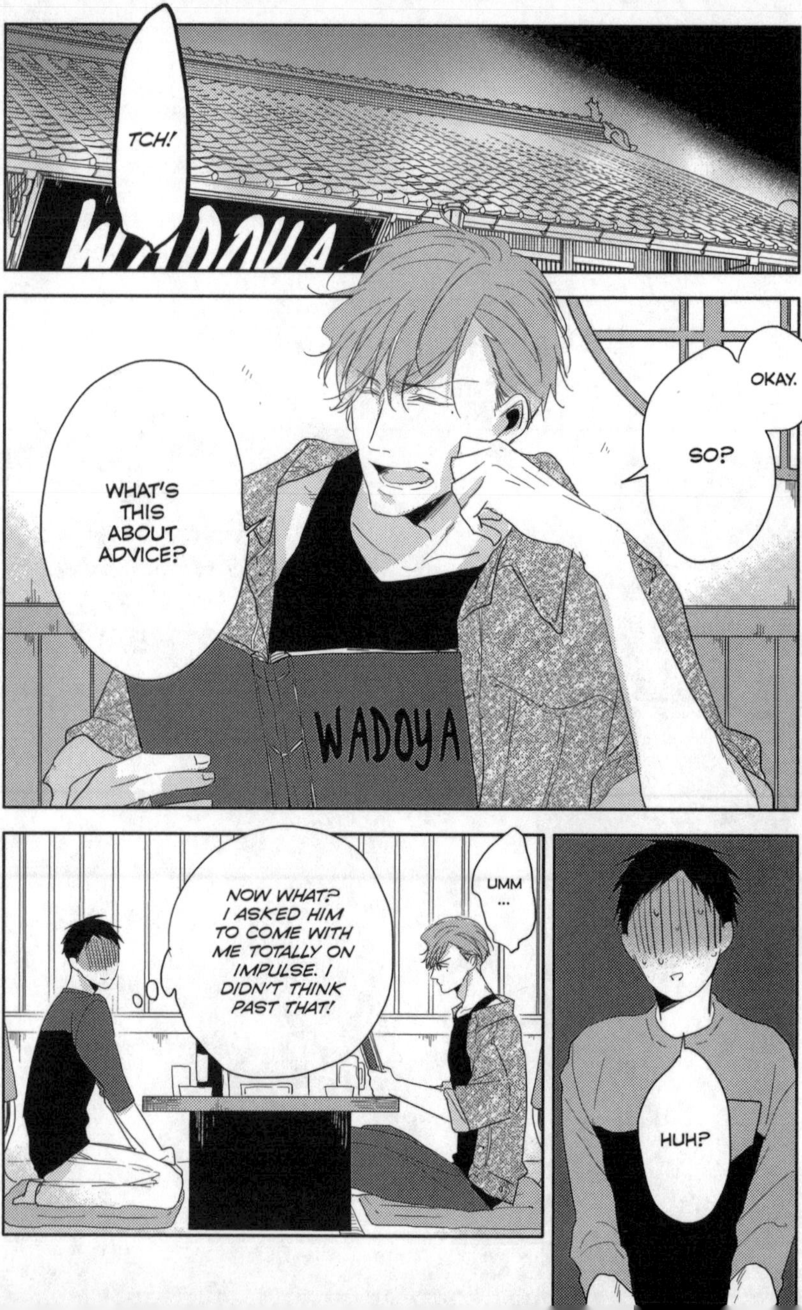
TCH!
OKAY.
SO?
WHAT'S THIS ABOUT ADVICE?
WADOYA
HUH?
UMM ...
NOW WHAT? I ASKED HIM TO COME WITH ME TOTALLY ON IMPULSE. I DIDN'T THINK PAST THAT!

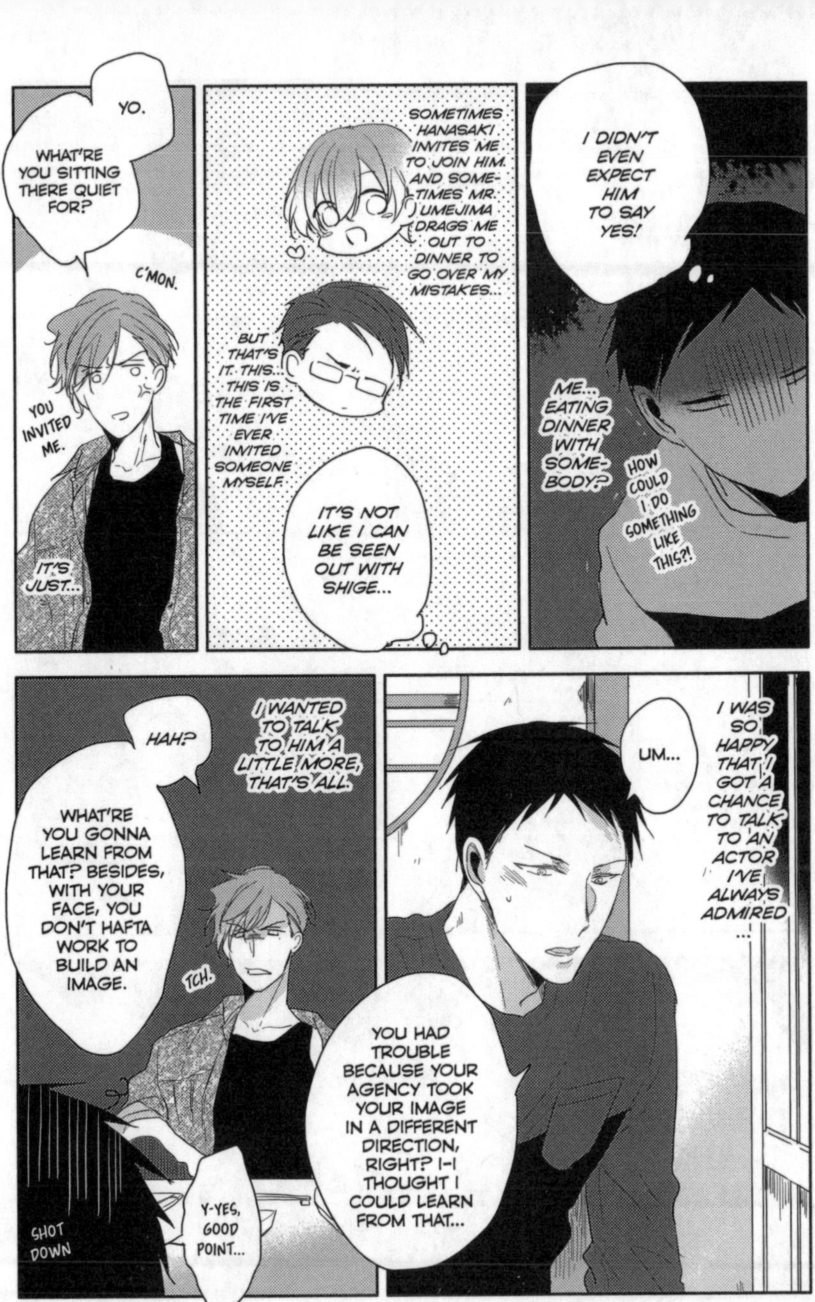
I DIDN'T EVEN EXPECT HIM TO SAY YES!
ME... EATING DINNER WITH SOME-BODY?
HOW COULD I DO SOMETHING LIKE THIS?!
SOMETIMES HANASAKI INVITES ME TO JOIN HIM. AND SOME-TIMES MR. UMEJIMA DRAGS ME OUT TO DINNER TO GO OVER MY MISTAKES...
BUT THAT'S IT. THIS... THIS IS THE FIRST TIME I'VE EVER INVITED SOMEONE MYSELF.
IT'S NOT LIKE I CAN BE SEEN OUT WITH SHIGE...
YO.
WHAT'RE YOU SITTING THERE QUIET FOR?
C'MON.
YOU INVITED ME.
IT'S JUST...
I WAS SO HAPPY THAT I GOT A CHANCE TO TALK TO AN ACTOR I'VE ALWAYS ADMIRED...
UM...
YOU HAD TROUBLE BECAUSE YOUR AGENCY TOOK YOUR IMAGE IN A DIFFERENT DIRECTION, RIGHT? I-I THOUGHT I COULD LEARN FROM THAT...
I WANTED TO TALK TO HIM A LITTLE MORE, THAT'S ALL.
HAH?
WHAT'RE YOU GONNA LEARN FROM THAT? BESIDES, WITH YOUR FACE, YOU DON'T HAFTA WORK TO BUILD AN IMAGE.
TCH.
Y-YES, GOOD POINT...
SHOT DOWN

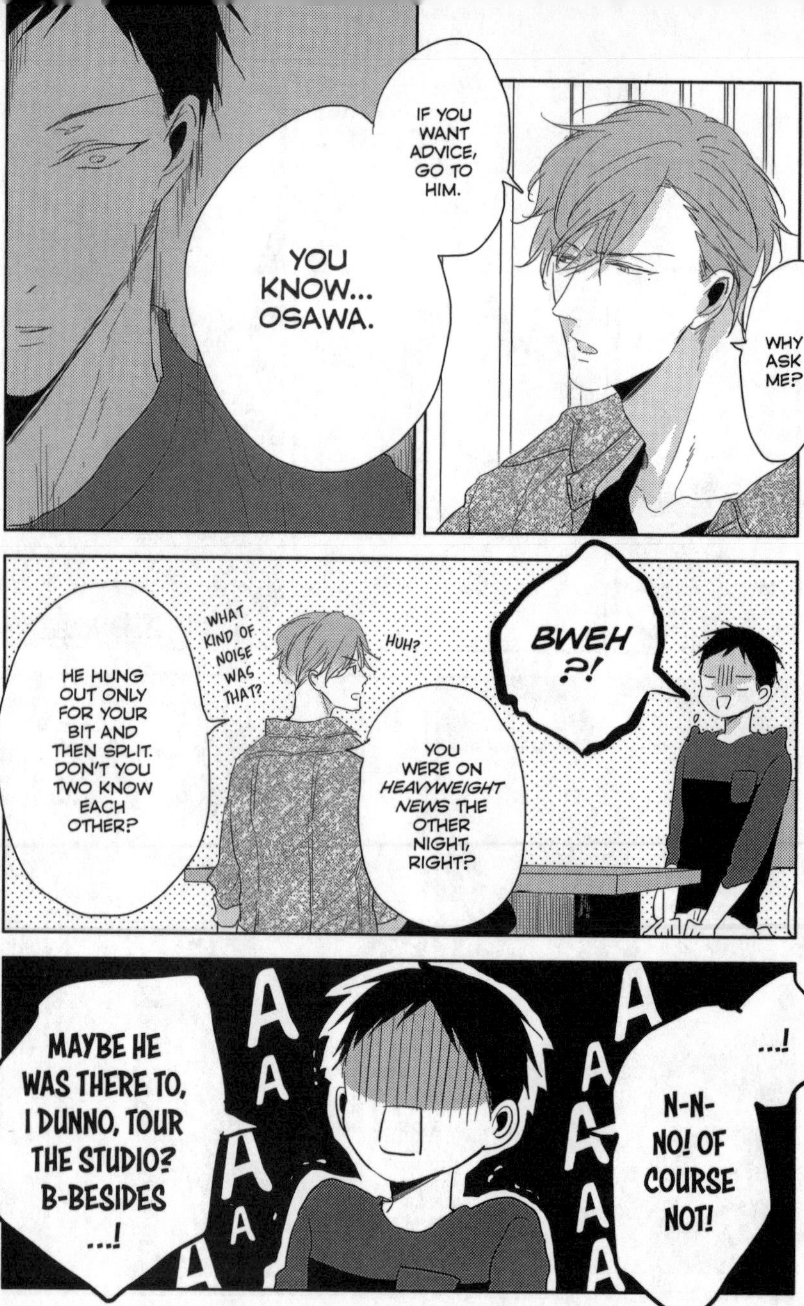
WHY ASK ME?
IF YOU WANT ADVICE, GO TO HIM.
YOU KNOW... OSAWA.
BWEH ?!
HUH?
WHAT KIND OF NOISE WAS THAT?
YOU WERE ON HEAVYWEIGHT NEWS THE OTHER NIGHT, RIGHT?
HE HUNG OUT ONLY FOR YOUR BIT AND THEN SPLIT. DON'T YOU TWO KNOW EACH OTHER?
...! N-N-NO! OF COURSE NOT!
AAAAAAAAAAA
MAYBE HE WAS THERE TO, I DUNNO, TOUR THE STUDIO? B-BESIDES ...!

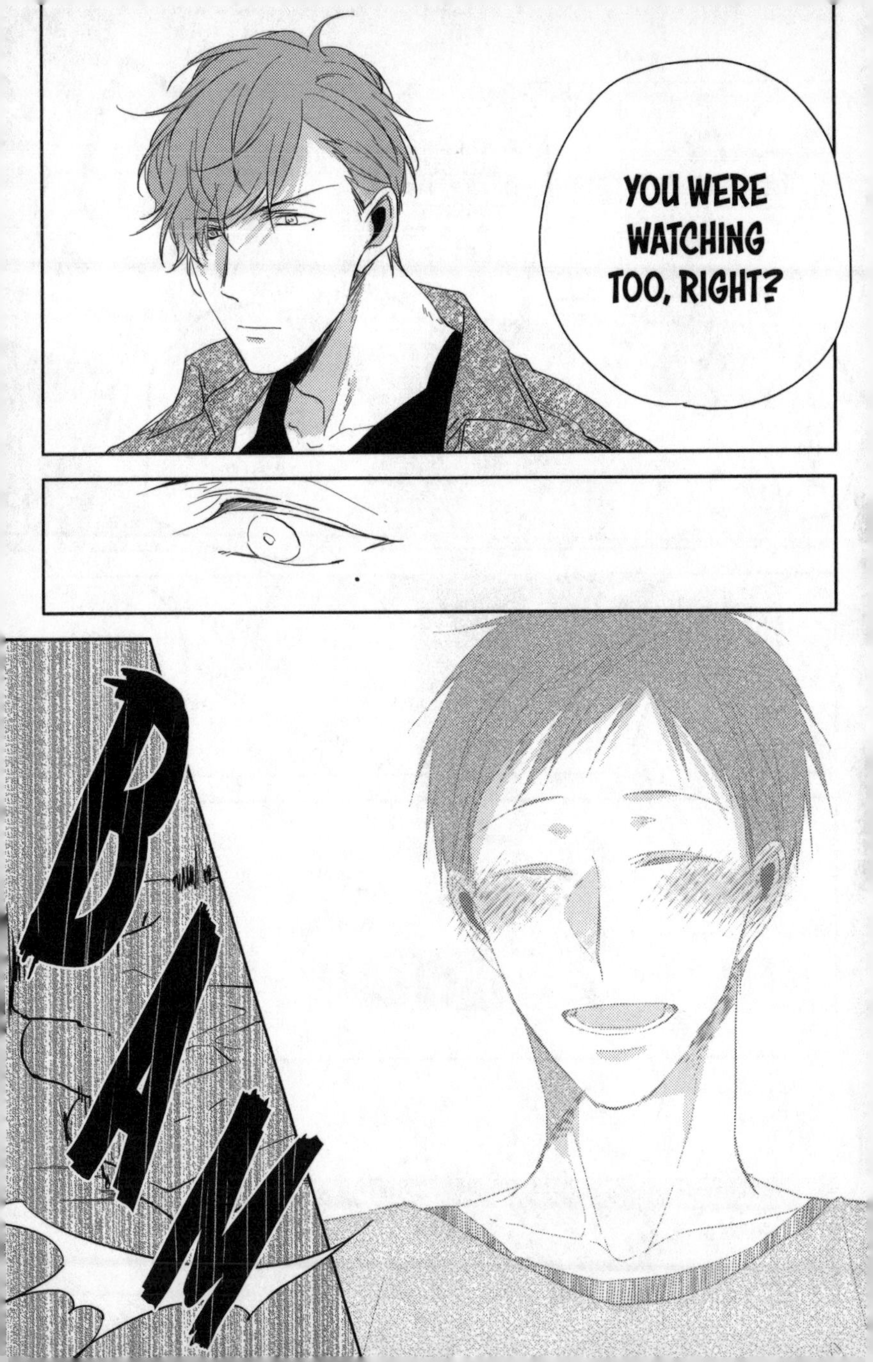
YOU WERE WATCHING TOO, RIGHT?
BAM

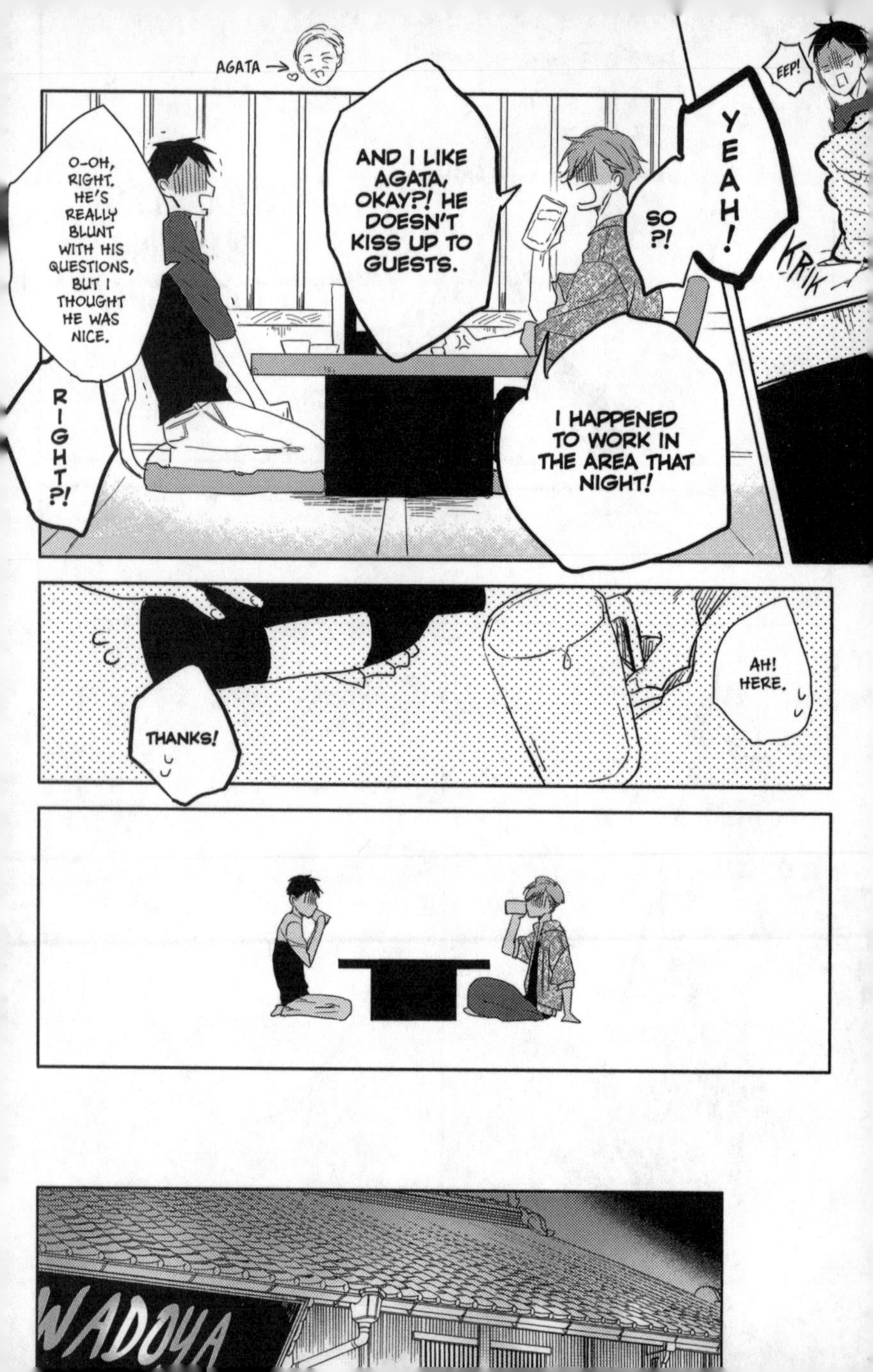
AGATA
EEP!
YEAH!
SO ?!
KRIK
AND I LIKE AGATA, OKAY?! HE DOESN'T KISS UP TO GUESTS.
I HAPPENED TO WORK IN THE AREA THAT NIGHT!
O-OH, RIGHT. HE'S REALLY BLUNT WITH HIS QUESTIONS, BUT I THOUGHT HE WAS NICE.
RIGHT?!
AH! HERE.
THANKS!
WADOYA

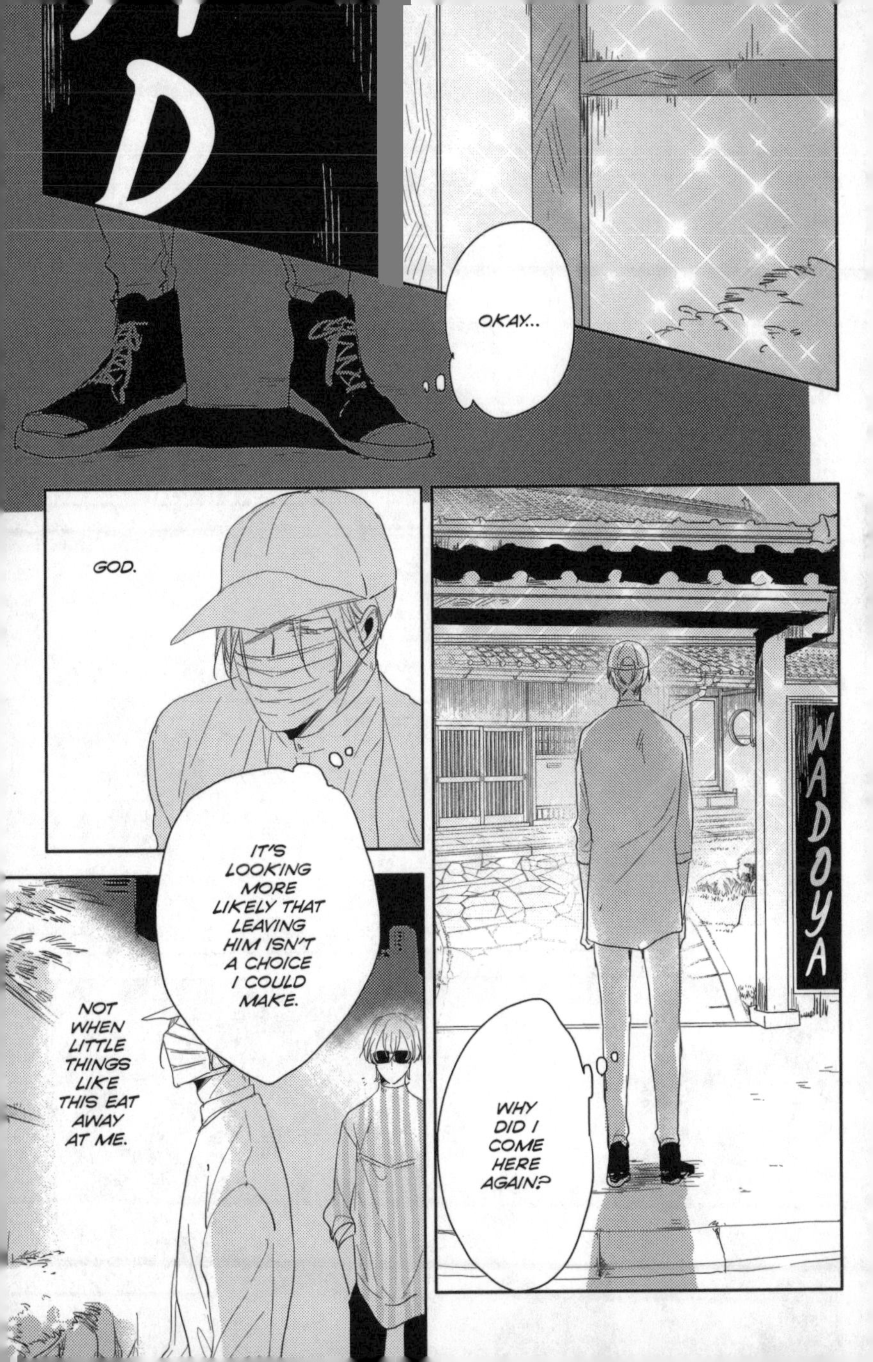
OKAY...
D
WADOYA
WHY DID I COME HERE AGAIN?
GOD.
IT'S LOOKING MORE LIKELY THAT LEAVING HIM ISN'T A CHOICE I COULD MAKE.
NOT WHEN LITTLE THINGS LIKE THIS EAT AWAY AT ME.

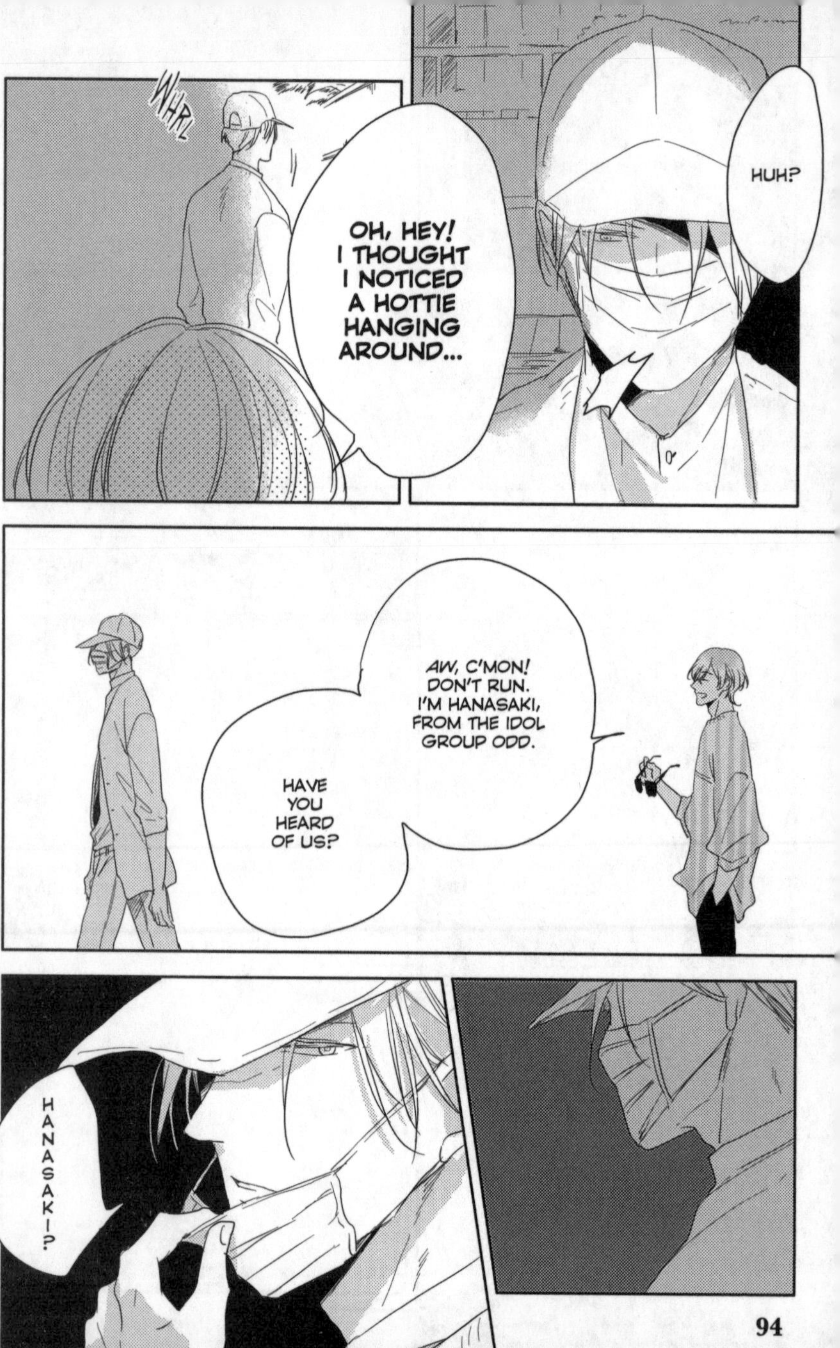
HUH?
WHRL
OH, HEY! I THOUGHT I NOTICED A HOTTIE HANGING AROUND...
AW, C'MON! DON'T RUN. I'M HANASAKI, FROM THE IDOL GROUP ODD.
HAVE YOU HEARD OF US?
HANASAKI?

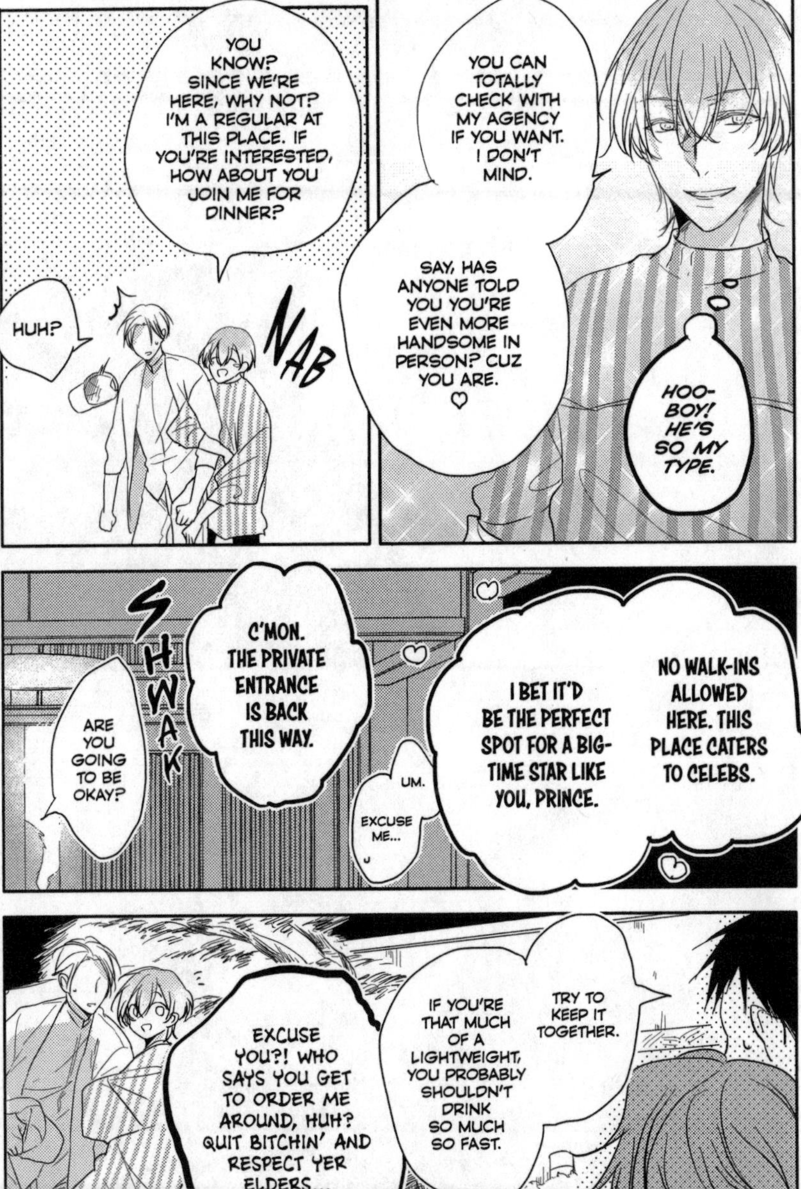
YOU CAN TOTALLY CHECK WITH MY AGENCY IF YOU WANT. I DON'T MIND.
SAY, HAS ANYONE TOLD YOU YOU'RE EVEN MORE HANDSOME IN PERSON? CUZ YOU ARE. ♡
HOO-BOY! HE'S SO MY TYPE.
YOU KNOW? SINCE WE'RE HERE, WHY NOT? I'M A REGULAR AT THIS PLACE. IF YOU'RE INTERESTED, HOW ABOUT YOU JOIN ME FOR DINNER?
NAB
HUH?
NO WALK-INS ALLOWED HERE. THIS PLACE CATERS TO CELEBS.
I BET IT'D BE THE PERFECT SPOT FOR A BIG-TIME STAR LIKE YOU, PRINCE.
UM.
EXCUSE ME...
C'MON. THE PRIVATE ENTRANCE IS BACK THIS WAY.
SHWAK
ARE YOU GOING TO BE OKAY?
TRY TO KEEP IT TOGETHER.
IF YOU'RE THAT MUCH OF A LIGHTWEIGHT, YOU PROBABLY SHOULDN'T DRINK SO MUCH SO FAST.
EXCUSE YOU?! WHO SAYS YOU GET TO ORDER ME AROUND, HUH? QUIT BITCHIN' AND RESPECT YER ELDERS...

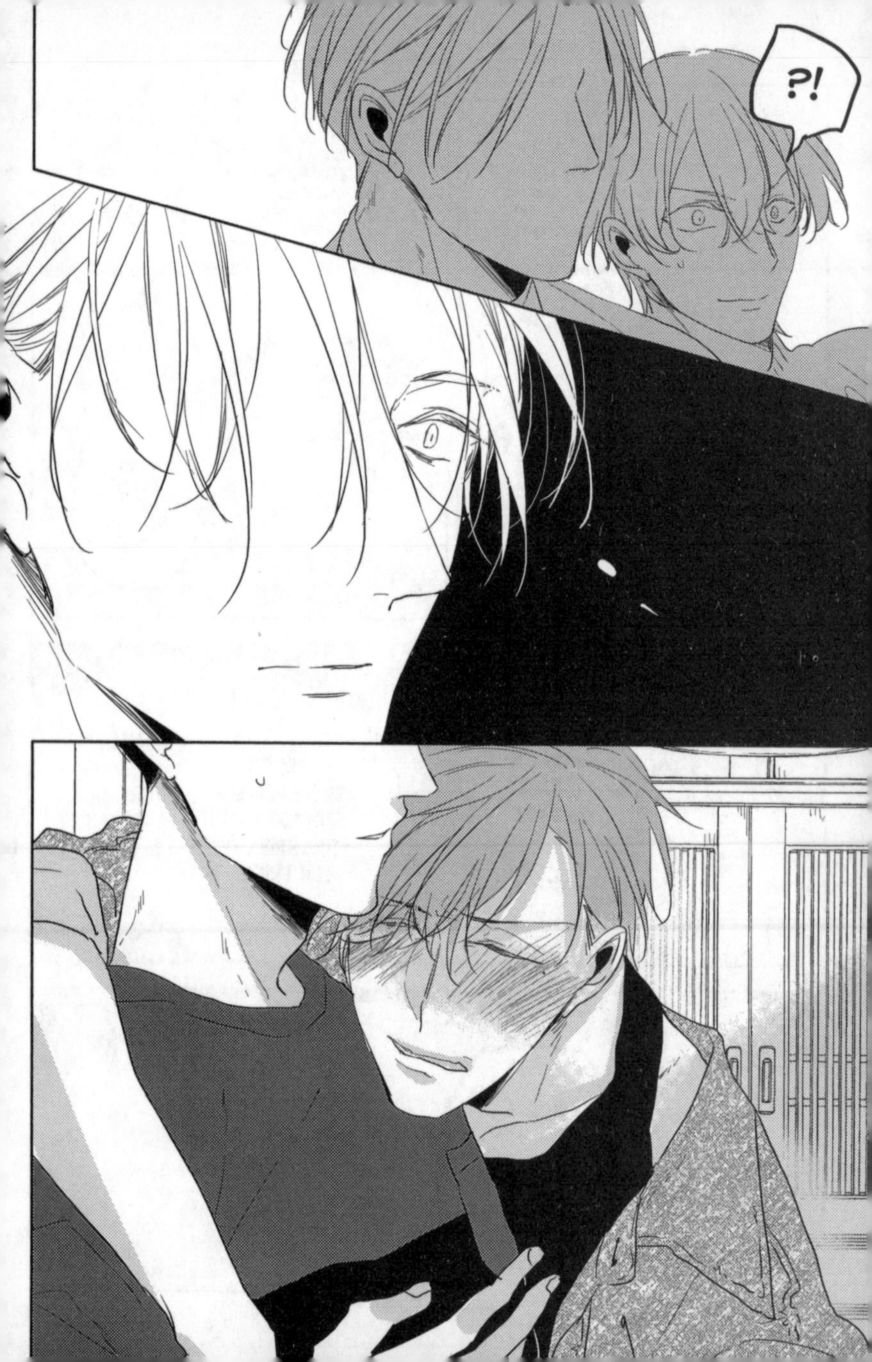
?!

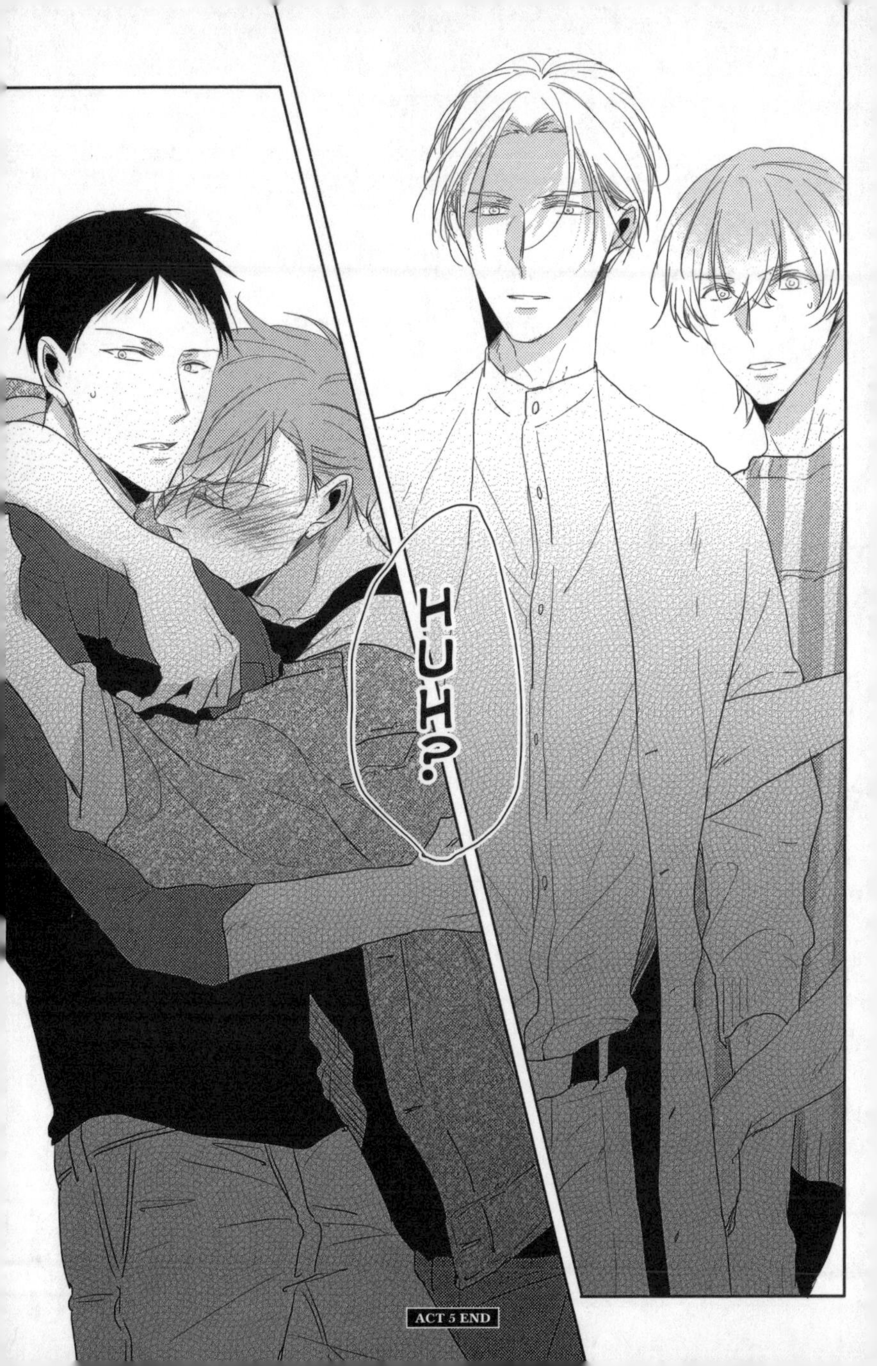
HUH?
ACT 5 END

Black
or White

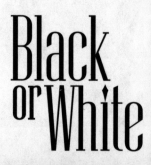

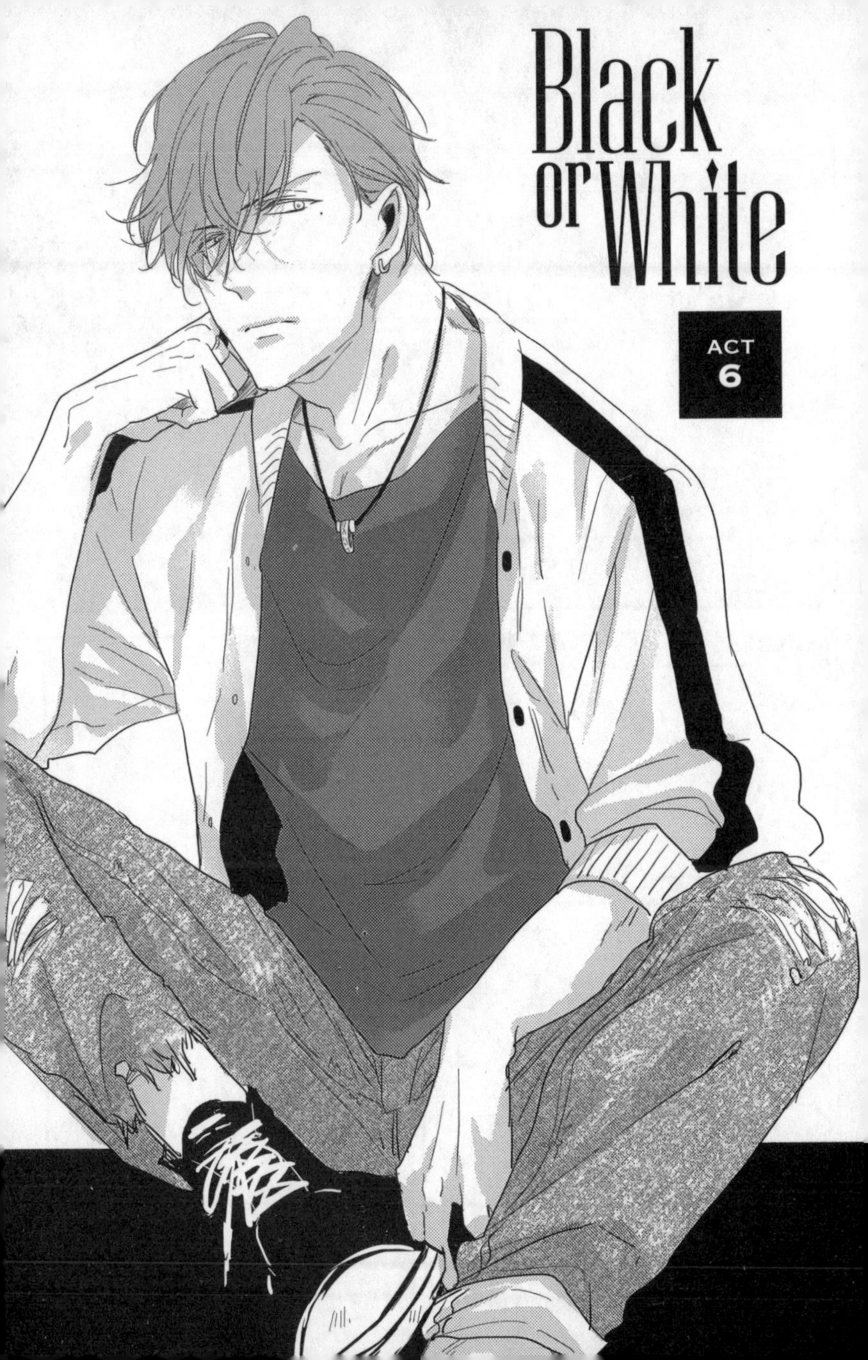
Black or White
ACT
6

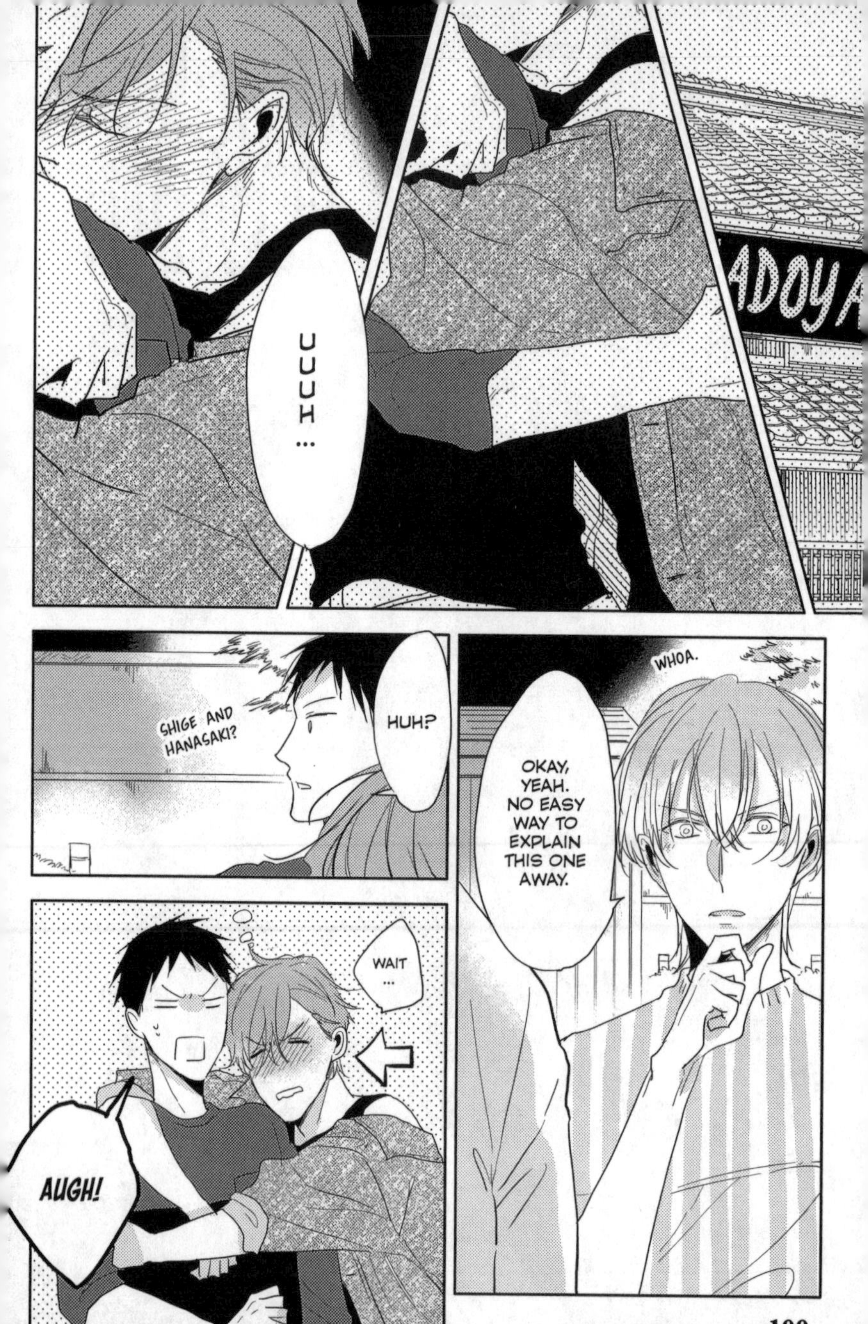
ADOYA
UUUH...
WHOA.
OKAY, YEAH. NO EASY WAY TO EXPLAIN THIS ONE AWAY.
HUH?
SHIGE AND HANASAKI?
WAIT...
AUGH!

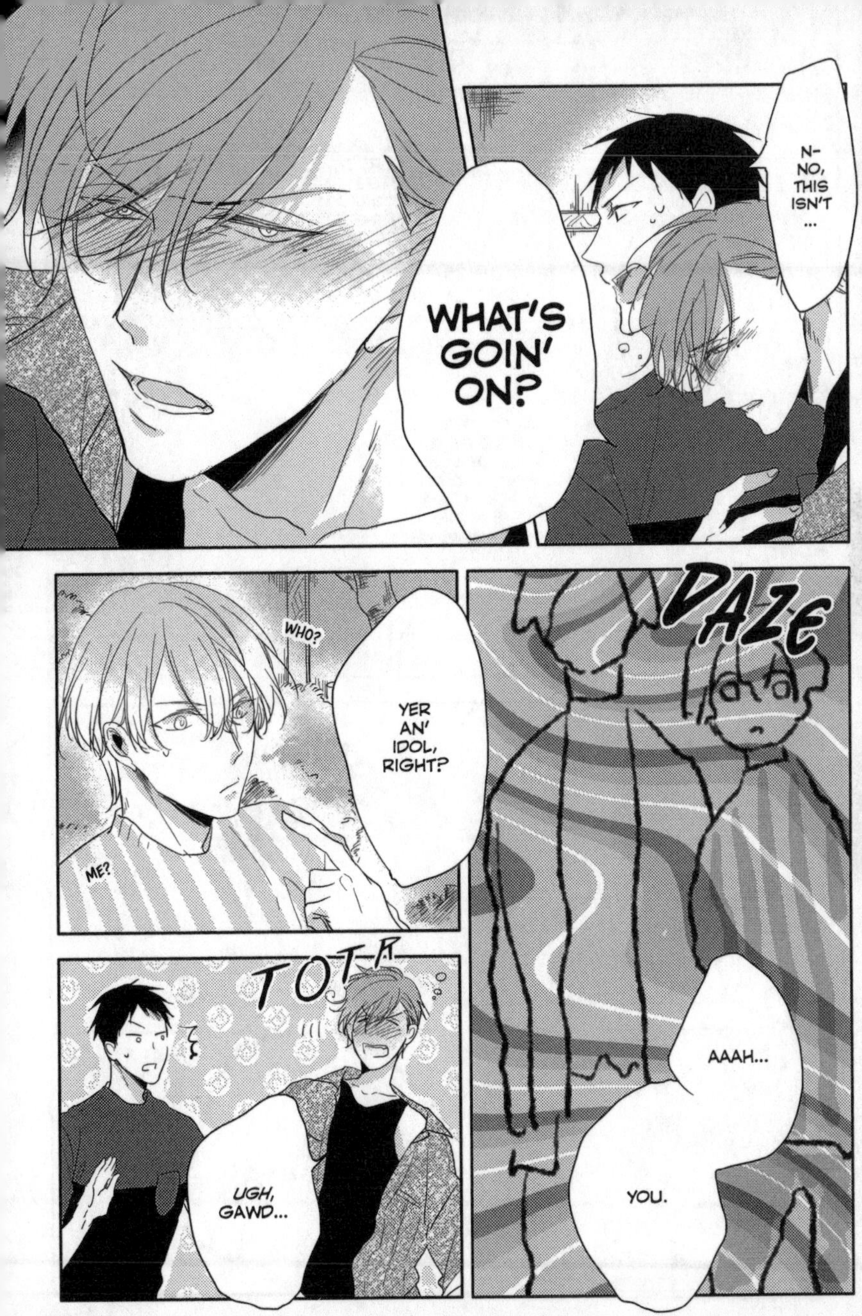
N-NO, THIS ISN'T ...
WHAT'S GOIN' ON?
DAZE
AAAH...
YOU.
YER AN' IDOL, RIGHT?
WHO?
ME?
TOTTR
UGH, GAWD...

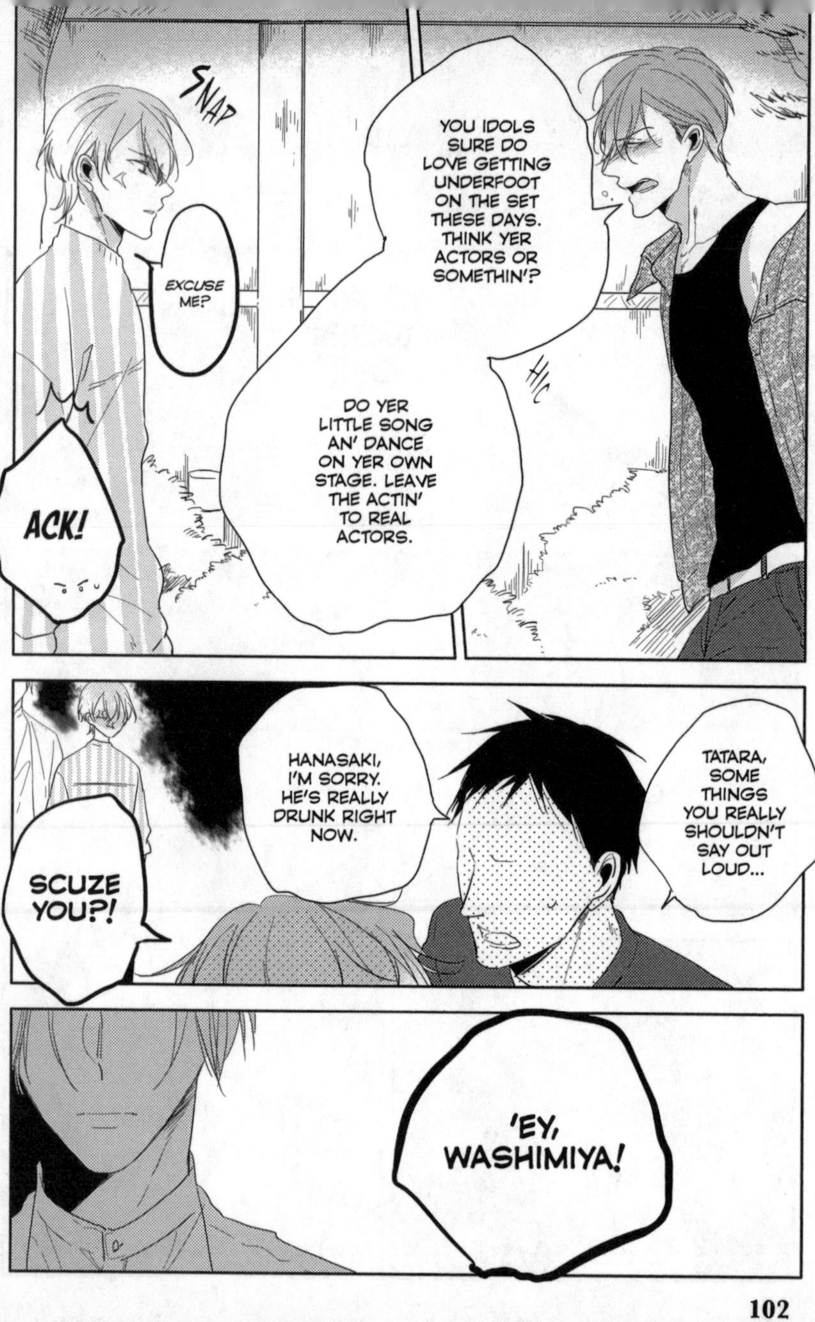
YOU IDOLS SURE DO LOVE GETTING UNDERFOOT ON THE SET THESE DAYS. THINK YER ACTORS OR SOMETHIN'?
HIC
DO YER LITTLE SONG AN' DANCE ON YER OWN STAGE. LEAVE THE ACTIN' TO REAL ACTORS.
SNAP
EXCUSE ME?
ACK!
TATARA, SOME THINGS YOU REALLY SHOULDN'T SAY OUT LOUD...
HANASAKI, I'M SORRY. HE'S REALLY DRUNK RIGHT NOW.
SCUZE YOU?!
'EY, WASHIMIYA!

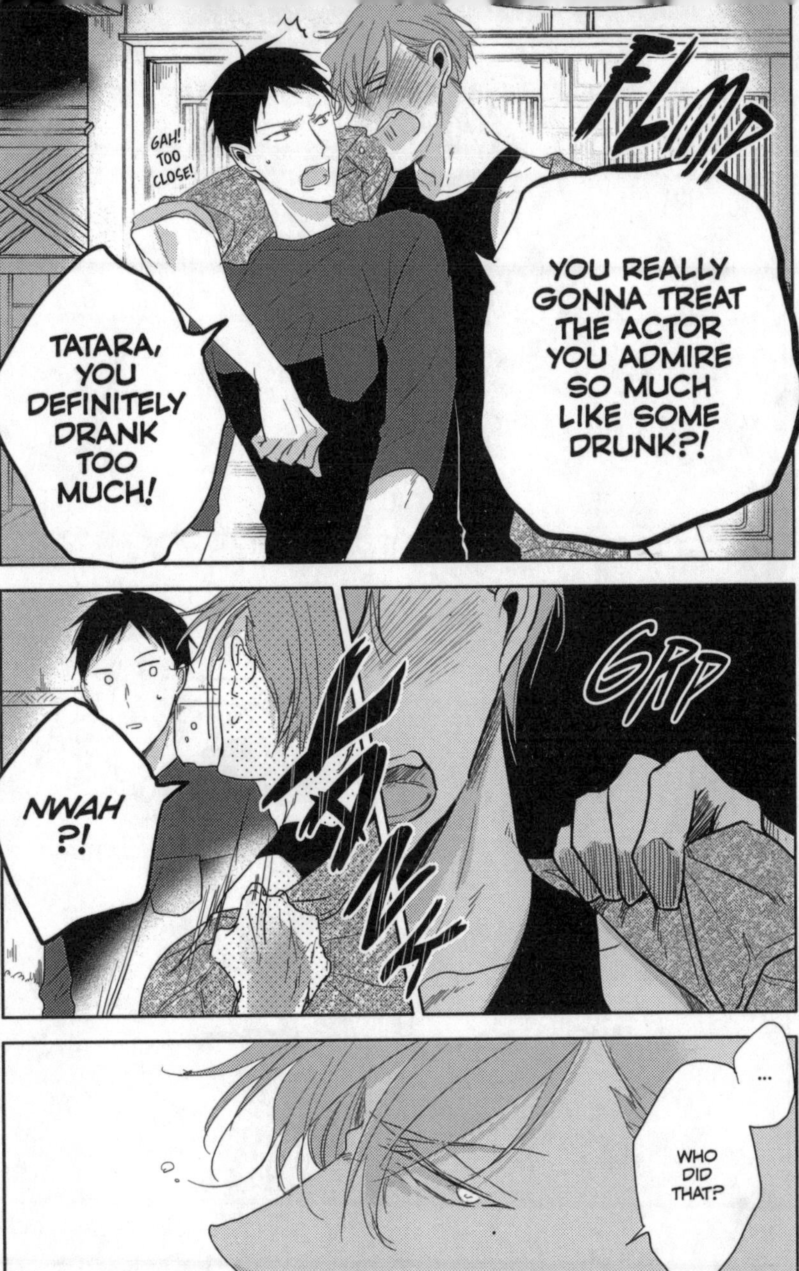
FLMP
YOU REALLY GONNA TREAT THE ACTOR YOU ADMIRE SO MUCH LIKE SOME DRUNK?!
GAH! TOO CLOSE!
TATARA, YOU DEFINITELY DRANK TOO MUCH!
GRPD
YANK
NWAH ?!
...
WHO DID THAT?

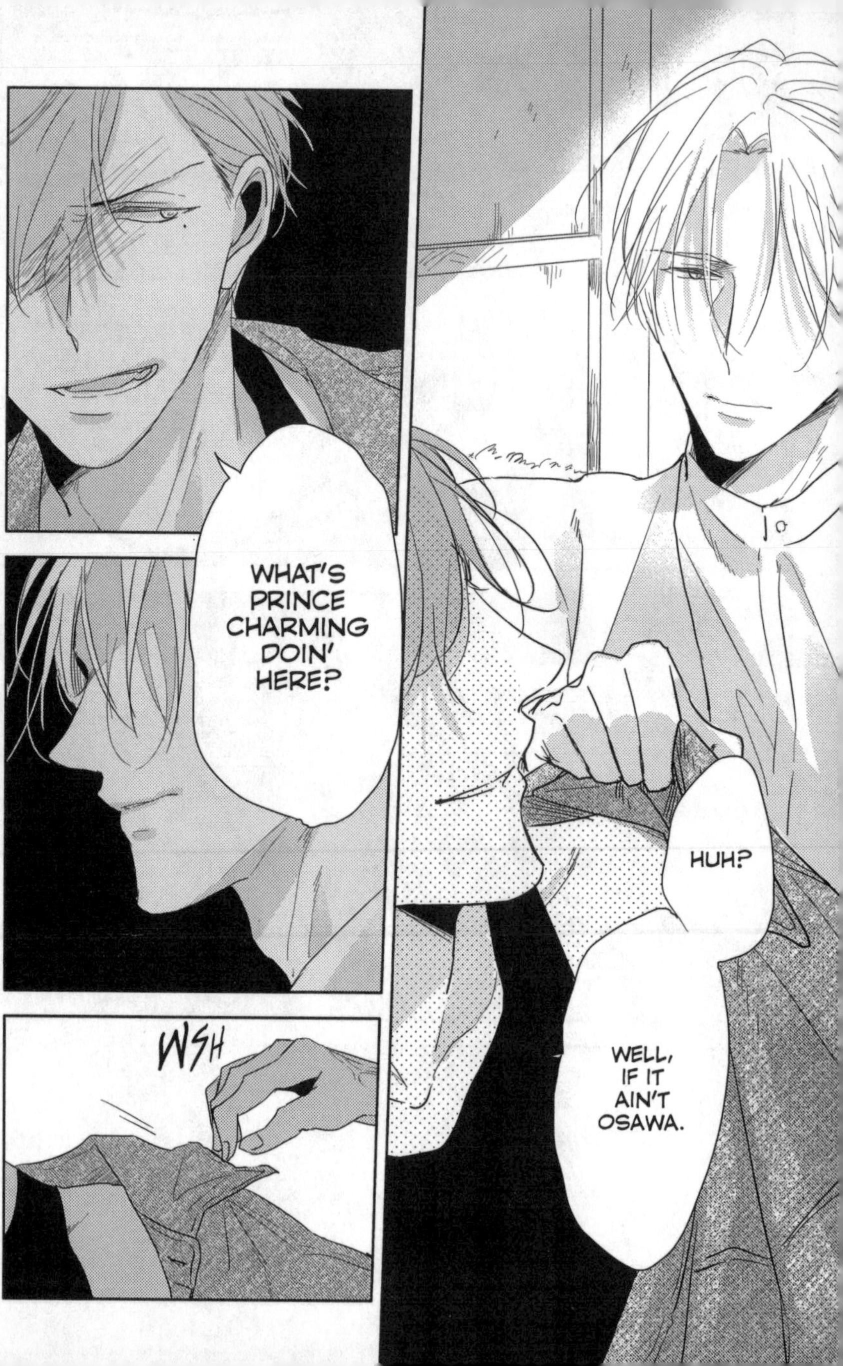
HUH?
WELL, IF IT AIN'T OSAWA.
WHAT'S PRINCE CHARMING DOIN' HERE?
WSH

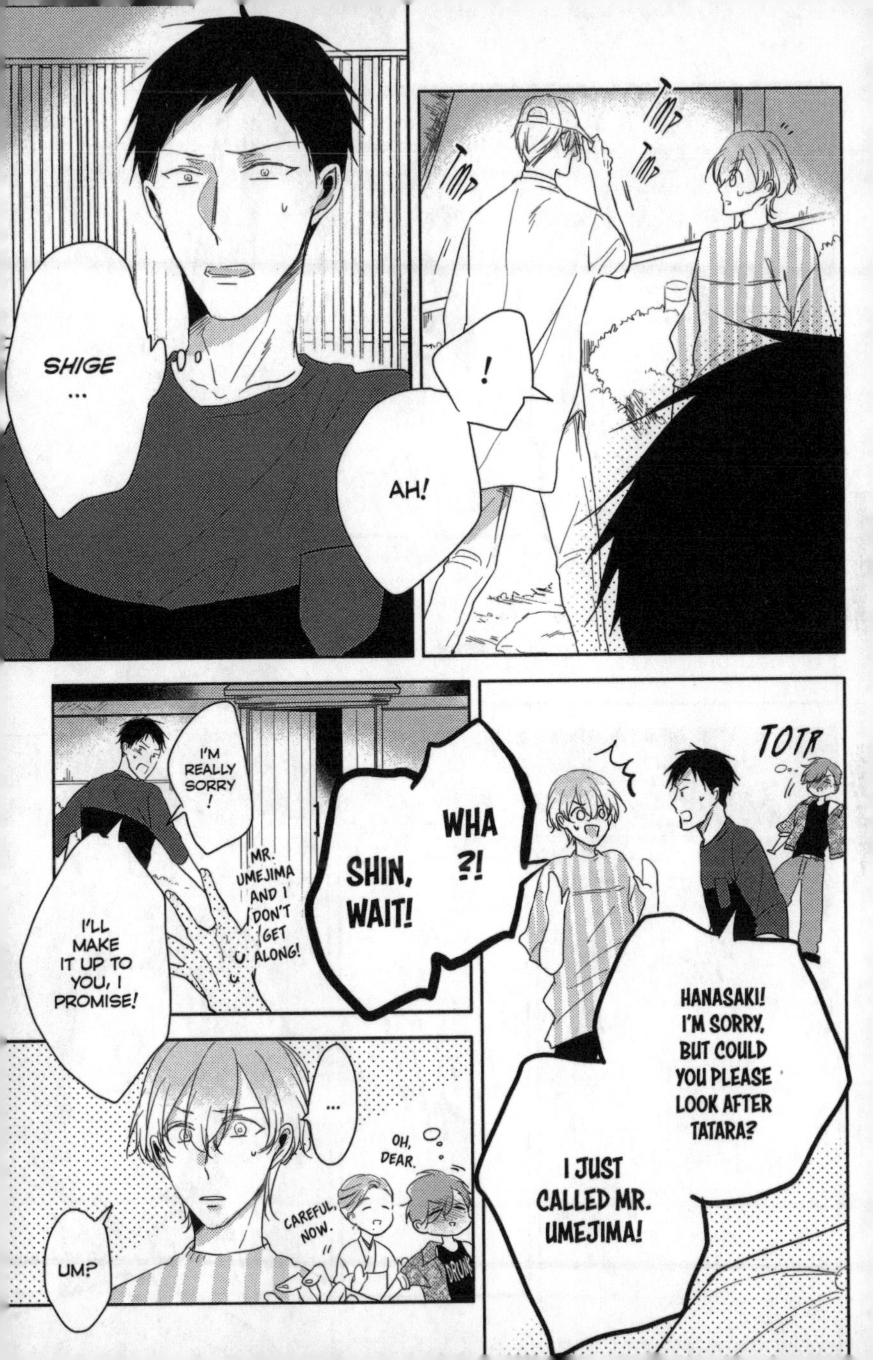

TMP TMP TMP TMP
!
AH!
SHIGE ...
TOTR
HANASAKI! I'M SORRY, BUT COULD YOU PLEASE LOOK AFTER TATARA?
I JUST CALLED MR. UMEJIMA!
WHA ?!
SHIN, WAIT!
I'M REALLY SORRY!
MR. UMEJIMA AND I DON'T GET ALONG!
I'LL MAKE IT UP TO YOU, I PROMISE!
...
OH, DEAR.
CAREFUL, NOW.
UM?

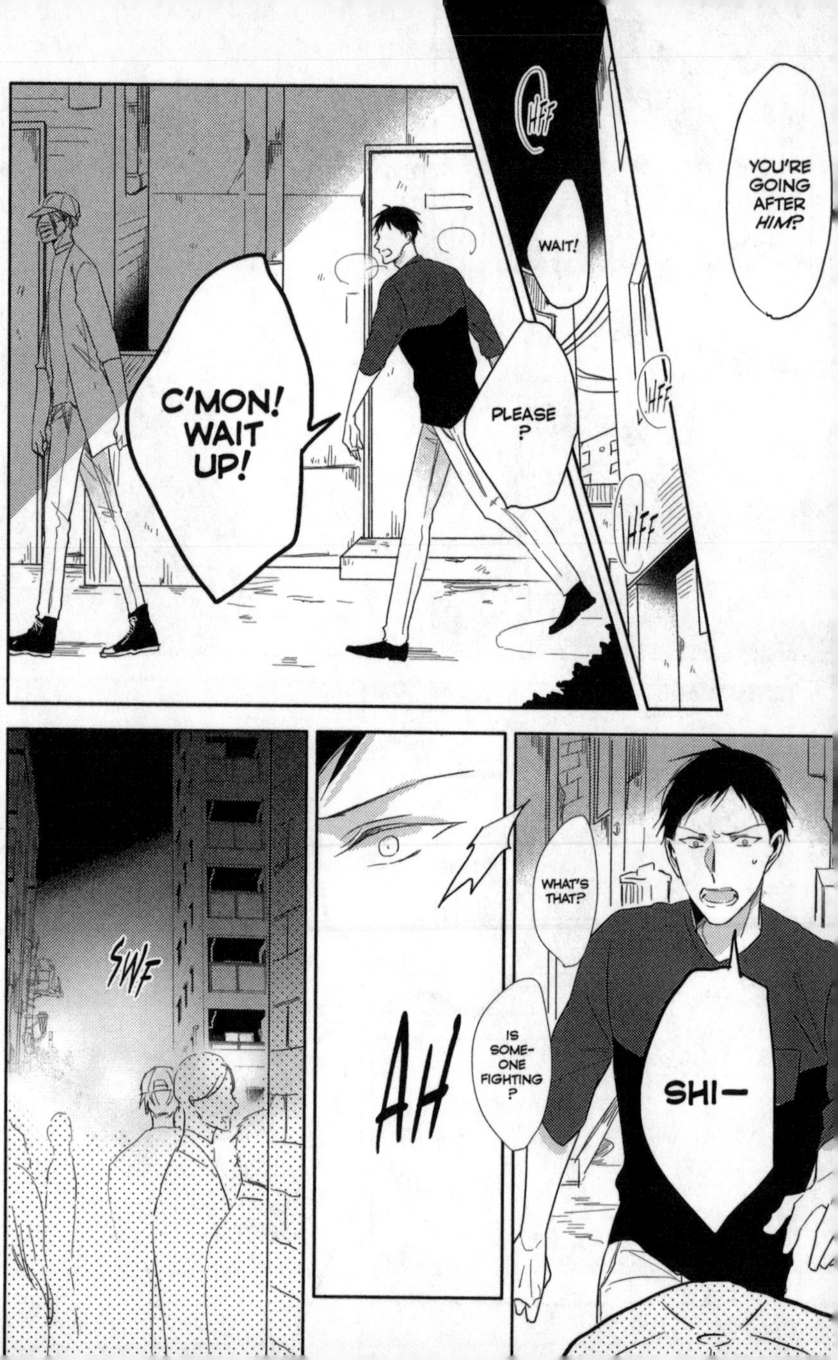
YOU'RE GOING AFTER *HIM*?
HFF
WAIT!
PLEASE?
HFF
HFF
C'MON! WAIT UP!
WHAT'S THAT?
IS SOME-ONE FIGHTING?
SHI—
AH
SWF

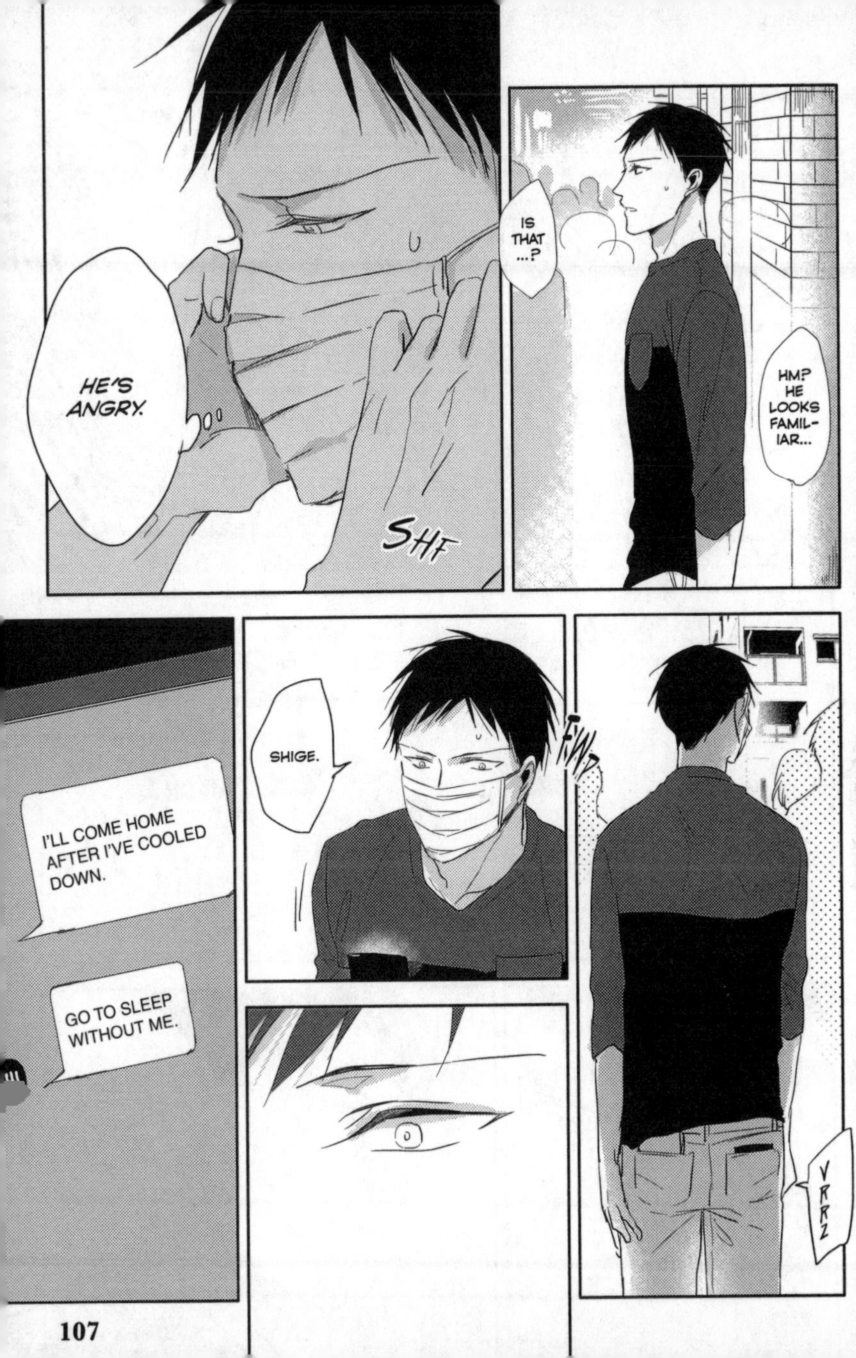
IS THAT ...?
HM? HE LOOKS FAMIL-IAR...
HE'S ANGRY.
SHF
VRRZ
FWD
SHIGE.
I'LL COME HOME AFTER I'VE COOLED DOWN.
GO TO SLEEP WITHOUT ME.

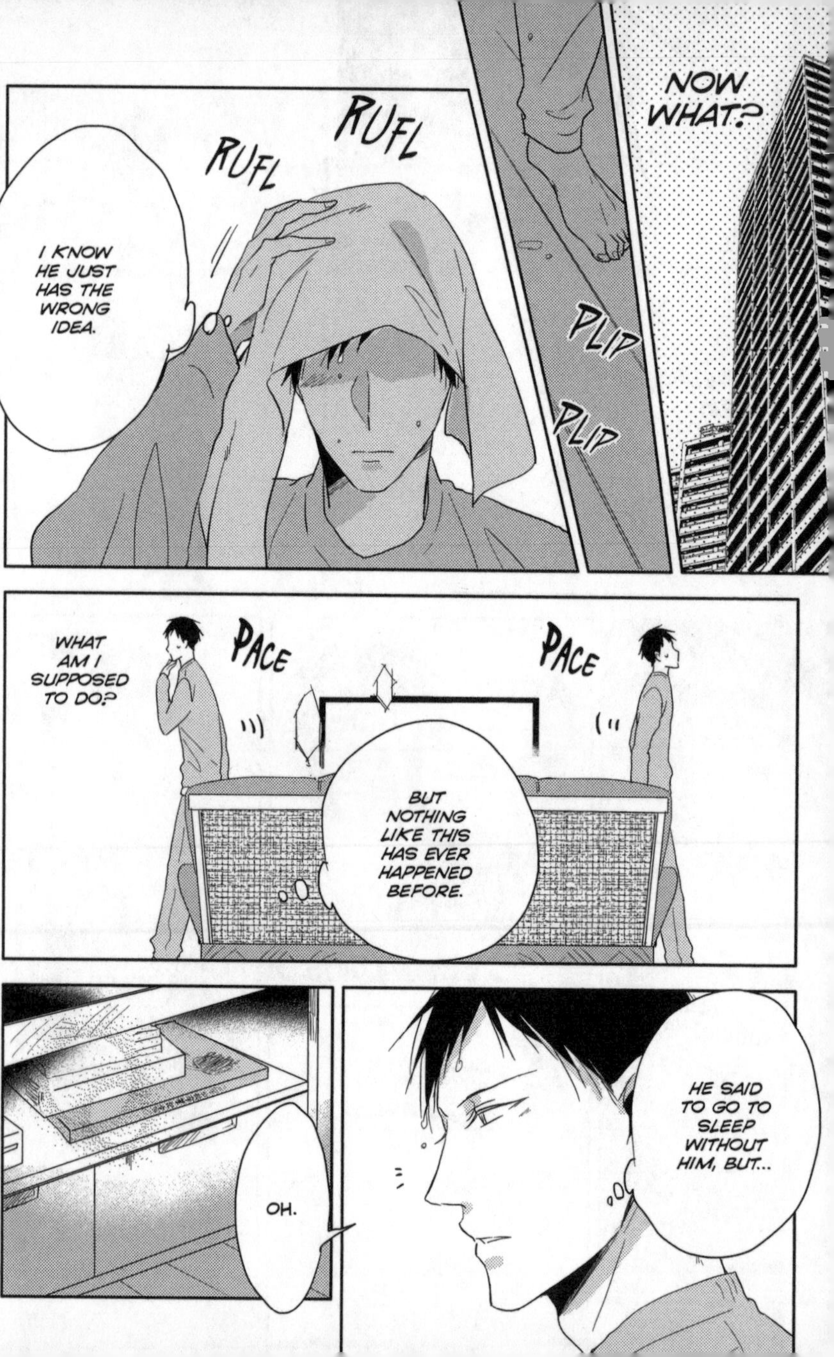
NOW WHAT?
PLIP
PLIP
RUFL
RUFL
I KNOW HE JUST HAS THE WRONG IDEA.
PACE
PACE
WHAT AM I SUPPOSED TO DO?
BUT NOTHING LIKE THIS HAS EVER HAPPENED BEFORE.
HE SAID TO GO TO SLEEP WITHOUT HIM, BUT...
OH.

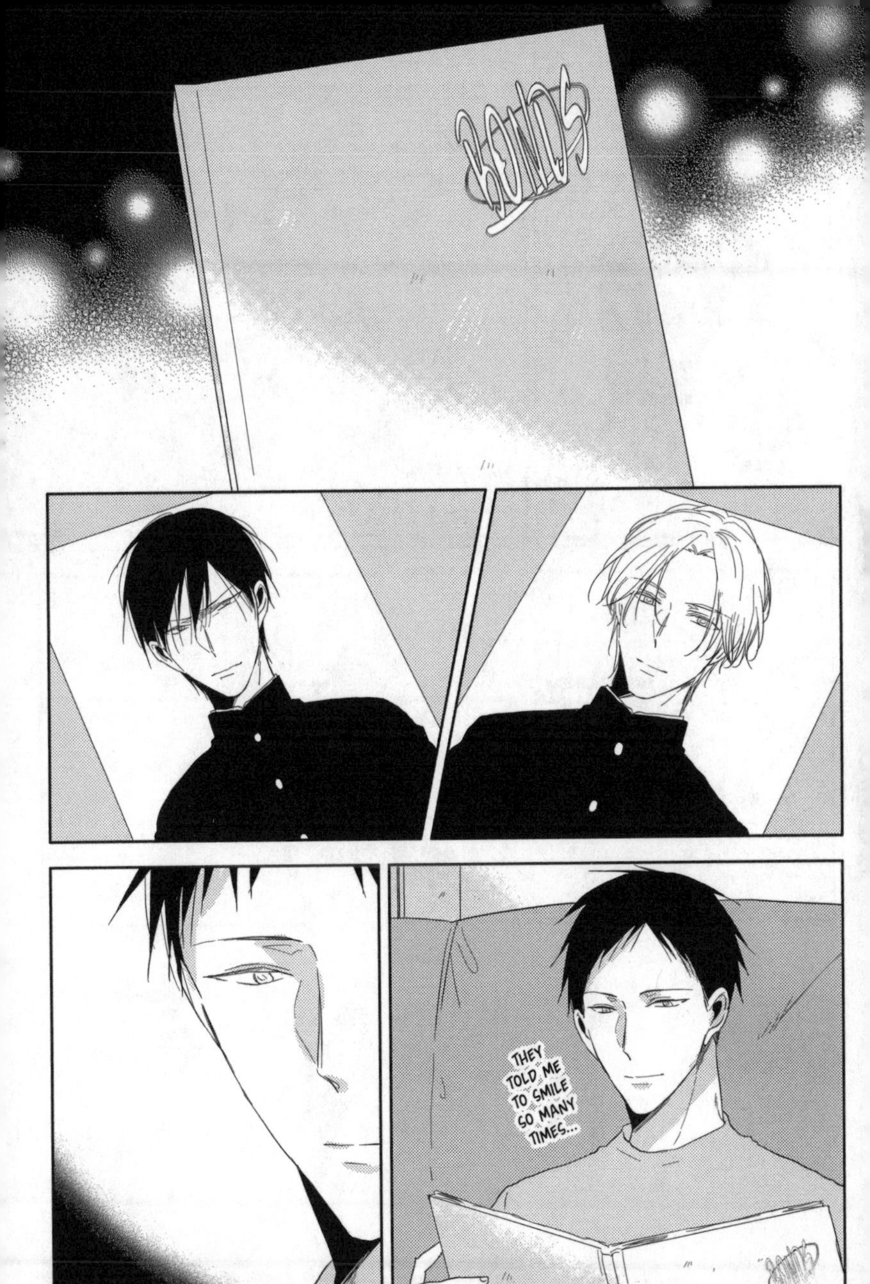
BONDS
THEY TOLD ME TO SMILE SO MANY TIMES...

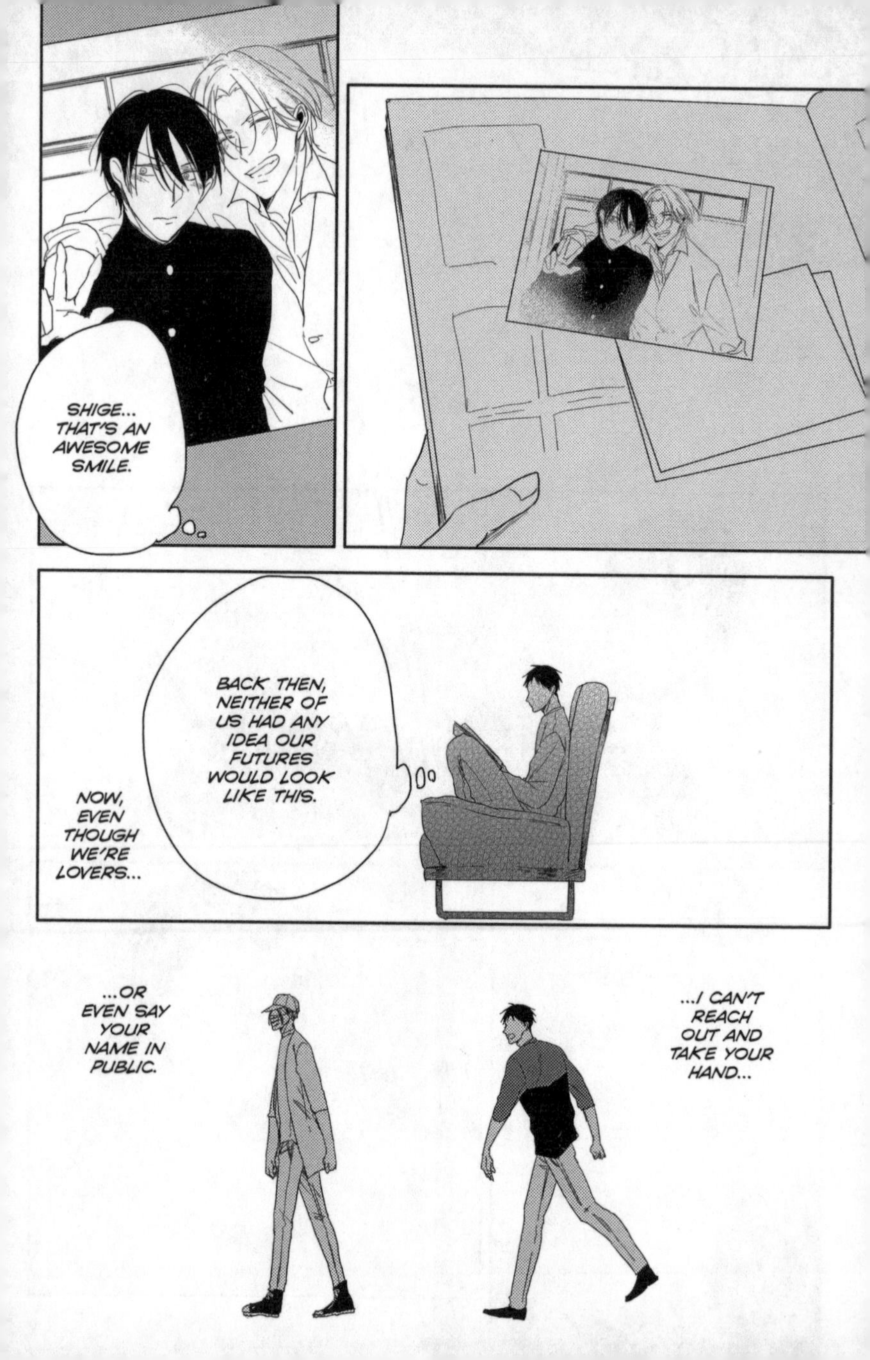
SHIGE... THAT'S AN AWESOME SMILE.
BACK THEN, NEITHER OF US HAD ANY IDEA OUR FUTURES WOULD LOOK LIKE THIS.
NOW, EVEN THOUGH WE'RE LOVERS...
...I CAN'T REACH OUT AND TAKE YOUR HAND...
...OR EVEN SAY YOUR NAME IN PUBLIC.

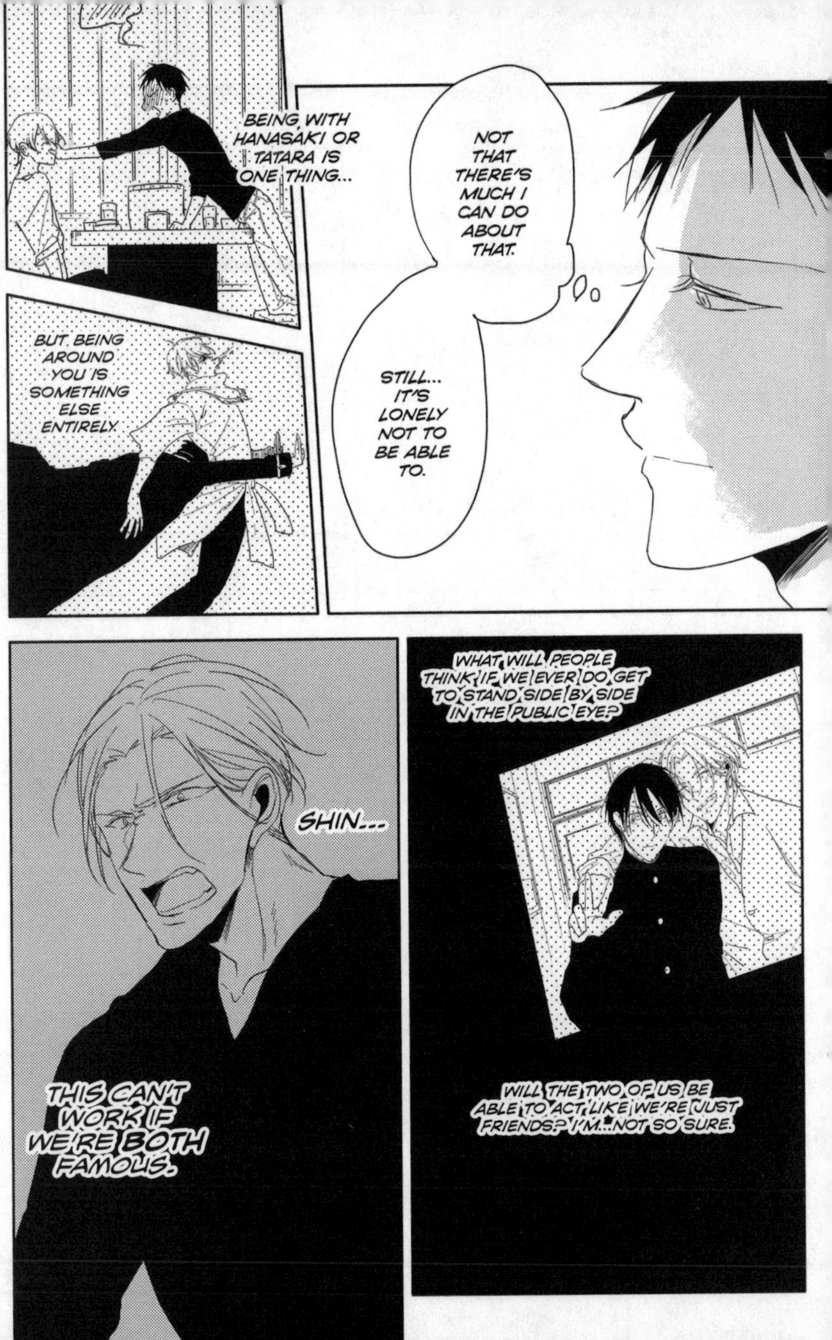
NOT THAT THERE'S MUCH I CAN DO ABOUT THAT.
STILL... IT'S LONELY NOT TO BE ABLE TO.
BEING WITH HANASAKI OR TATARA IS ONE THING...
BUT BEING AROUND YOU IS SOMETHING ELSE ENTIRELY.
WHAT WILL PEOPLE THINK IF WE EVER DO GET TO STAND SIDE BY SIDE IN THE PUBLIC EYE?
WILL THE TWO OF US BE ABLE TO ACT LIKE WE'RE JUST FRIENDS? I'M...NOT SO SURE.
SHIN...
THIS CAN'T WORK IF WE'RE BOTH FAMOUS.

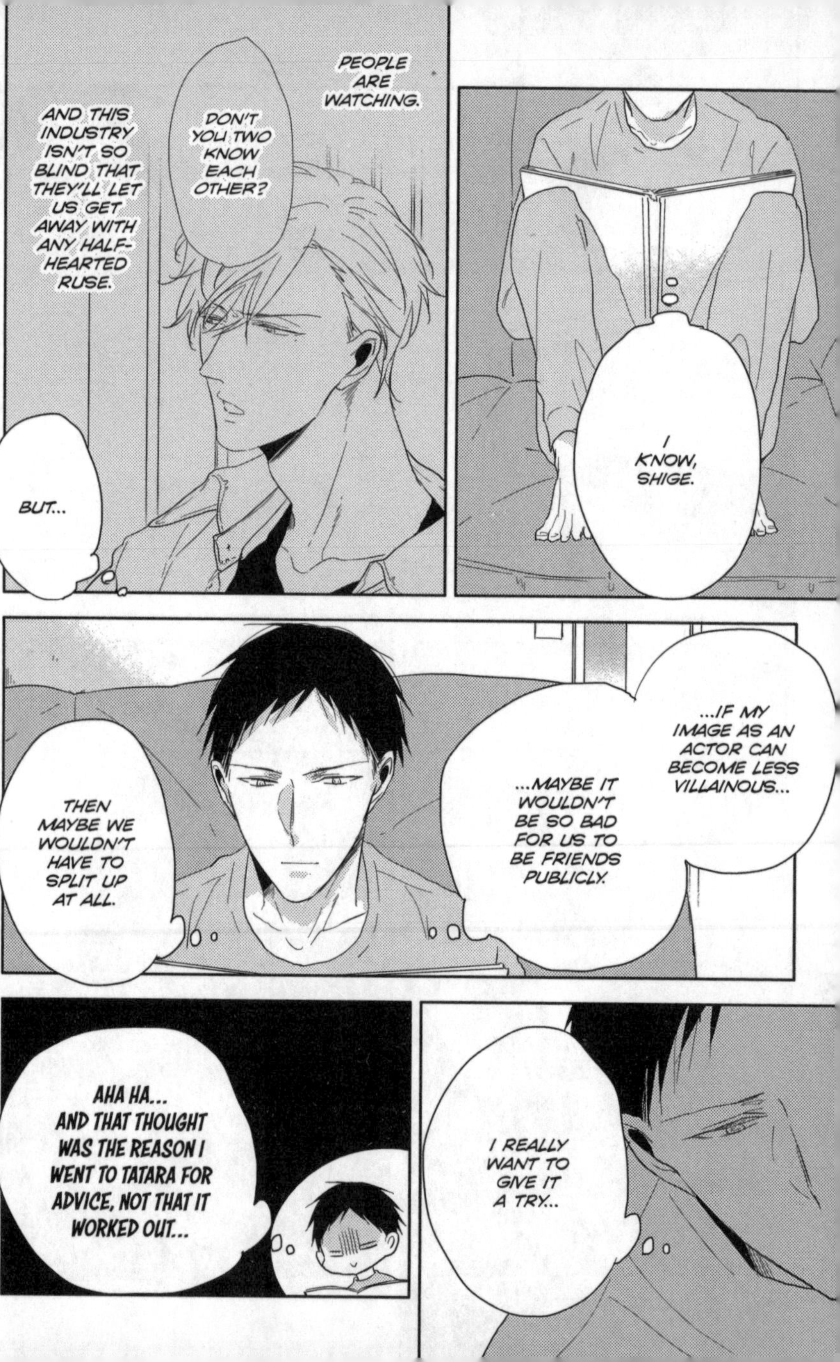
I KNOW, SHIGE.
PEOPLE ARE WATCHING.
DON'T YOU TWO KNOW EACH OTHER?
AND THIS INDUSTRY ISN'T SO BLIND THAT THEY'LL LET US GET AWAY WITH ANY HALF-HEARTED RUSE.
BUT...
...IF MY IMAGE AS AN ACTOR CAN BECOME LESS VILLAINOUS...
...MAYBE IT WOULDN'T BE SO BAD FOR US TO BE FRIENDS PUBLICLY.
THEN MAYBE WE WOULDN'T HAVE TO SPLIT UP AT ALL.
I REALLY WANT TO GIVE IT A TRY...
AHA HA... AND THAT THOUGHT WAS THE REASON I WENT TO TATARA FOR ADVICE, NOT THAT IT WORKED OUT...

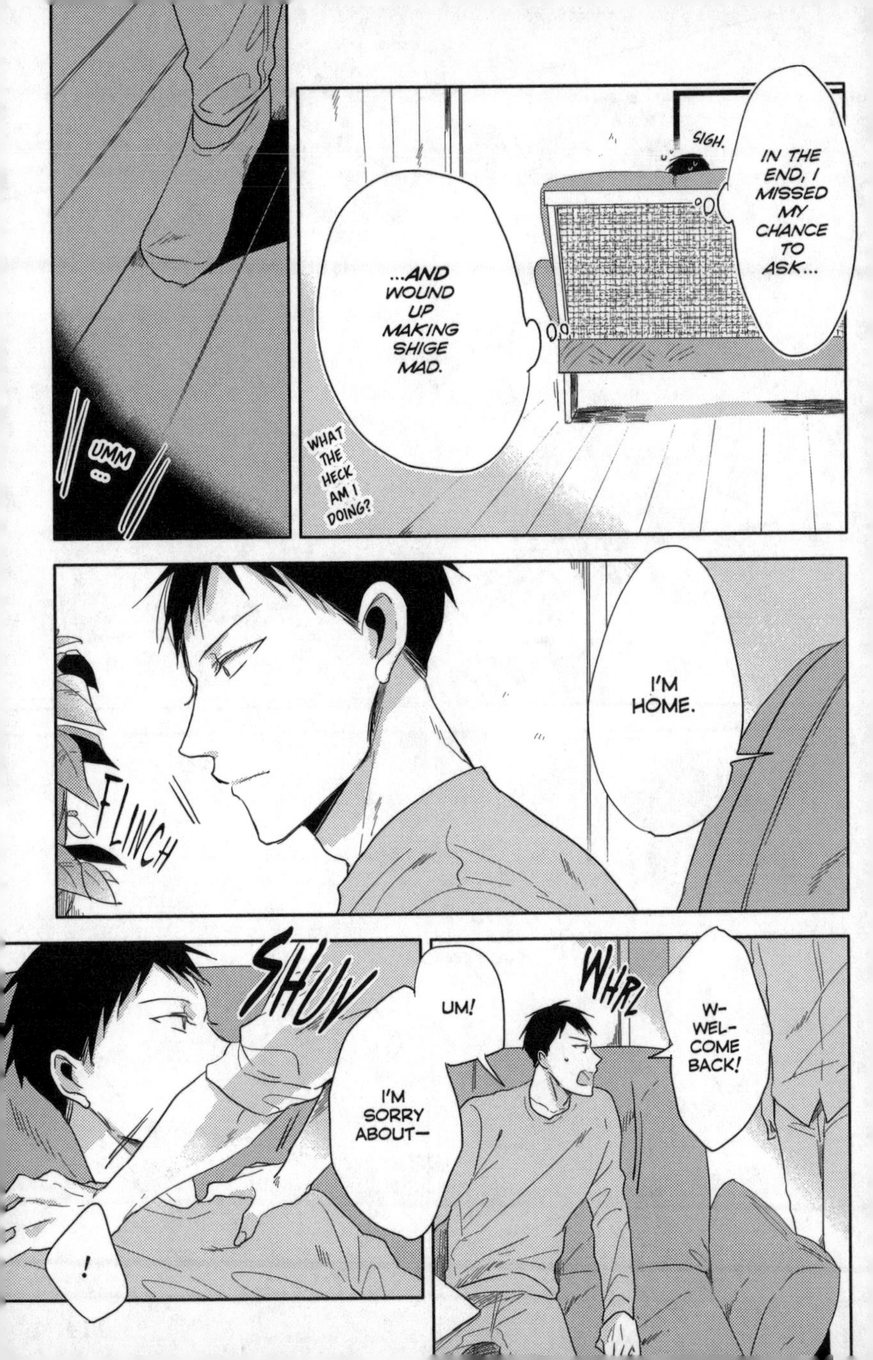
SIGH.
IN THE END, I MISSED MY CHANCE TO ASK...
...AND WOUND UP MAKING SHIGE MAD.
WHAT THE HECK AM I DOING?
UMM...
I'M HOME.
FLINCH
WHRL
W- WEL- COME BACK!
UM!
I'M SORRY ABOUT—
SHUV
!

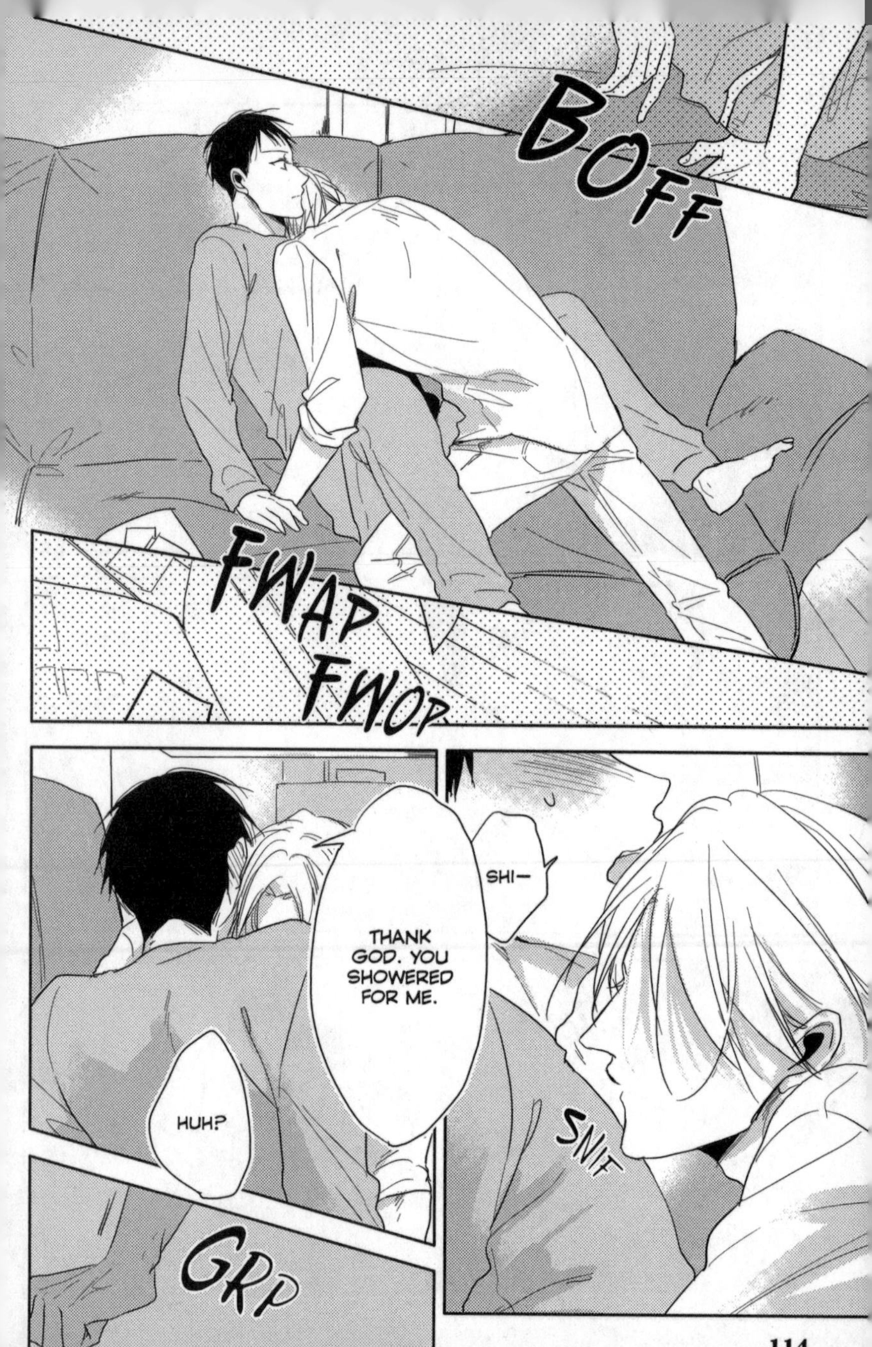
BOFF
FWAP
FWOP
SHI—
SNIF
THANK GOD. YOU SHOWERED FOR ME.
HUH?
GRP

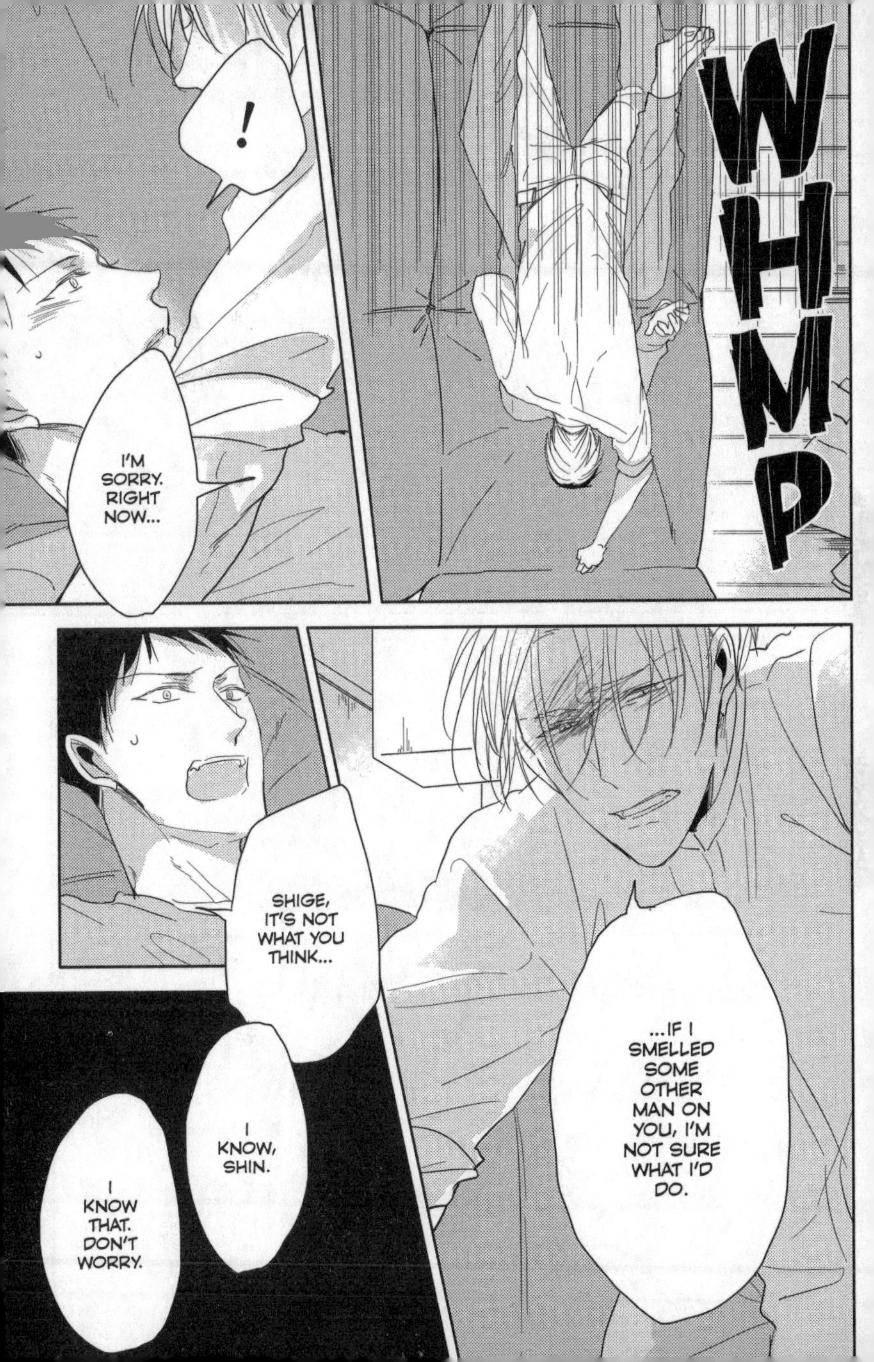
WHMP
!
I'M SORRY. RIGHT NOW...
SHIGE, IT'S NOT WHAT YOU THINK...
I KNOW, SHIN.
I KNOW THAT. DON'T WORRY.
...IF I SMELLED SOME OTHER MAN ON YOU, I'M NOT SURE WHAT I'D DO.

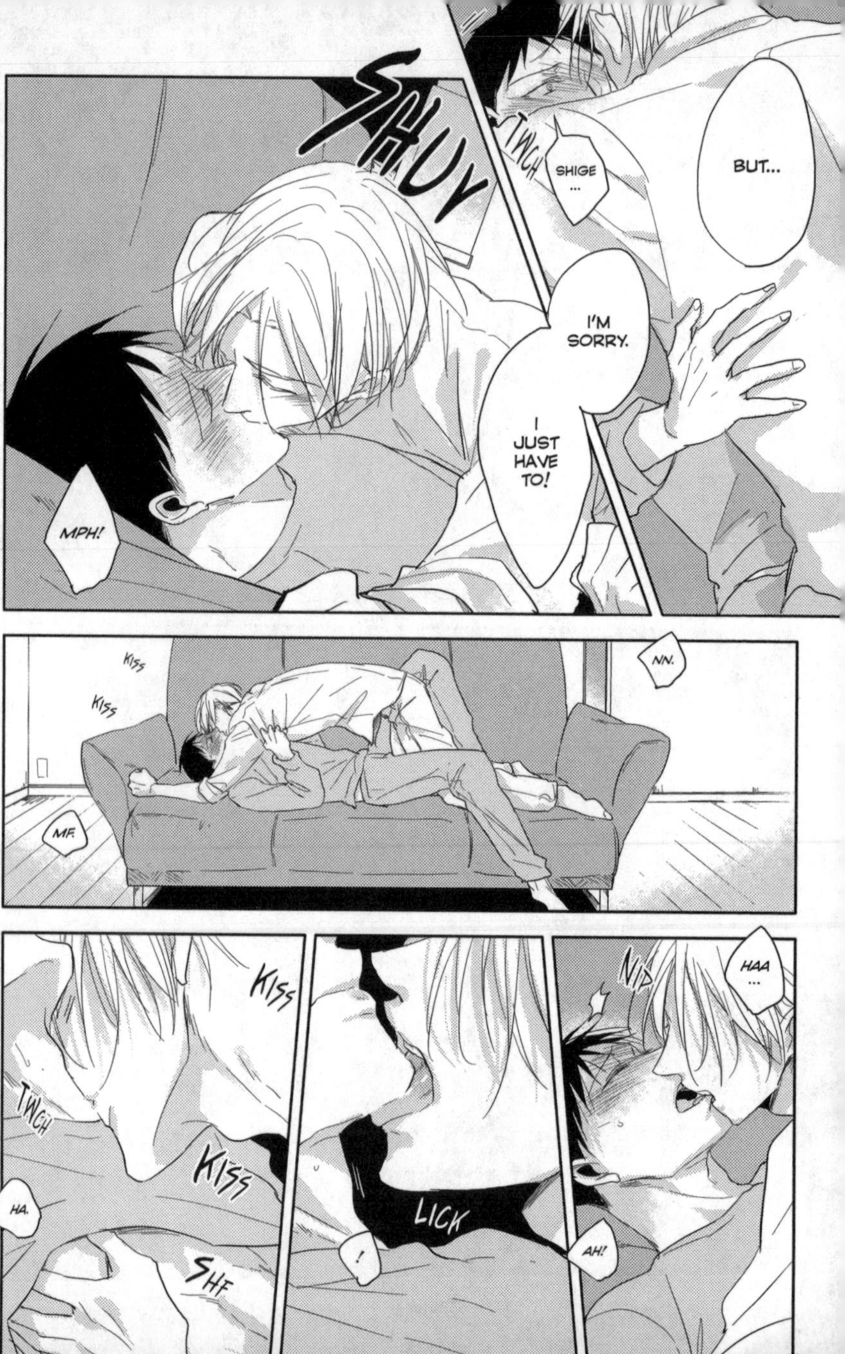
BUT...
SHIGE ...
TWCH
SHUV
I'M SORRY.
I JUST HAVE TO!
MPH!
NN.
KISS
KISS
MF.
HAA ...
NIP
AH!
LICK
!
KISS
TWCH
KISS
HA.
SHF

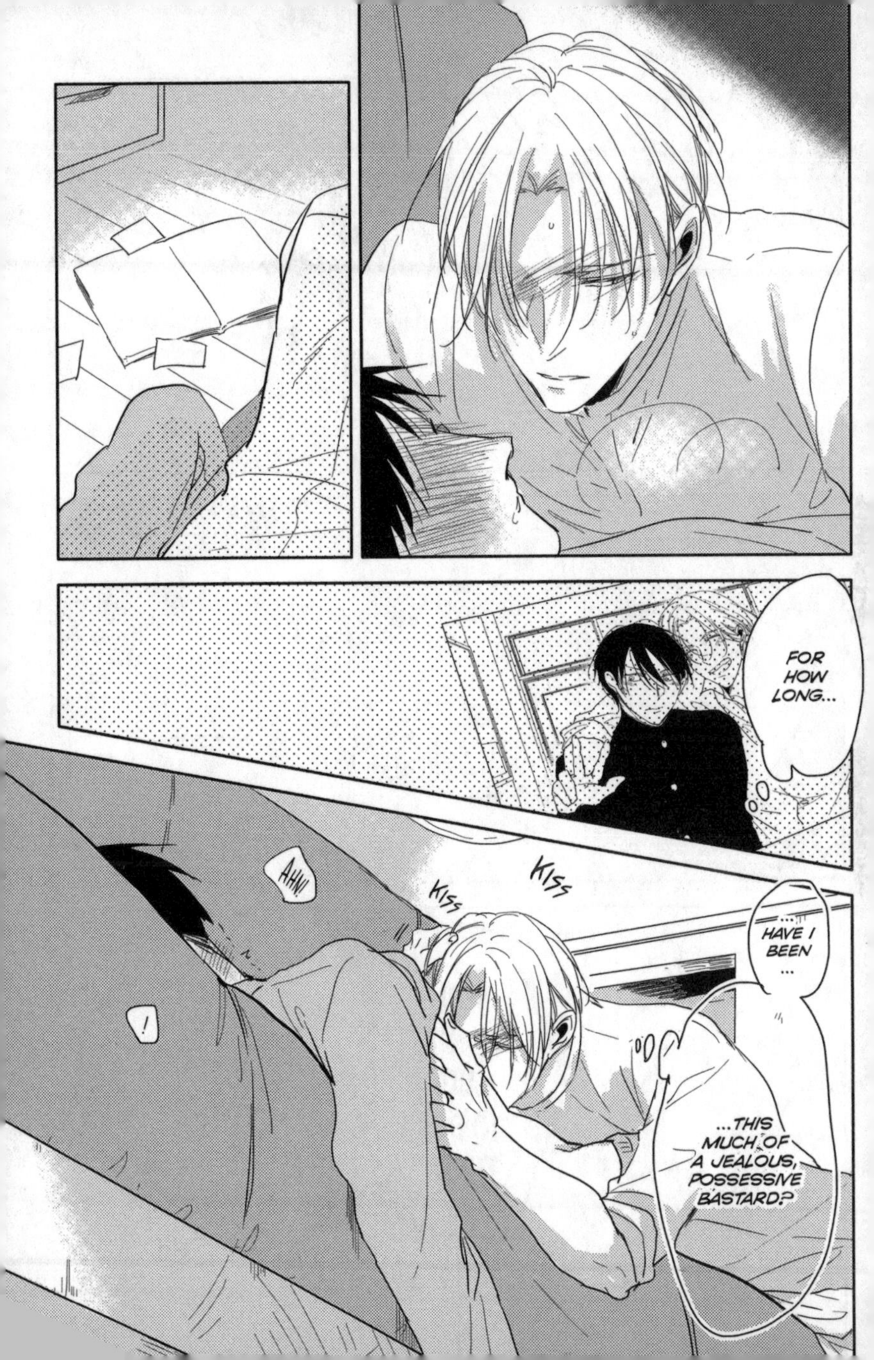
FOR HOW LONG...
...HAVE I BEEN ...
KISS
KISS
AHN!
!
...THIS MUCH OF A JEALOUS, POSSESSIVE BASTARD?

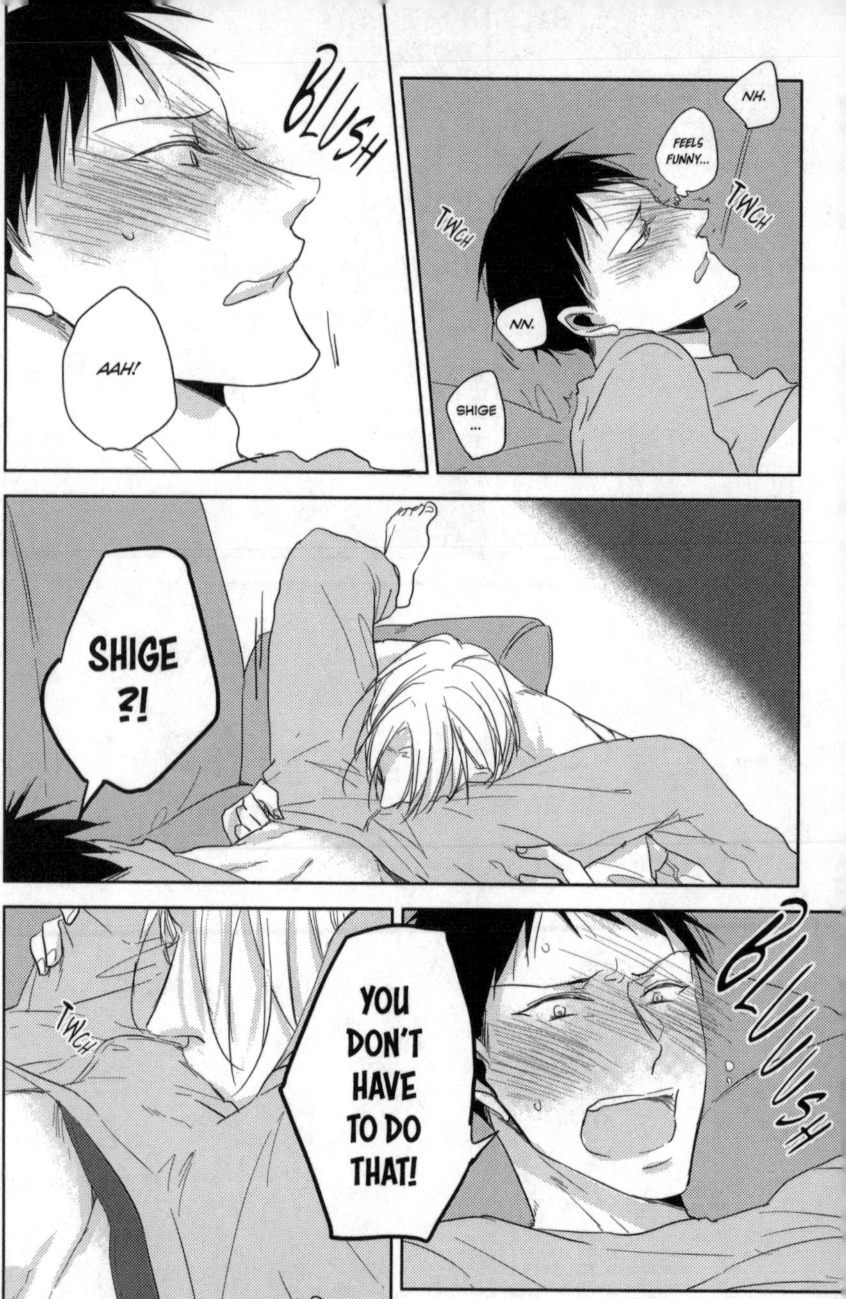
NH.
FEELS FUNNY...
TWCH
TWCH
NN.
SHIGE ...
BLUSH
AAH!
SHIGE ?!
BLUUUSH
YOU DON'T HAVE TO DO THAT!
TWCH

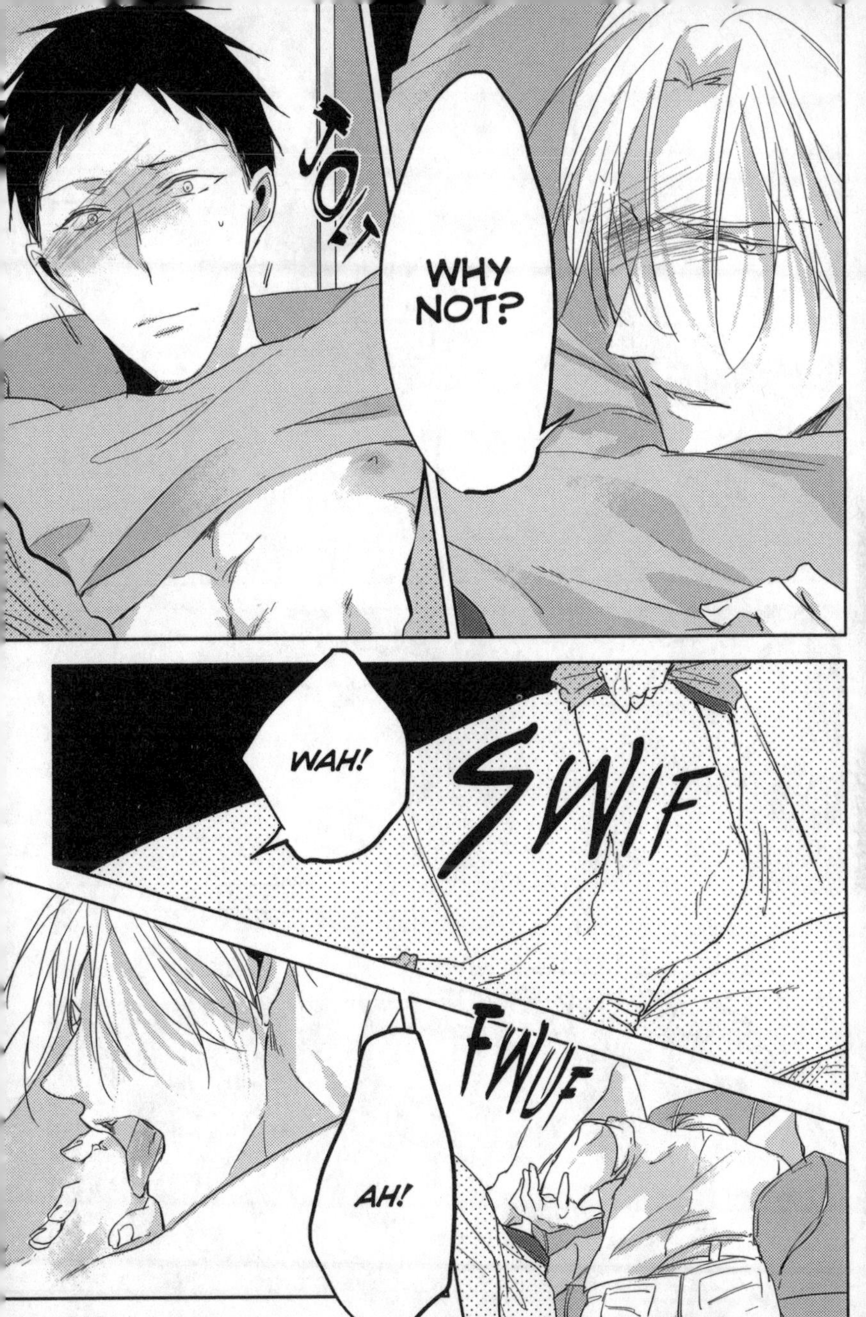
WHY NOT?
JOLT
SWIF
WAH!
FWUF
AH!

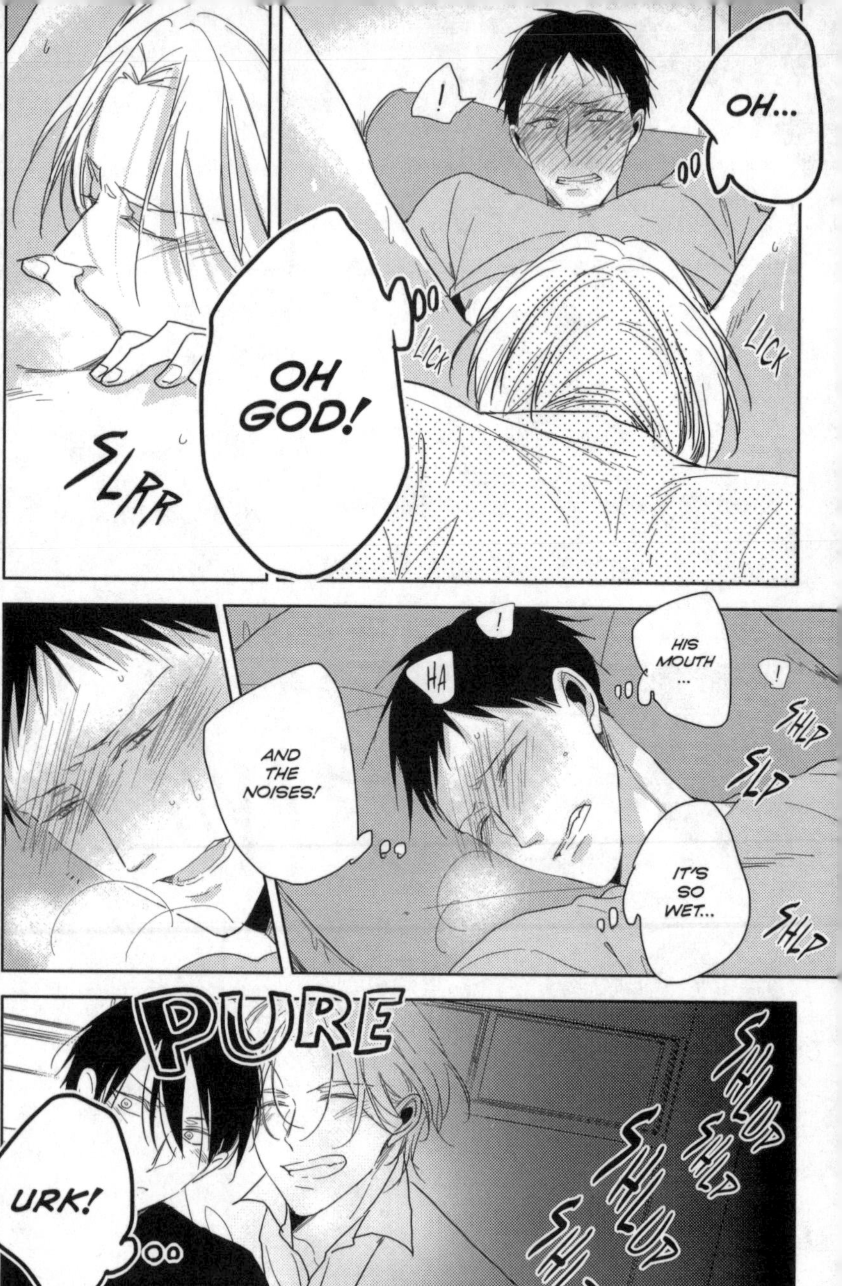
!
OH...
LICK
LICK
OH GOD!
SLRR
!
HIS MOUTH ...
!
HA
SHLP
SLP
IT'S SO WET...
SHLP
AND THE NOISES!
PURE
SHLUP
SHLP
SHLUP
SHLP
URK!

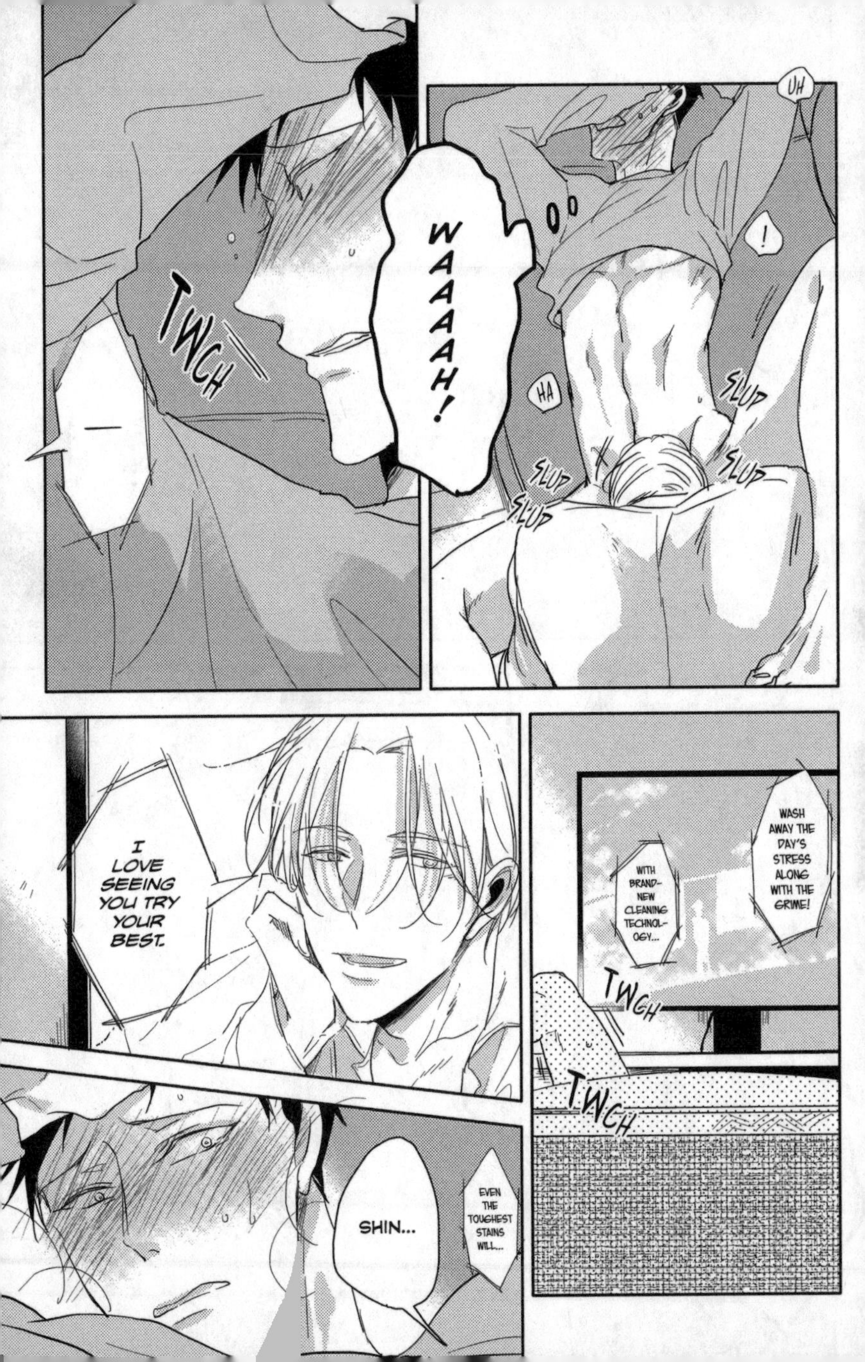
UH
!
HA
SLUP
SLUP
SLUP
SLUP
WAAAAAH!
TWCH
WASH AWAY THE DAY'S STRESS ALONG WITH THE GRIME!
WITH BRAND-NEW CLEANING TECHNOLOGY...
TWCH
TWCH
I LOVE SEEING YOU TRY YOUR BEST.
EVEN THE TOUGHEST STAINS WILL...
SHIN...

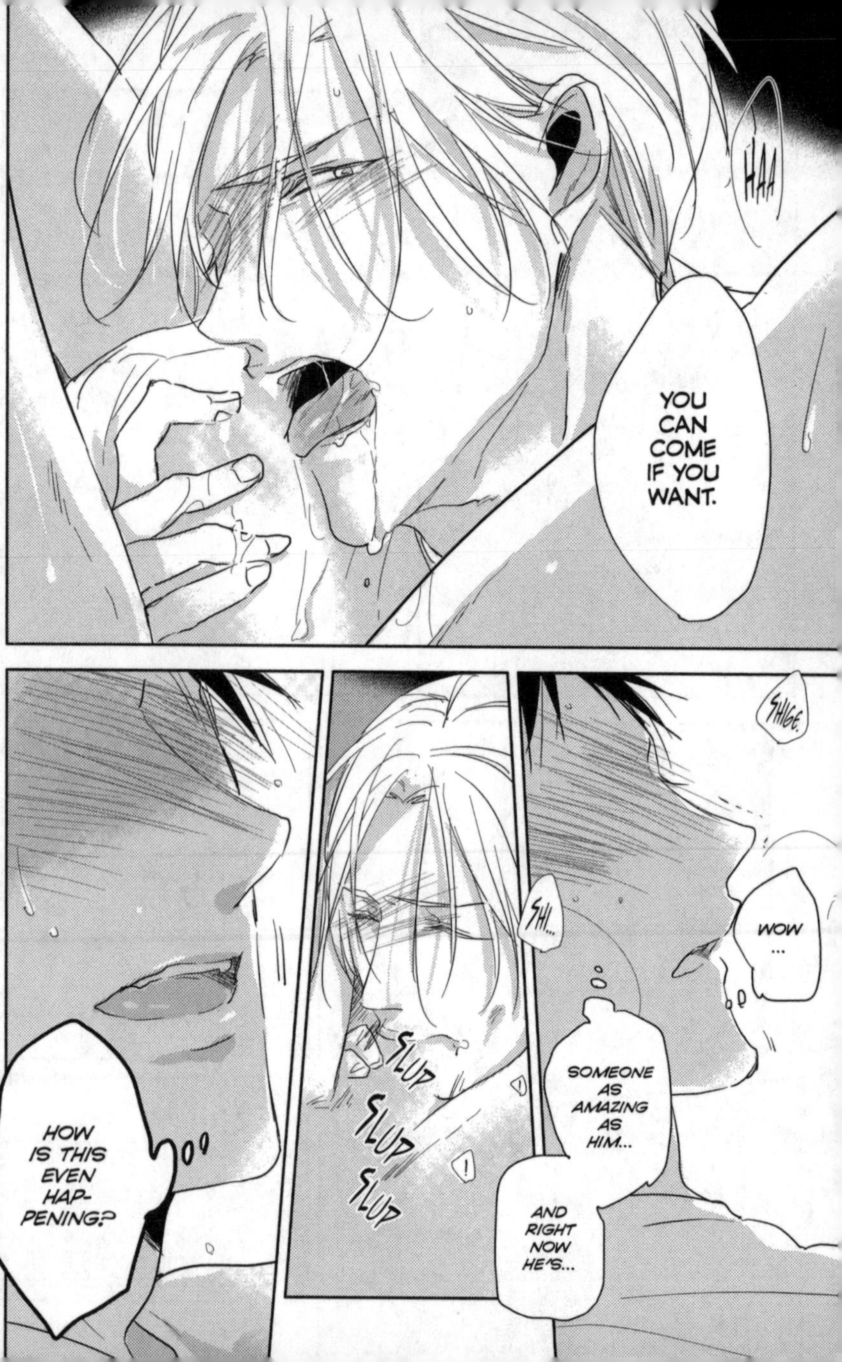
HAA
YOU CAN COME IF YOU WANT.
SHIGE.
WOW...
SOMEONE AS AMAZING AS HIM...
AND RIGHT NOW HE'S...
SHI...
SLUP
SLUP
SLUP
SLUP
HOW IS THIS EVEN HAP-PENING?

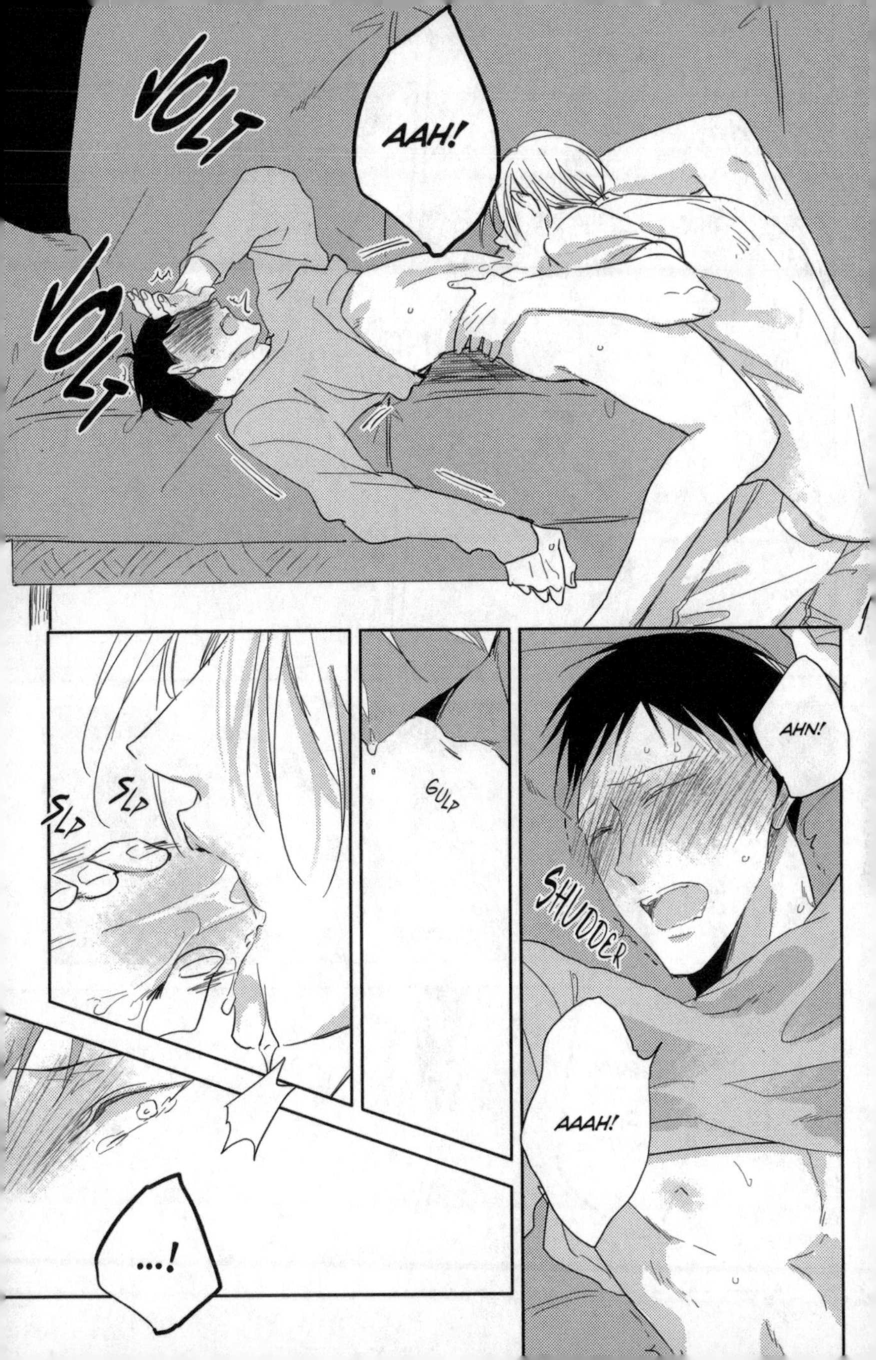
AAH!
JOLT
JOLT
AHN!
SHUDDER
AAAH!
GULP
SLP
SLP
...!

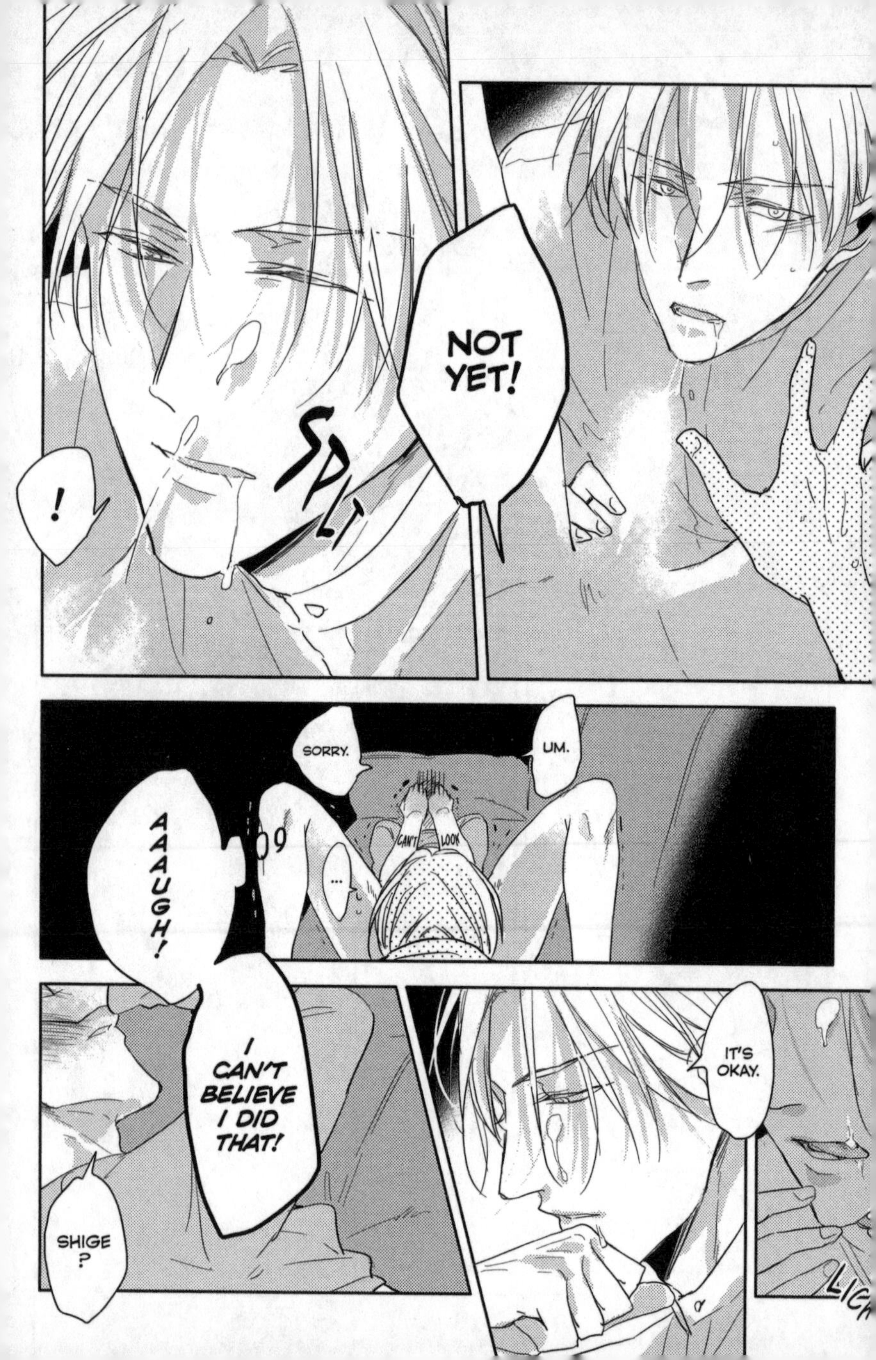
NOT YET!
SPLT
!
UM.
SORRY.
CAN'T LOOK
...
AAAUGH!
LIC
IT'S OKAY.
I CAN'T BELIEVE I DID THAT!
SHIGE?

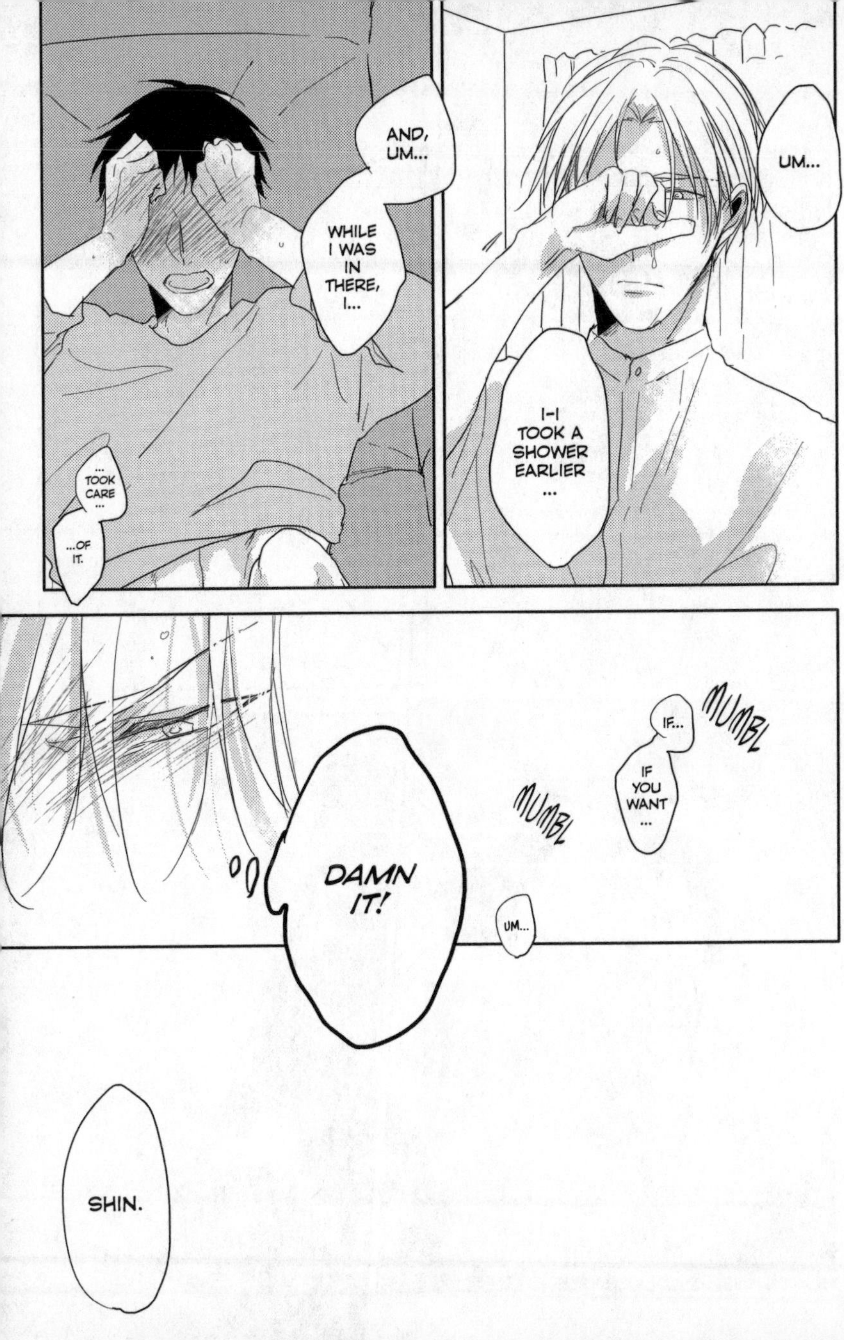
UM...
I-I TOOK A SHOWER EARLIER ...
AND, UM...
WHILE I WAS IN THERE, I...
...TOOK CARE ...
...OF IT.
MUMBL
IF...
IF YOU WANT ...
MUMBL
UM...
DAMN IT!
SHIN.

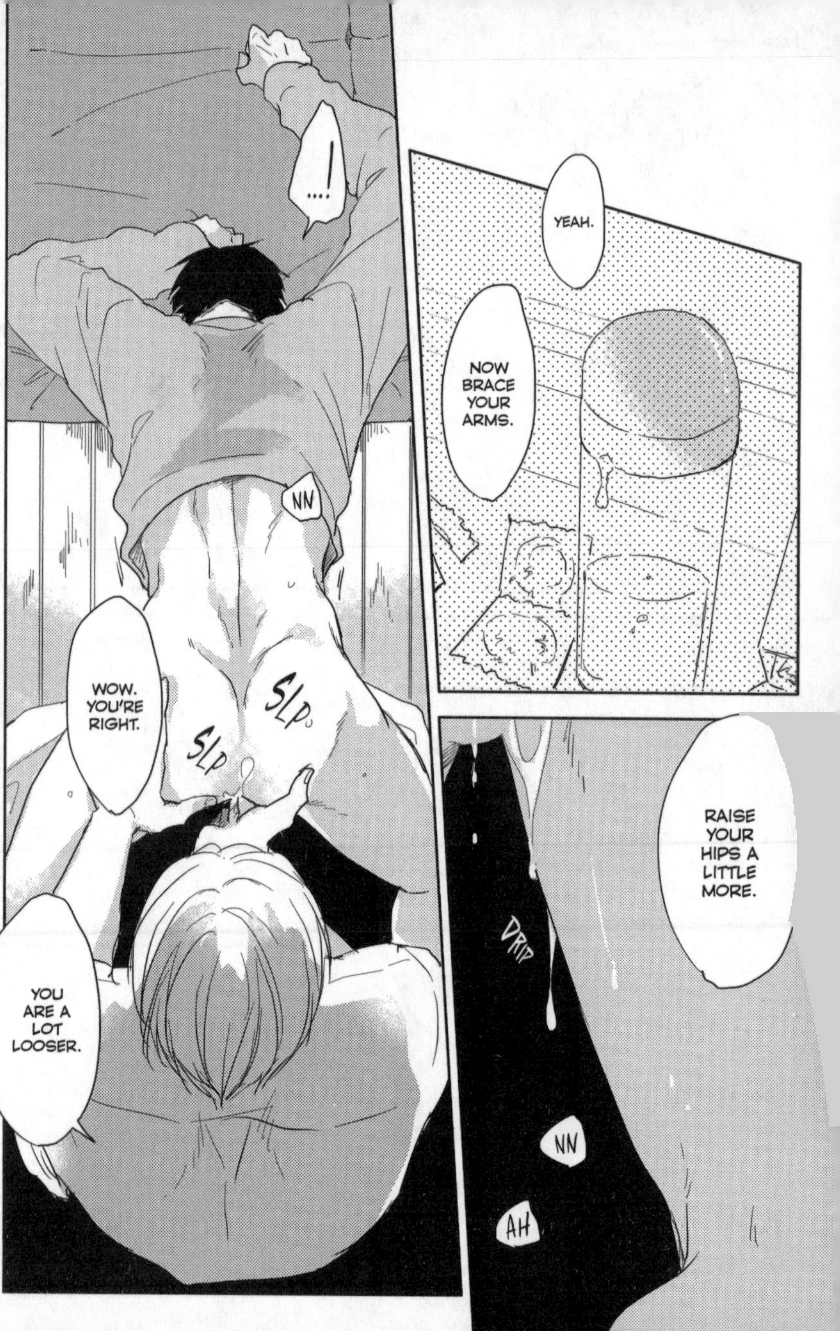
YEAH.
NOW BRACE YOUR ARMS.
RAISE YOUR HIPS A LITTLE MORE.
DRIP
NN
AH
....!
NN
WOW. YOU'RE RIGHT.
SLP
SLP
YOU ARE A LOT LOOSER.

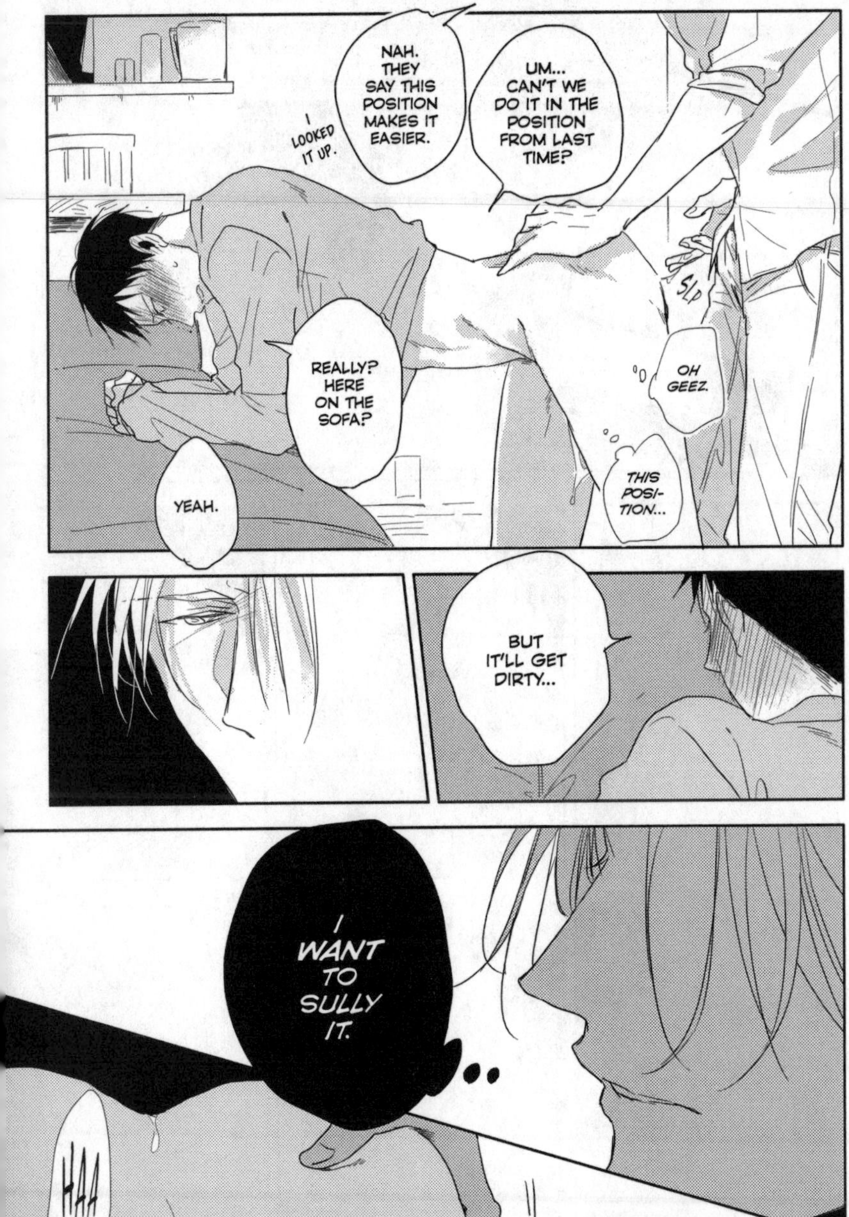
UM... CAN'T WE DO IT IN THE POSITION FROM LAST TIME?
NAH. THEY SAY THIS POSITION MAKES IT EASIER.
I LOOKED IT UP.
SLP
OH GEEZ.
THIS POSI-TION...
REALLY? HERE ON THE SOFA?
YEAH.
BUT IT'LL GET DIRTY...
I WANT TO SULLY IT.
HAA

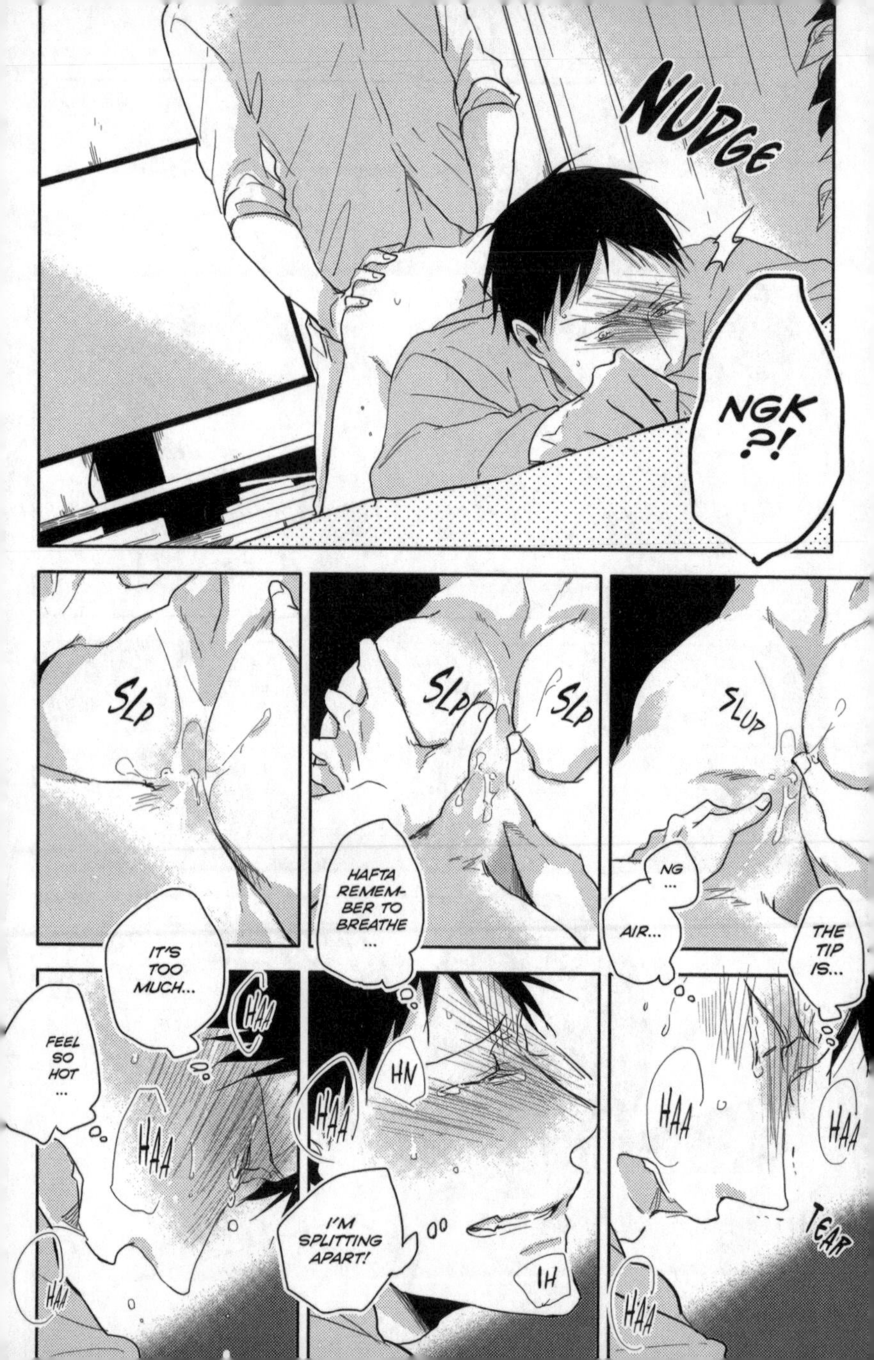
NUDGE
NGK ?!
SLUP
THE TIP IS...
NG ...
AIR...
SLP
SLP
HAFTA REMEMBER TO BREATHE ...
SLP
HAA
HAA
TEAR
HAA
HN
HAA
I'M SPLITTING APART!
IH
IT'S TOO MUCH...
HAA
FEEL SO HOT ...
HAA
HAA

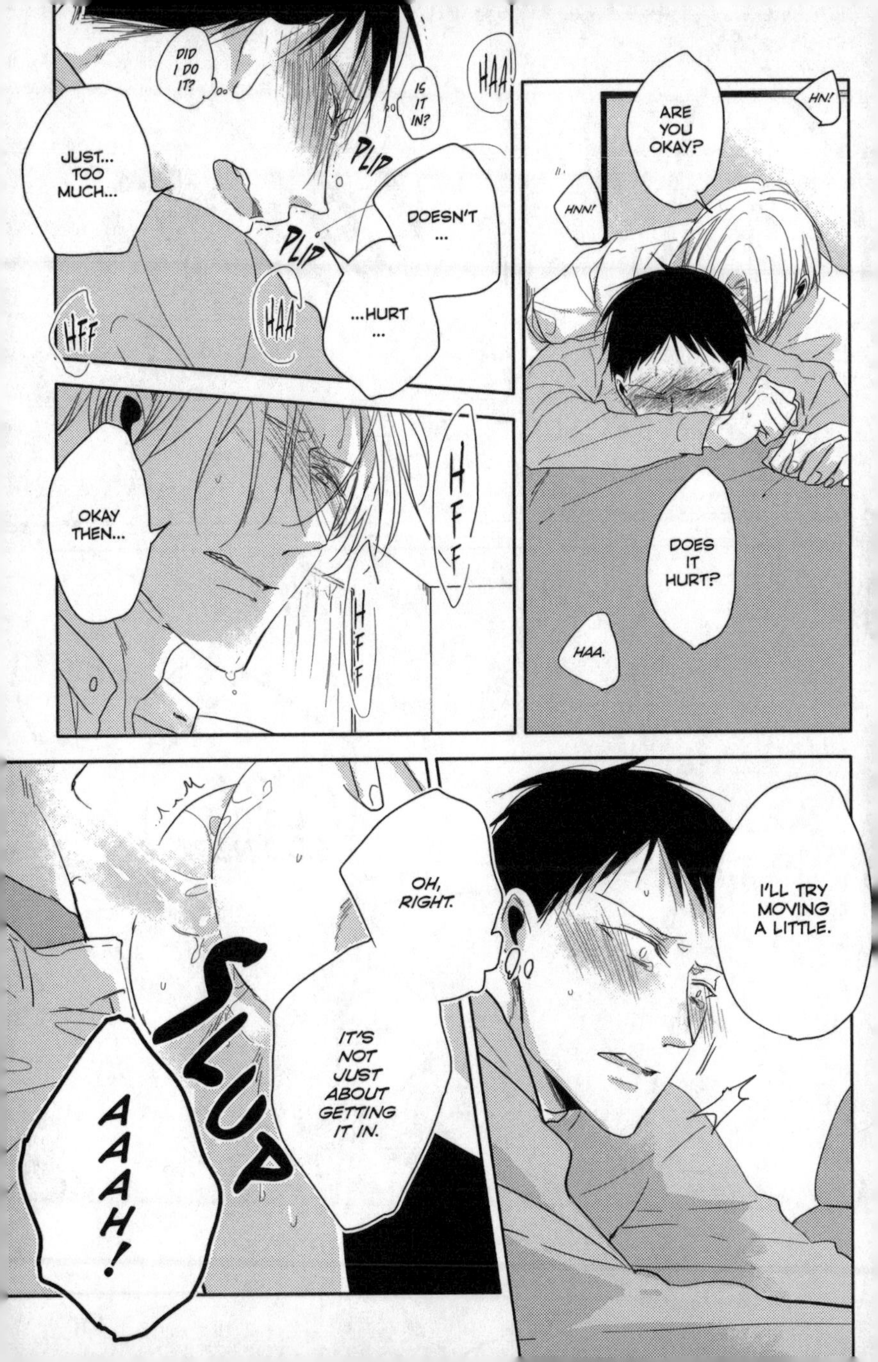
HN!
ARE YOU OKAY?
HNN!
DOES IT HURT?
HAA.
HAA!
IS IT IN?
DID I DO IT?
PLIP
DOESN'T ...
...HURT ...
JUST... TOO MUCH...
PLIP
HAA
HFF
HFF
HFF
OKAY THEN...
I'LL TRY MOVING A LITTLE.
OH, RIGHT.
IT'S NOT JUST ABOUT GETTING IT IN.
SLUP
AAAH!

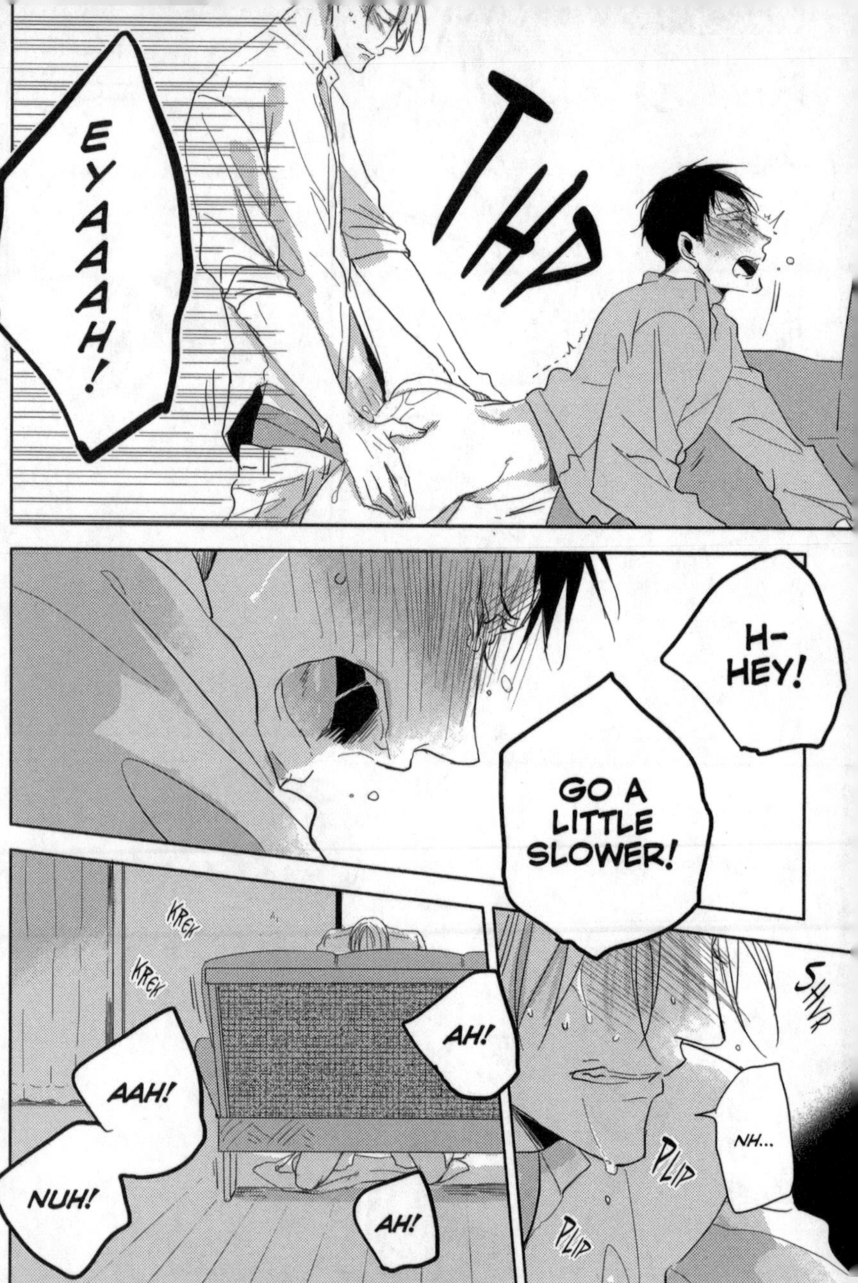
THP
EYAAAAH!
H-HEY!
GO A LITTLE SLOWER!
SHVR
NH...
PLIP
PLIP
AH!
KREK
KREK
AAH!
NUH!
AH!

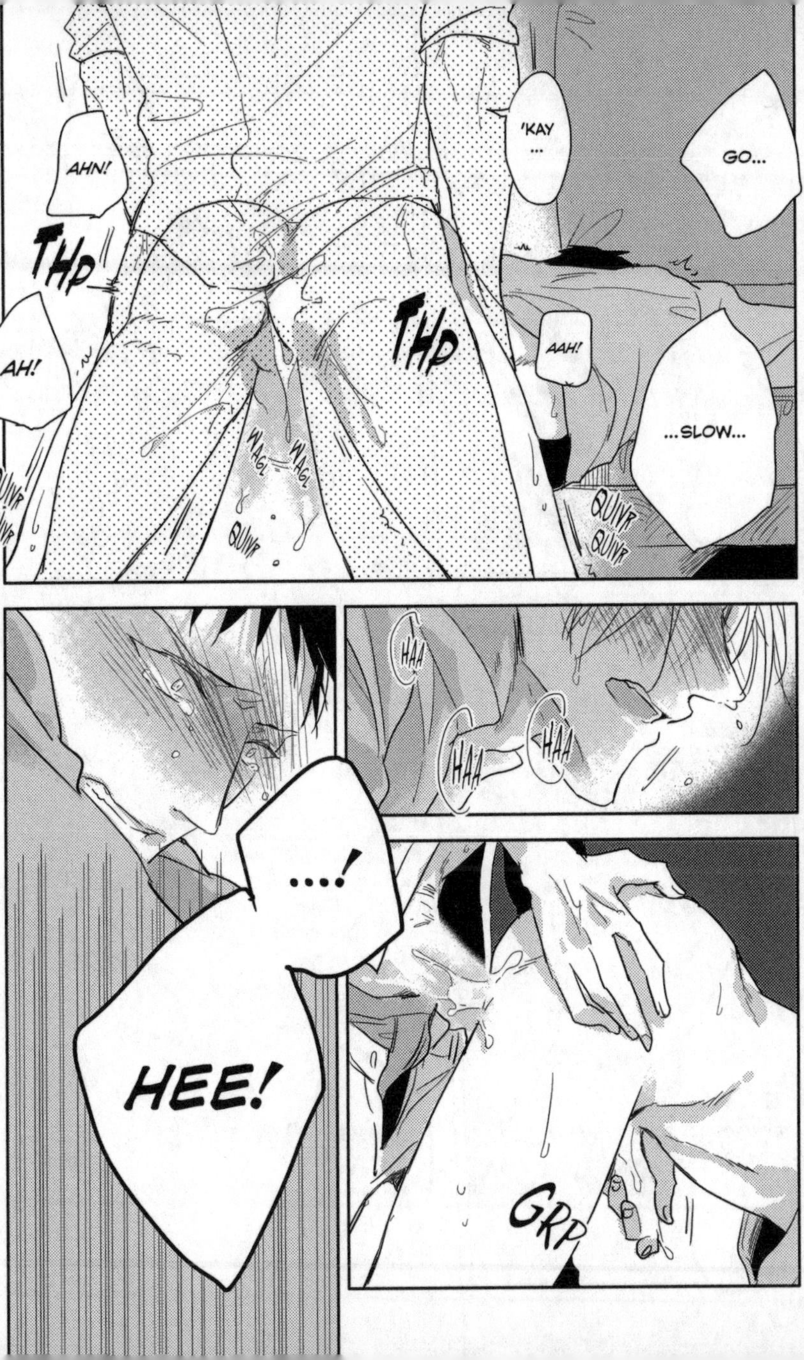
GO...
'KAY ...
AHN!
THP
THP
...SLOW...
AAH!
AH!
QUIVR QUIVR
WAGL WAGL
QUIVR
QUIVR QUIVR
HAA
HAA
HAA
GRP
...!
HEE!

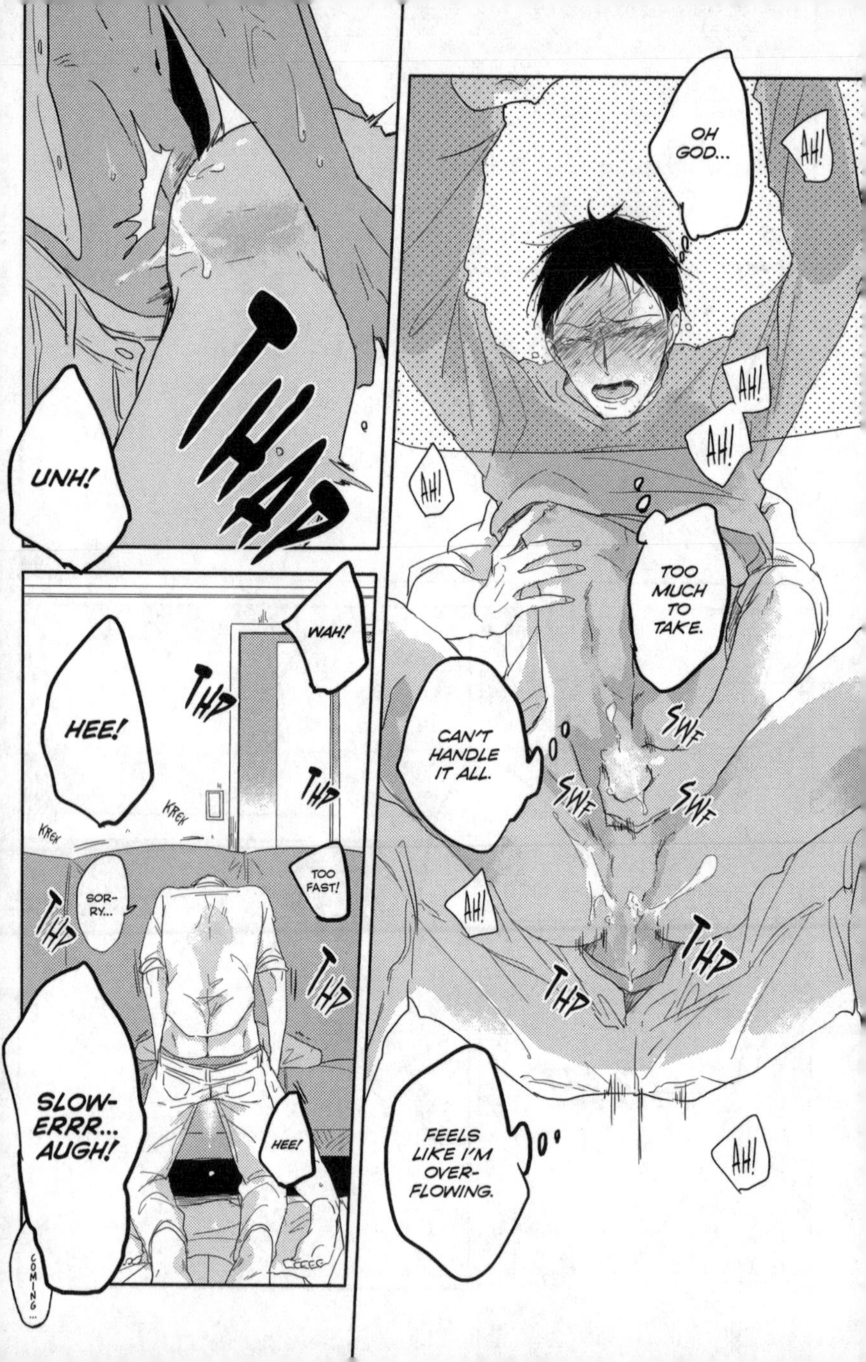
AH!
OH GOD...
AH!
AH!
AH!
TOO MUCH TO TAKE.
CAN'T HANDLE IT ALL.
SWF
SWF
SWF
AH!
THP
THP
AH!
FEELS LIKE I'M OVER-FLOWING.
THAP
UNH!
WAH!
THP
HEE!
THP
KREK
KREK
TOO FAST!
SOR-RY...
THP
THP
HEE!
SLOW-ERRR... AUGH!
COMING...

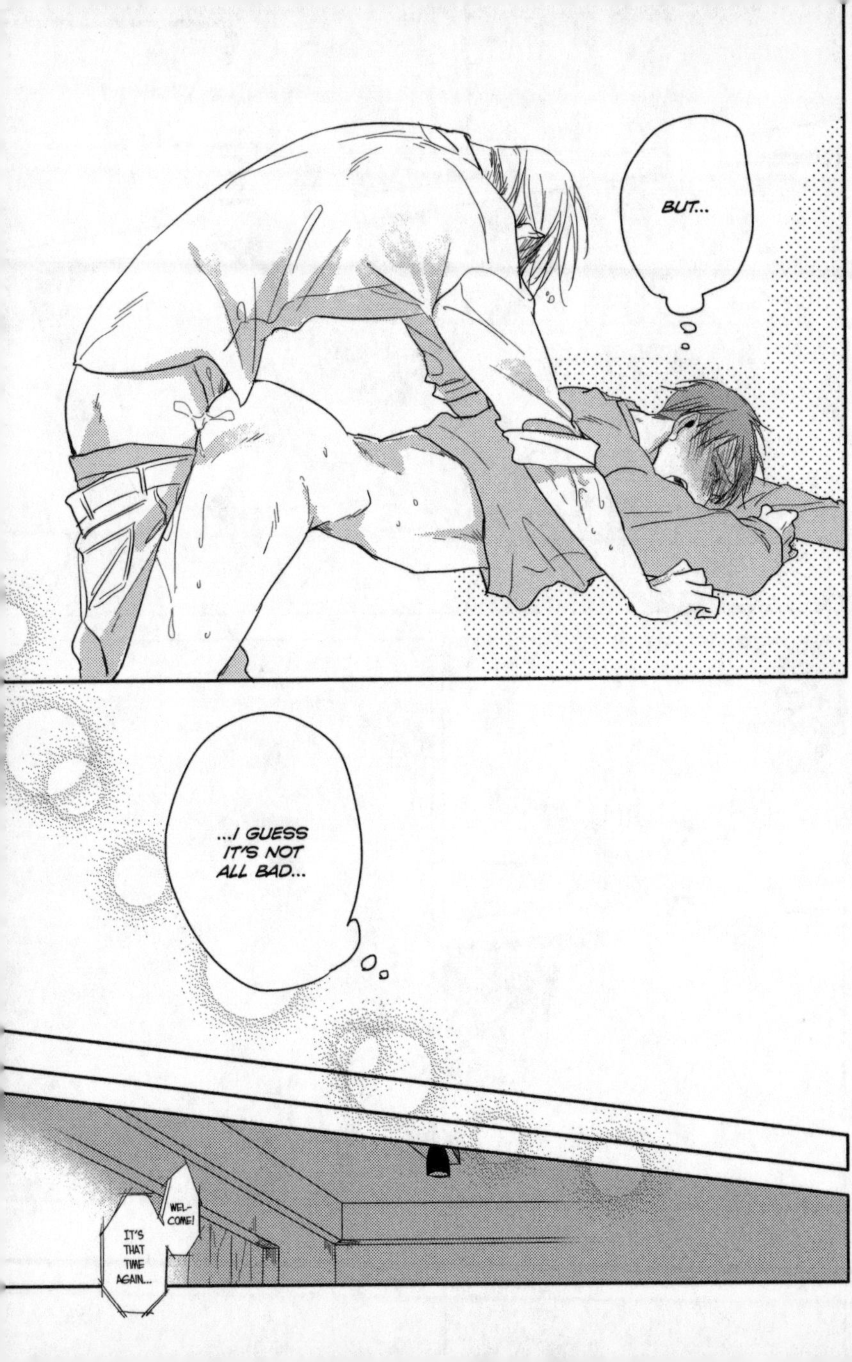
BUT...
...I GUESS IT'S NOT ALL BAD...
WEL-COME!
IT'S THAT TIME AGAIN...

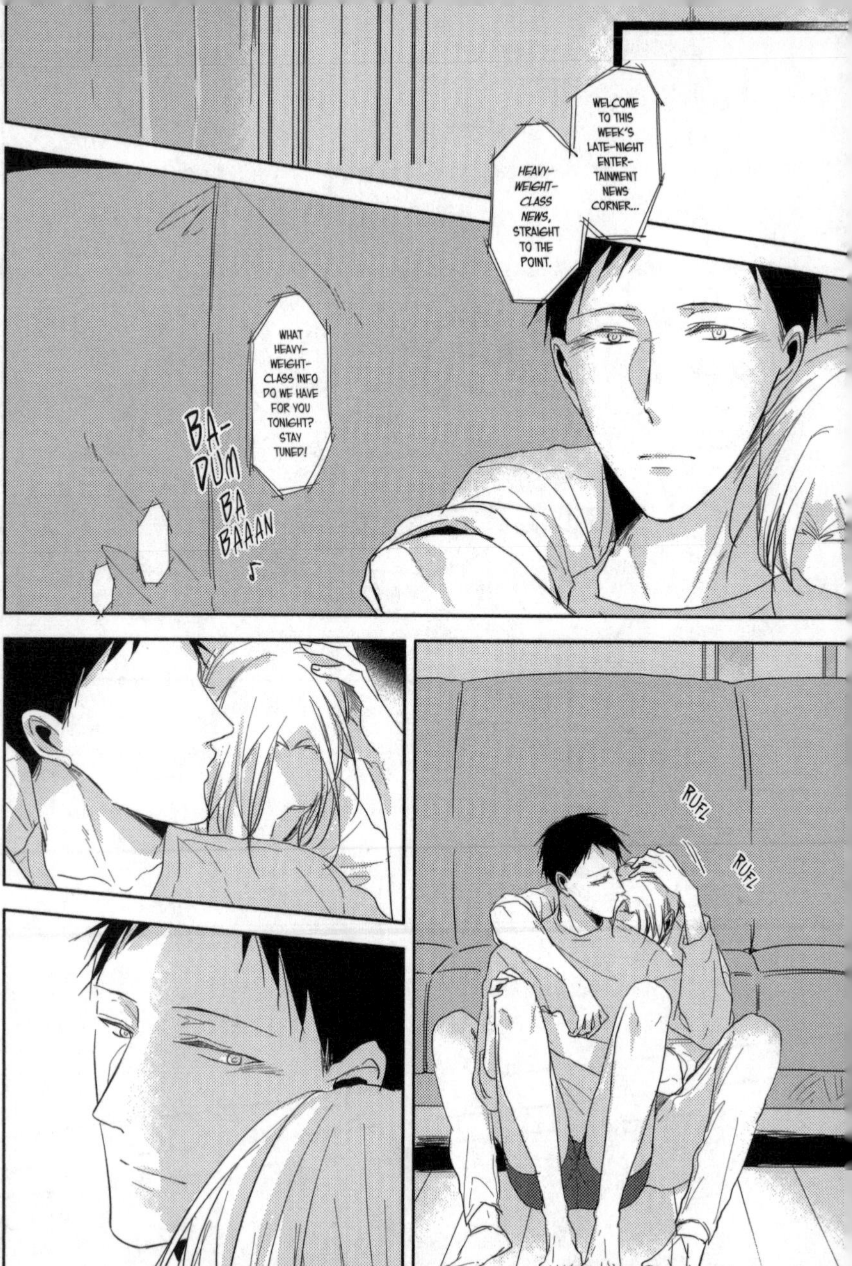
WELCOME TO THIS WEEK'S LATE-NIGHT ENTER-TAINMENT NEWS CORNER...
HEAVY-WEIGHT-CLASS NEWS, STRAIGHT TO THE POINT.
WHAT HEAVY-WEIGHT-CLASS INFO DO WE HAVE FOR YOU TONIGHT? STAY TUNED!
BA-DUM BA BAAAN ♪
RUFL
RUFL

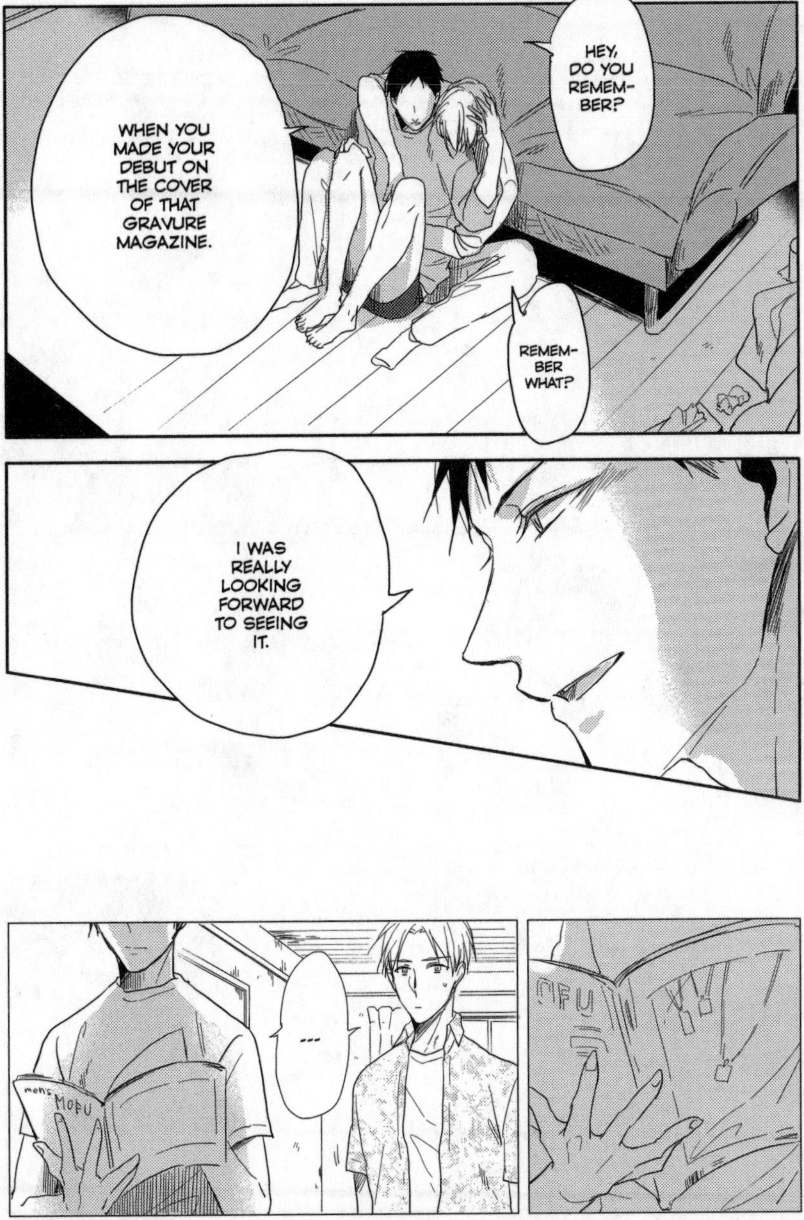
HEY, DO YOU REMEMBER?
REMEMBER WHAT?
WHEN YOU MADE YOUR DEBUT ON THE COVER OF THAT GRAVURE MAGAZINE.
I WAS REALLY LOOKING FORWARD TO SEEING IT.
...
men's MOFU

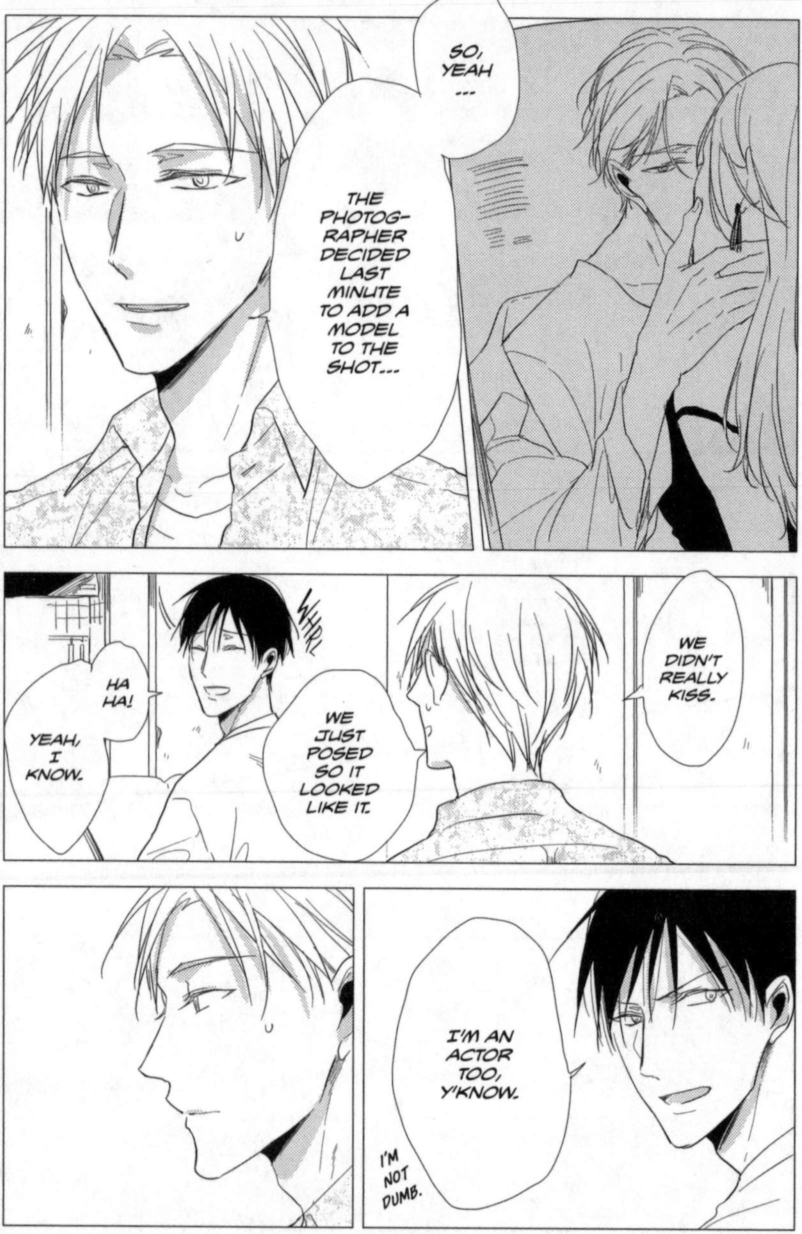
SO, YEAH...
THE PHOTOGRAPHER DECIDED LAST MINUTE TO ADD A MODEL TO THE SHOT...
WE DIDN'T REALLY KISS.
WE JUST POSED SO IT LOOKED LIKE IT.
WHIRL
HA HA!
YEAH, I KNOW.
I'M AN ACTOR TOO, Y'KNOW.
I'M NOT DUMB.

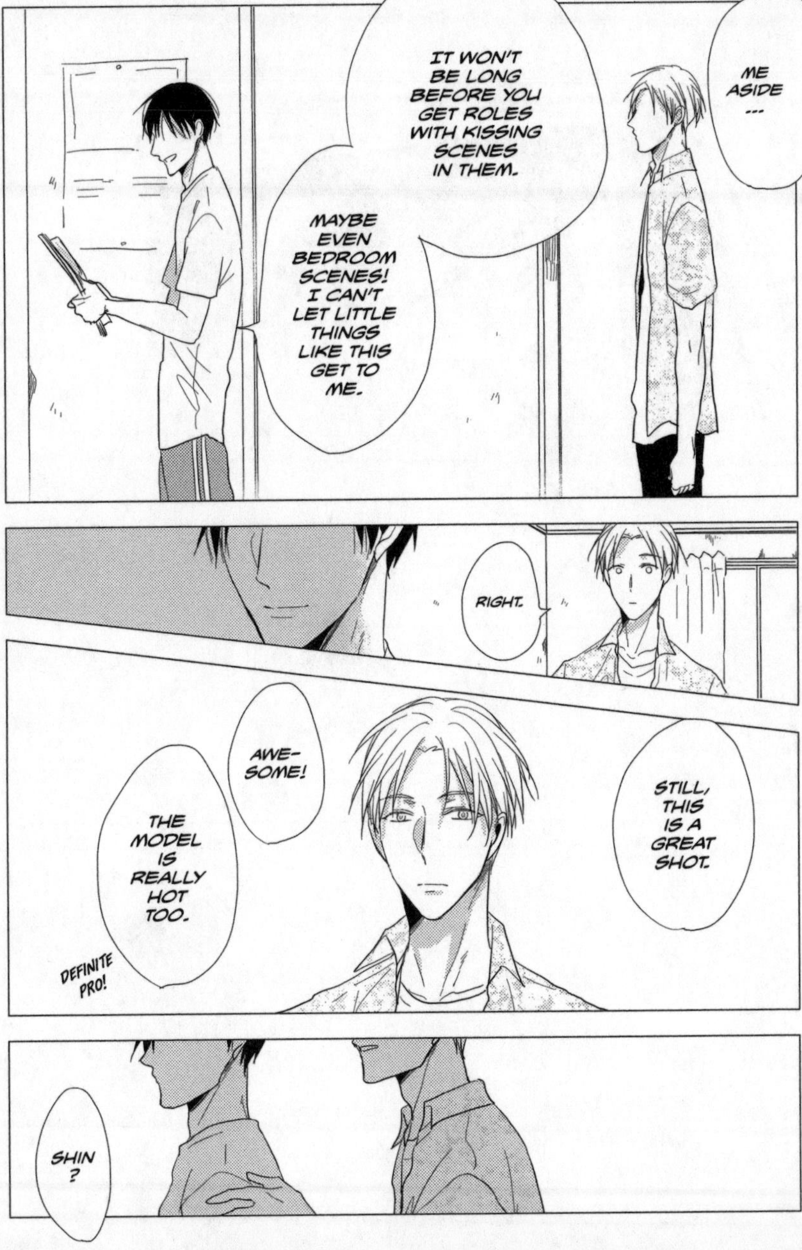
ME ASIDE---
IT WON'T BE LONG BEFORE YOU GET ROLES WITH KISSING SCENES IN THEM.
MAYBE EVEN BEDROOM SCENES! I CAN'T LET LITTLE THINGS LIKE THIS GET TO ME.
RIGHT.
STILL, THIS IS A GREAT SHOT.
AWE-SOME!
THE MODEL IS REALLY HOT TOO.
DEFINITE PRO!
SHIN?

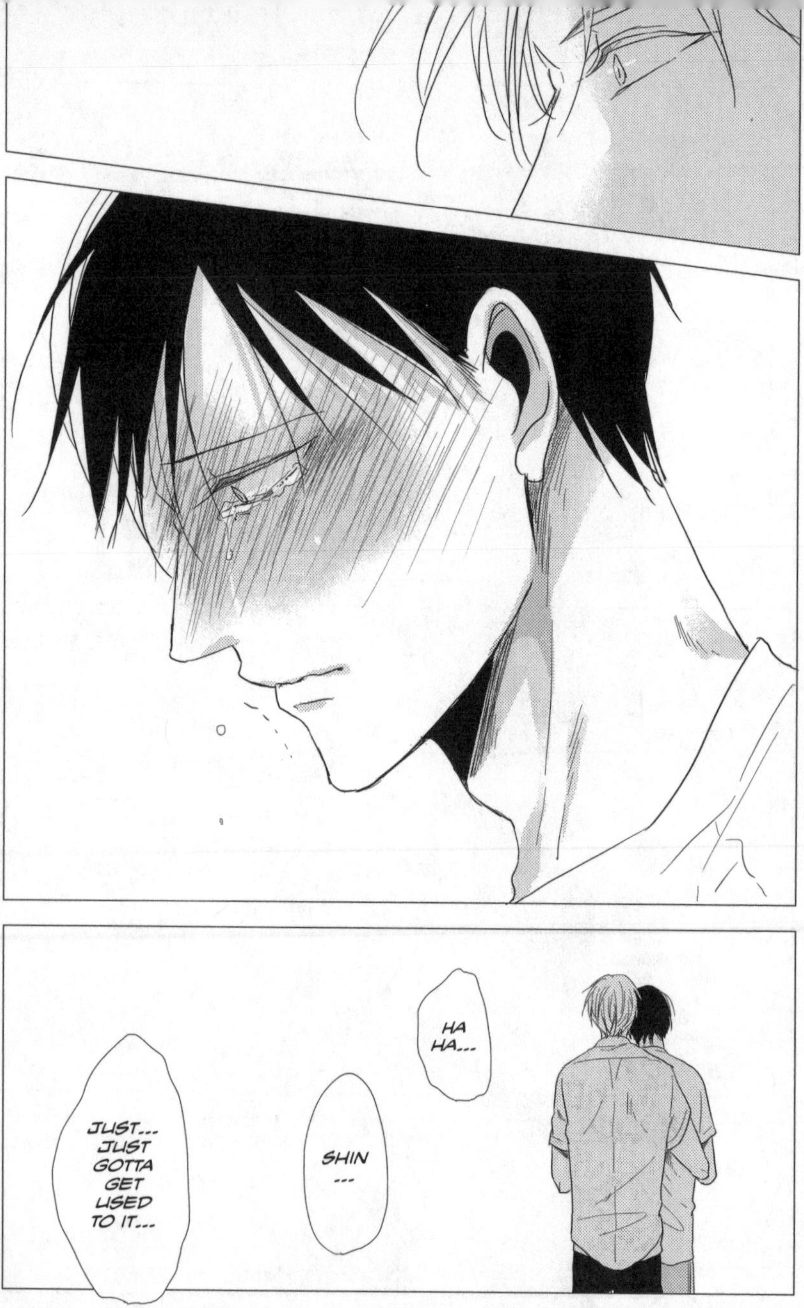
HA HA...
SHIN ---
JUST... JUST GOTTA GET USED TO IT...

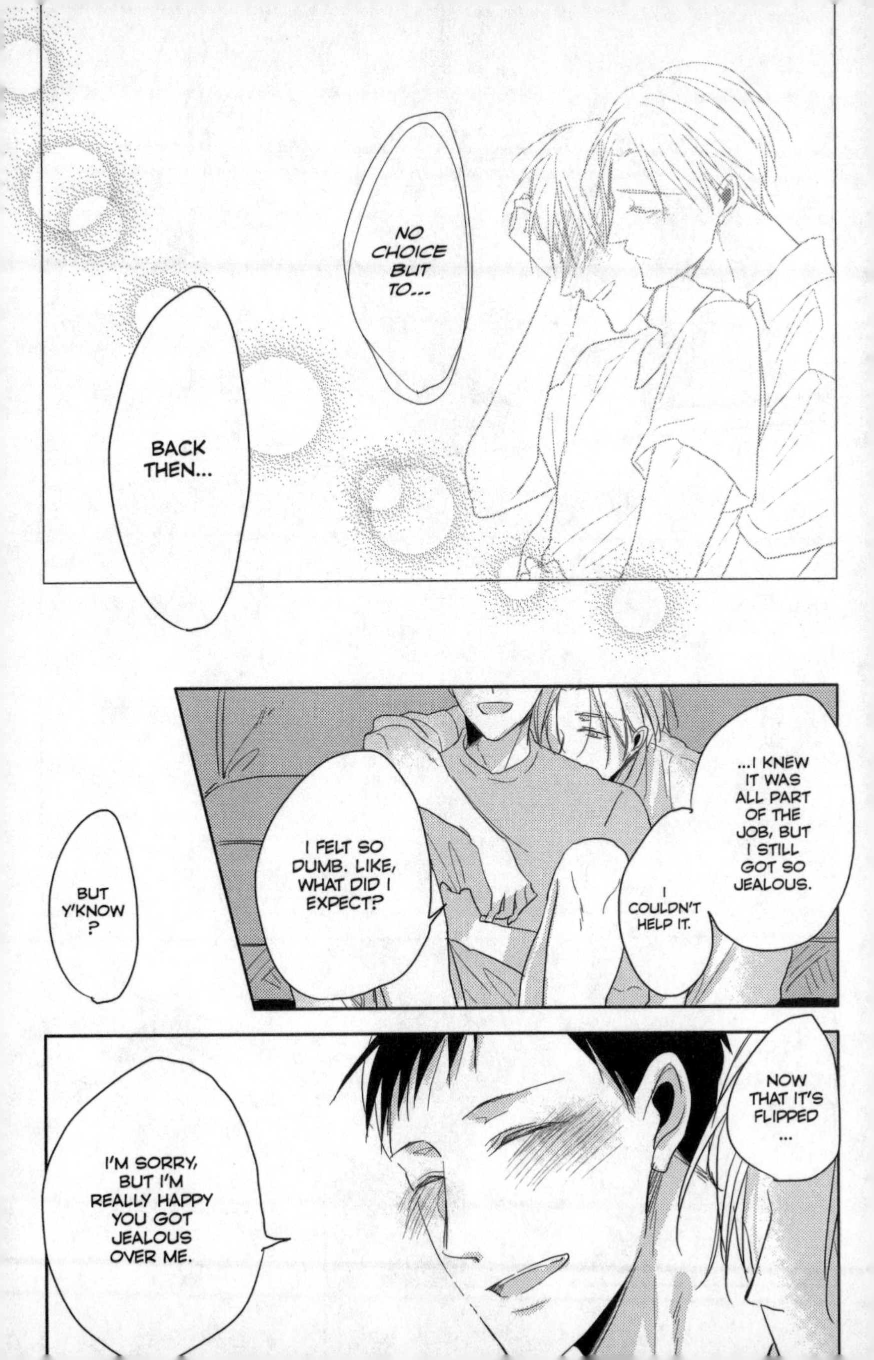
NO CHOICE BUT TO...
BACK THEN...
...I KNEW IT WAS ALL PART OF THE JOB, BUT I STILL GOT SO JEALOUS.
I COULDN'T HELP IT.
I FELT SO DUMB. LIKE, WHAT DID I EXPECT?
BUT Y'KNOW?
NOW THAT IT'S FLIPPED...
I'M SORRY, BUT I'M REALLY HAPPY YOU GOT JEALOUS OVER ME.

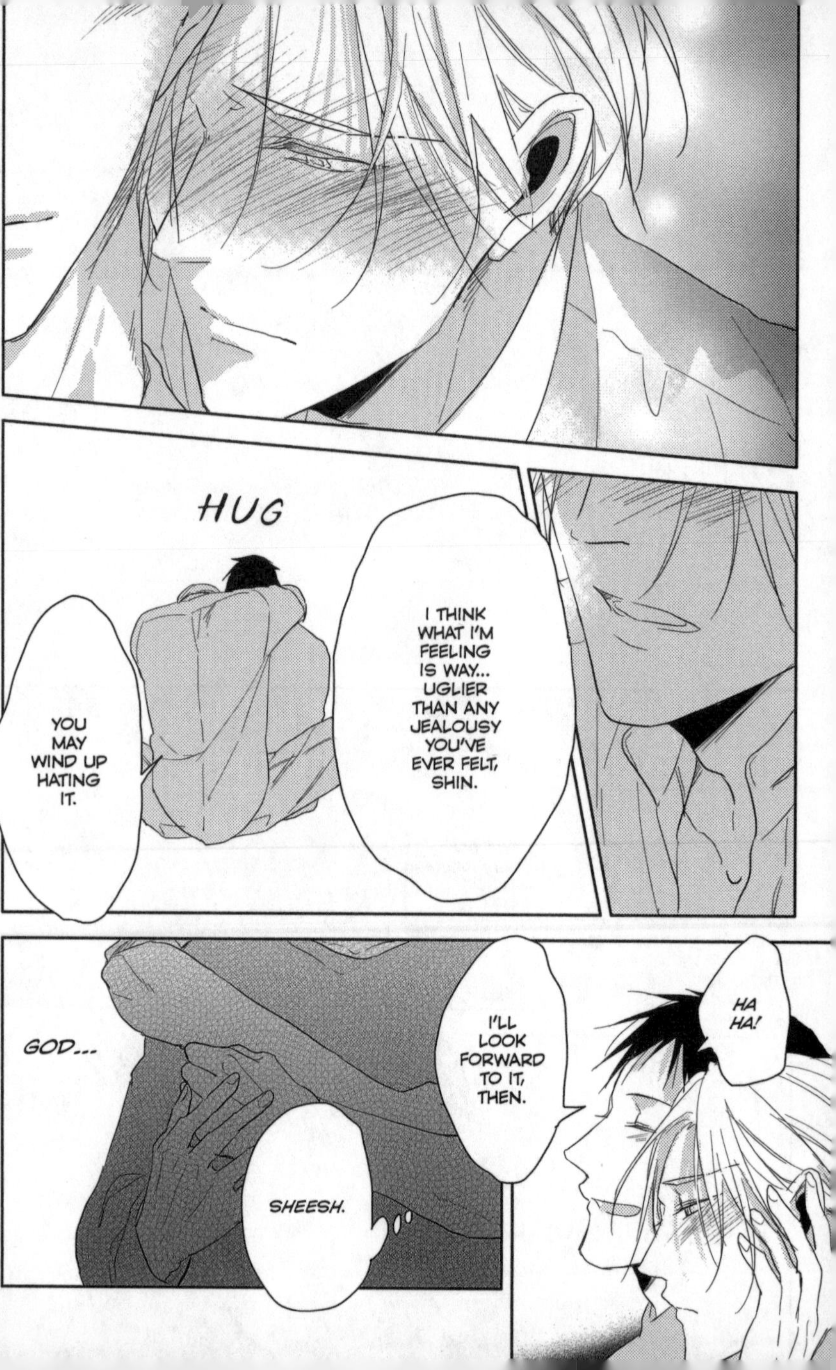
I THINK WHAT I'M FEELING IS WAY... UGLIER THAN ANY JEALOUSY YOU'VE EVER FELT, SHIN.
HUG
YOU MAY WIND UP HATING IT.
HA HA!
I'LL LOOK FORWARD TO IT, THEN.
GOD...
SHEESH.

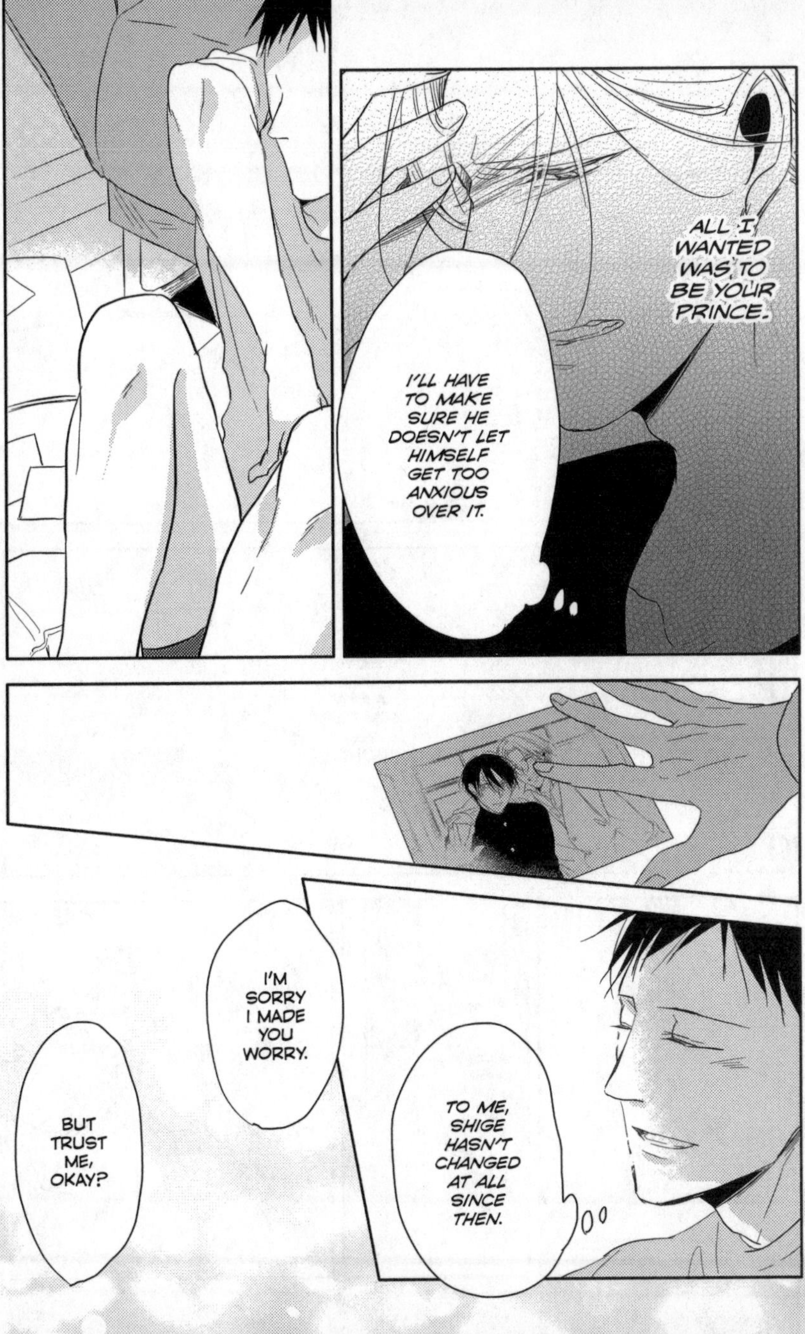
ALL I WANTED WAS TO BE YOUR PRINCE.
I'LL HAVE TO MAKE SURE HE DOESN'T LET HIMSELF GET TOO ANXIOUS OVER IT.
TO ME, SHIGE HASN'T CHANGED AT ALL SINCE THEN.
I'M SORRY I MADE YOU WORRY.
BUT TRUST ME, OKAY?

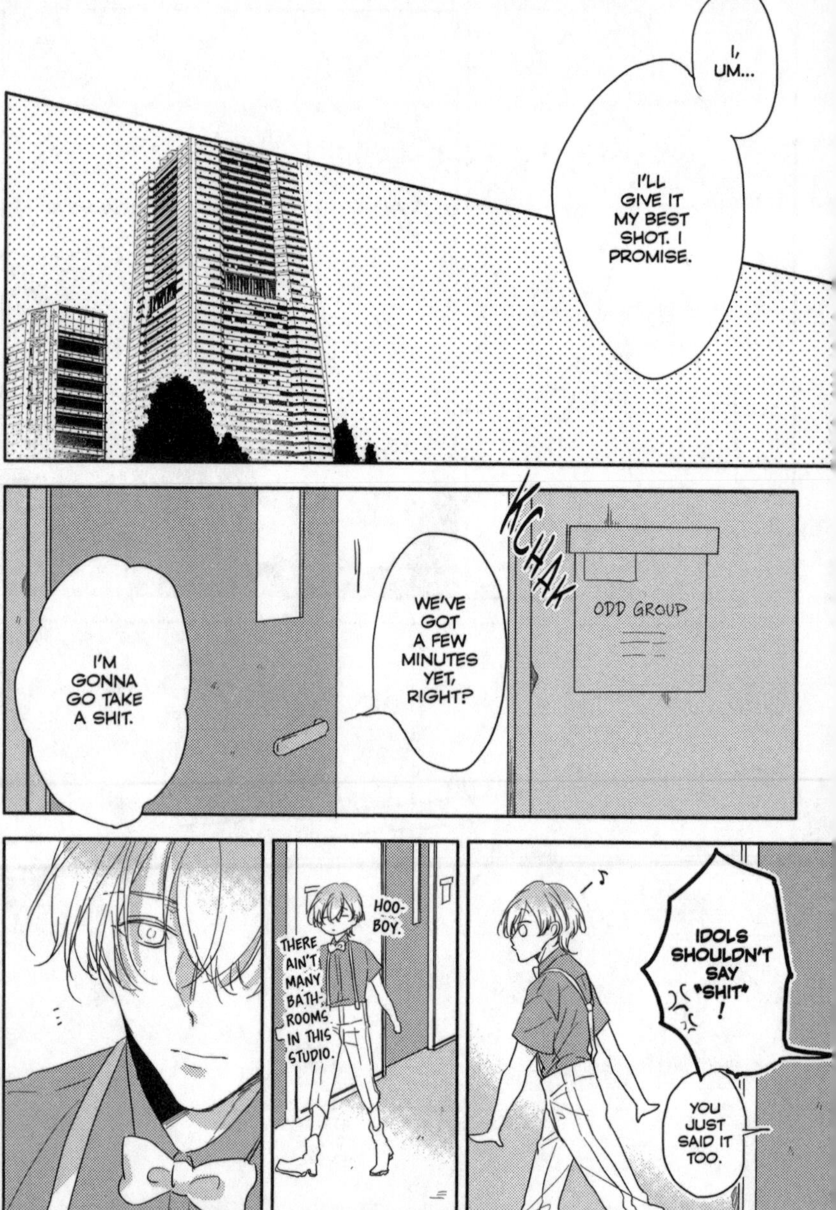
I, UM...
I'LL GIVE IT MY BEST SHOT. I PROMISE.
KCHAK
ODD GROUP
WE'VE GOT A FEW MINUTES YET, RIGHT?
I'M GONNA GO TAKE A SHIT.
IDOLS SHOULDN'T SAY "SHIT"!
YOU JUST SAID IT TOO.
HOO-BOY.
THERE AIN'T MANY BATHROOMS IN THIS STUDIO.

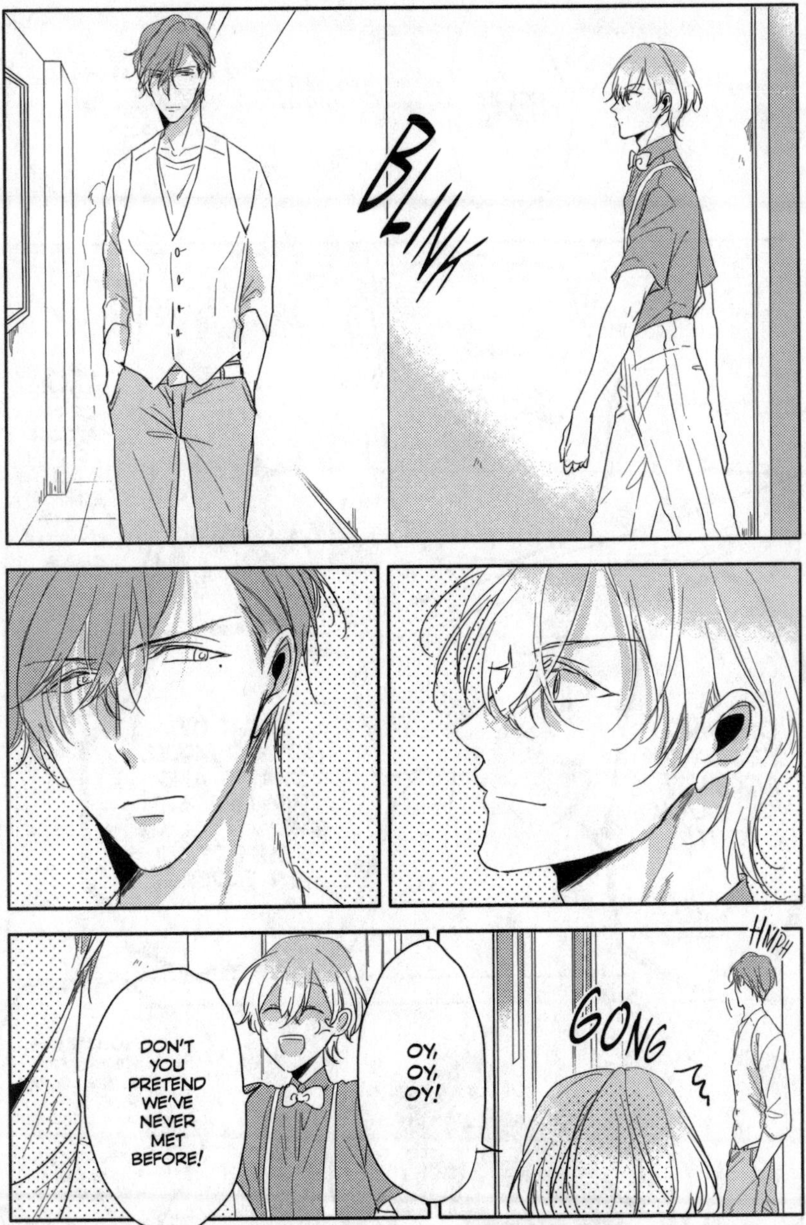
BLINK
HMPH
GONG
OY, OY, OY!
DON'T YOU PRETEND WE'VE NEVER MET BEFORE!

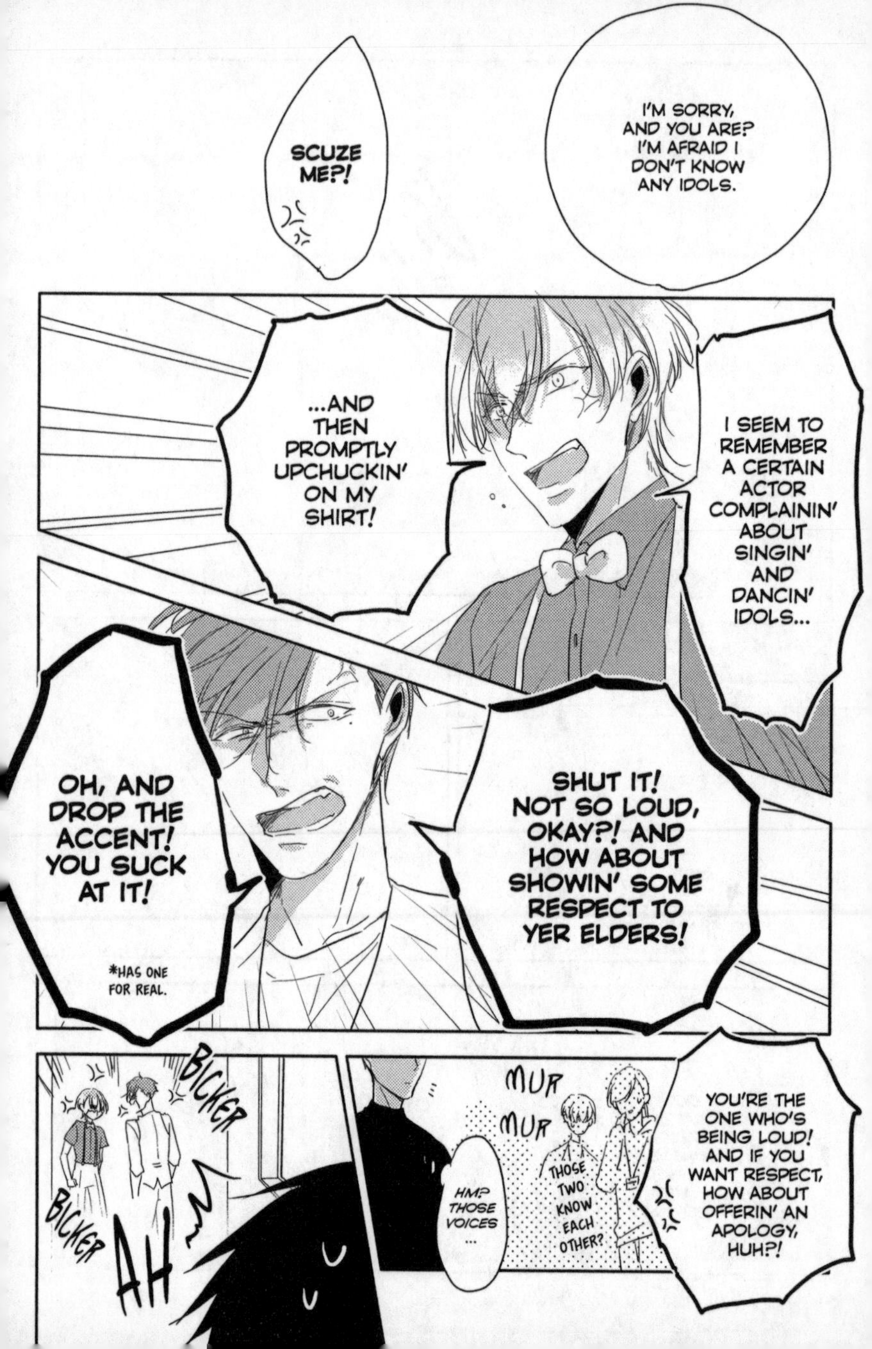
I'M SORRY, AND YOU ARE? I'M AFRAID I DON'T KNOW ANY IDOLS.
SCUZE ME?!
I SEEM TO REMEMBER A CERTAIN ACTOR COMPLAININ' ABOUT SINGIN' AND DANCIN' IDOLS...
...AND THEN PROMPTLY UPCHUCKIN' ON MY SHIRT!
SHUT IT! NOT SO LOUD, OKAY?! AND HOW ABOUT SHOWIN' SOME RESPECT TO YER ELDERS!
OH, AND DROP THE ACCENT! YOU SUCK AT IT!
*HAS ONE FOR REAL.
YOU'RE THE ONE WHO'S BEING LOUD! AND IF YOU WANT RESPECT, HOW ABOUT OFFERIN' AN APOLOGY, HUH?!
MUR
MUR
THOSE TWO KNOW EACH OTHER?
HM? THOSE VOICES...
BICKER
BICKER
AH

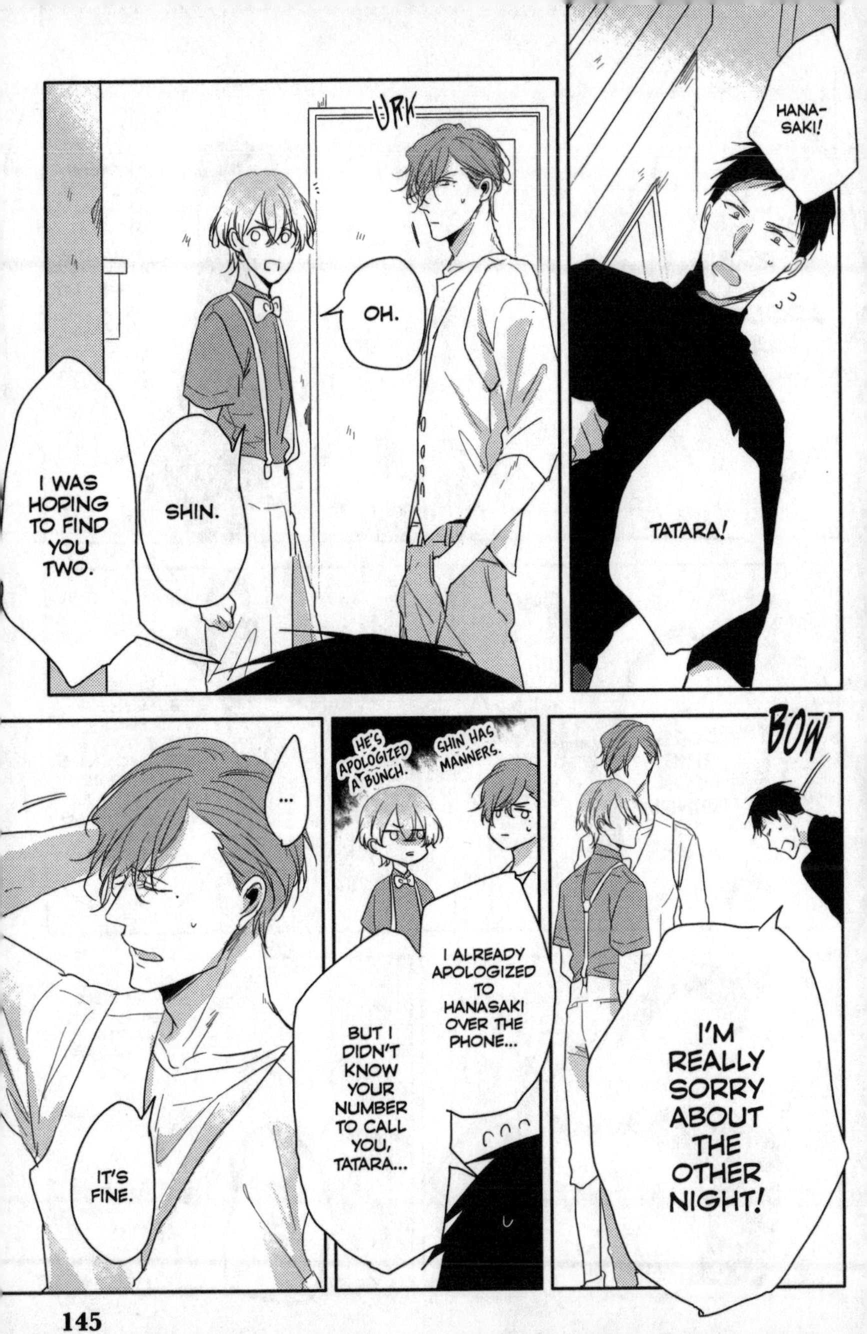
HANA-SAKI!
TATARA!
URK
OH.
SHIN.
I WAS HOPING TO FIND YOU TWO.
BOW
I'M REALLY SORRY ABOUT THE OTHER NIGHT!
SHIN HAS MANNERS.
HE'S APOLOGIZED A BUNCH.
I ALREADY APOLOGIZED TO HANASAKI OVER THE PHONE...
BUT I DIDN'T KNOW YOUR NUMBER TO CALL YOU, TATARA...
...
IT'S FINE.

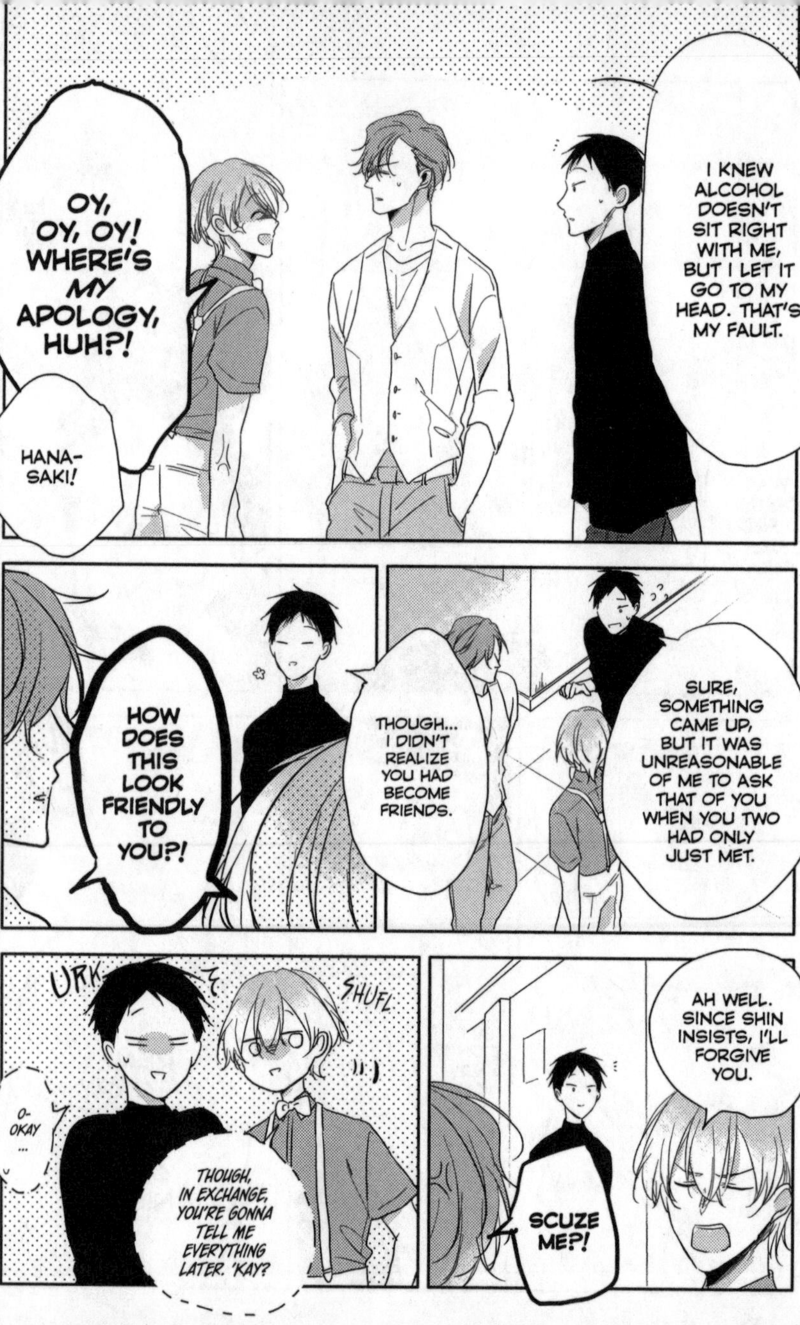
I KNEW ALCOHOL DOESN'T SIT RIGHT WITH ME, BUT I LET IT GO TO MY HEAD. THAT'S MY FAULT.
OY, OY, OY! WHERE'S *MY* APOLOGY, HUH?!
HANA-SAKI!
SURE, SOMETHING CAME UP, BUT IT WAS UNREASONABLE OF ME TO ASK THAT OF YOU WHEN YOU TWO HAD ONLY JUST MET.
THOUGH... I DIDN'T REALIZE YOU HAD BECOME FRIENDS.
HOW DOES THIS LOOK FRIENDLY TO YOU?!
AH WELL. SINCE SHIN INSISTS, I'LL FORGIVE YOU.
SCUZE ME?!
SHUFL
URK
THOUGH, IN EXCHANGE, YOU'RE GONNA TELL ME EVERYTHING LATER. 'KAY?
O-OKAY...

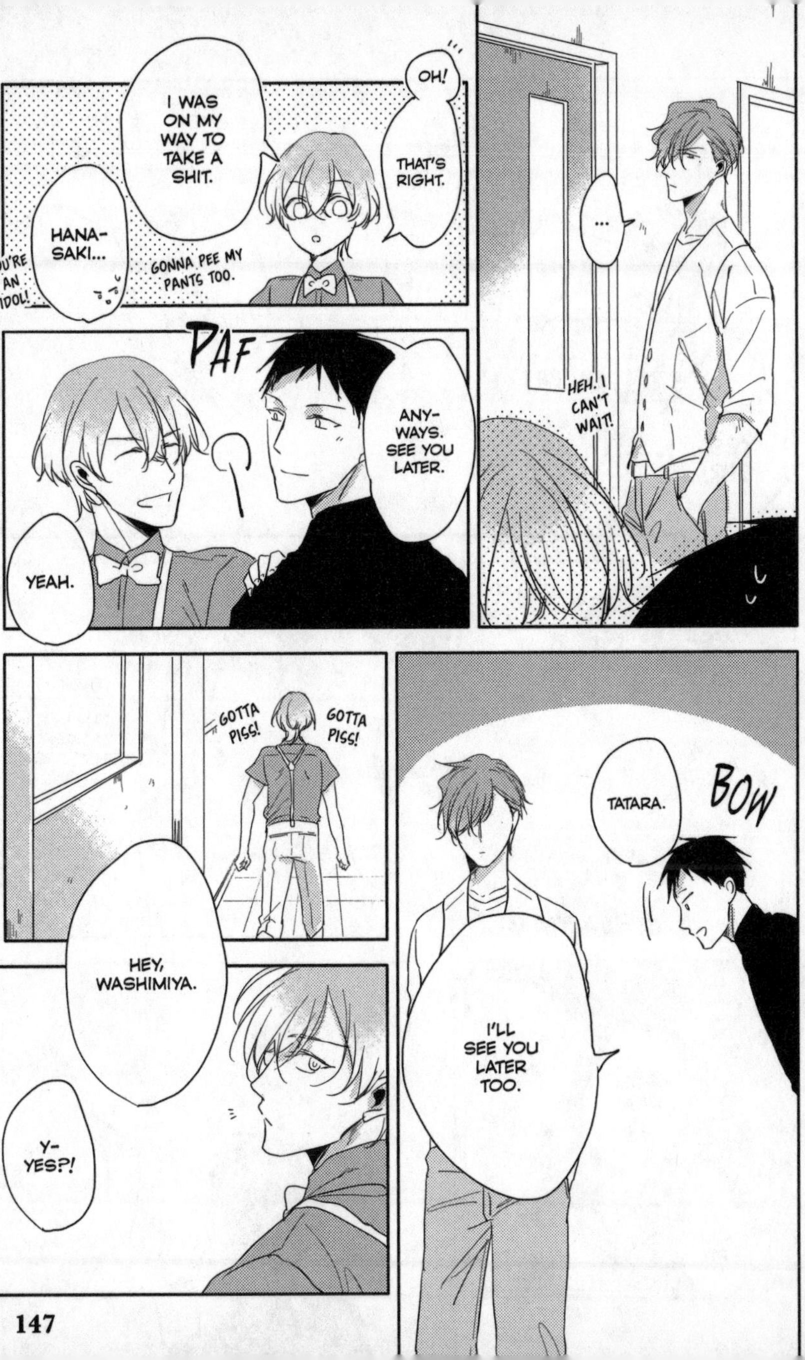
...
HEH. I CAN'T WAIT!
OH! THAT'S RIGHT.
I WAS ON MY WAY TO TAKE A SHIT.
GONNA PEE MY PANTS TOO.
HANA-SAKI...
YOU'RE AN IDOL!
PAF
ANY-WAYS. SEE YOU LATER.
YEAH.
TATARA.
BOW
I'LL SEE YOU LATER TOO.
GOTTA PISS!
GOTTA PISS!
HEY, WASHIMIYA.
Y-YES?!

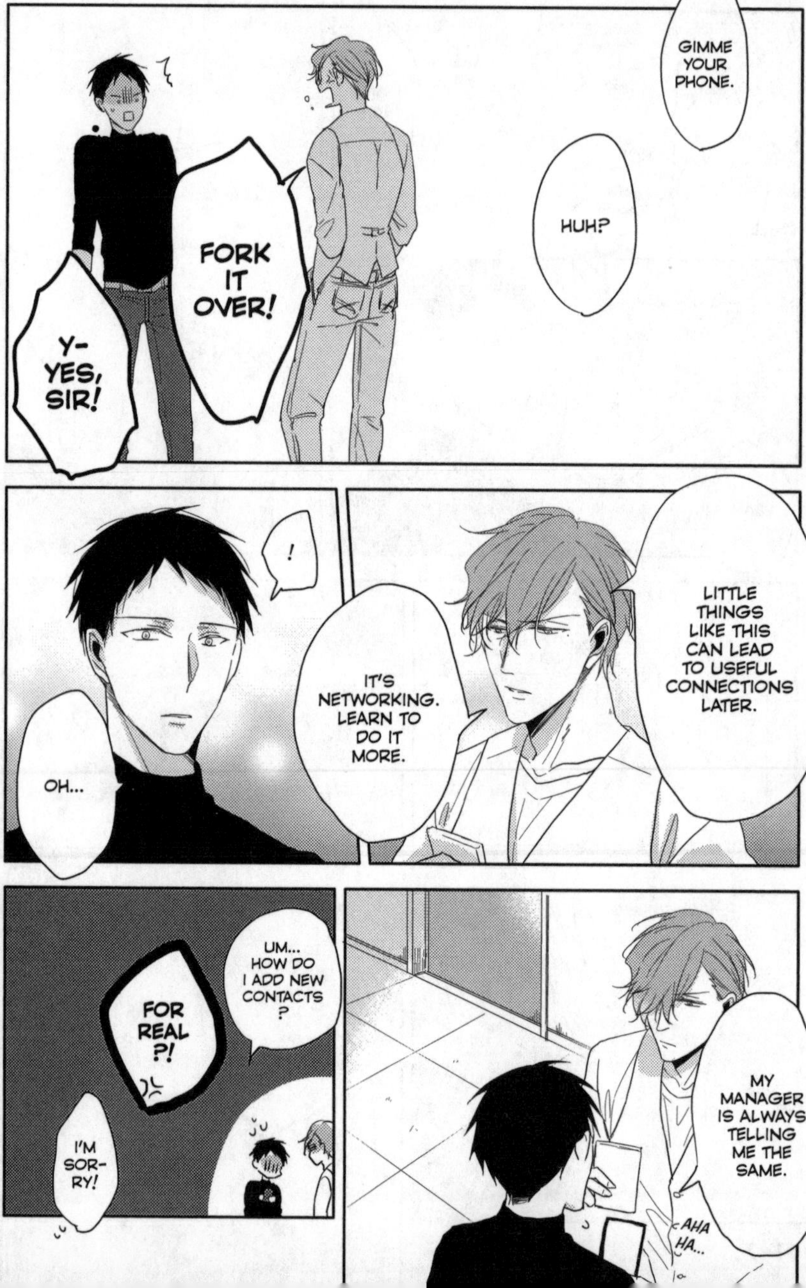
GIMME YOUR PHONE.
HUH?
FORK IT OVER!
Y- YES, SIR!
LITTLE THINGS LIKE THIS CAN LEAD TO USEFUL CONNECTIONS LATER.
IT'S NETWORKING. LEARN TO DO IT MORE.
!
OH...
MY MANAGER IS ALWAYS TELLING ME THE SAME.
AHA HA...
UM... HOW DO I ADD NEW CONTACTS?
FOR REAL?!
I'M SOR-RY!

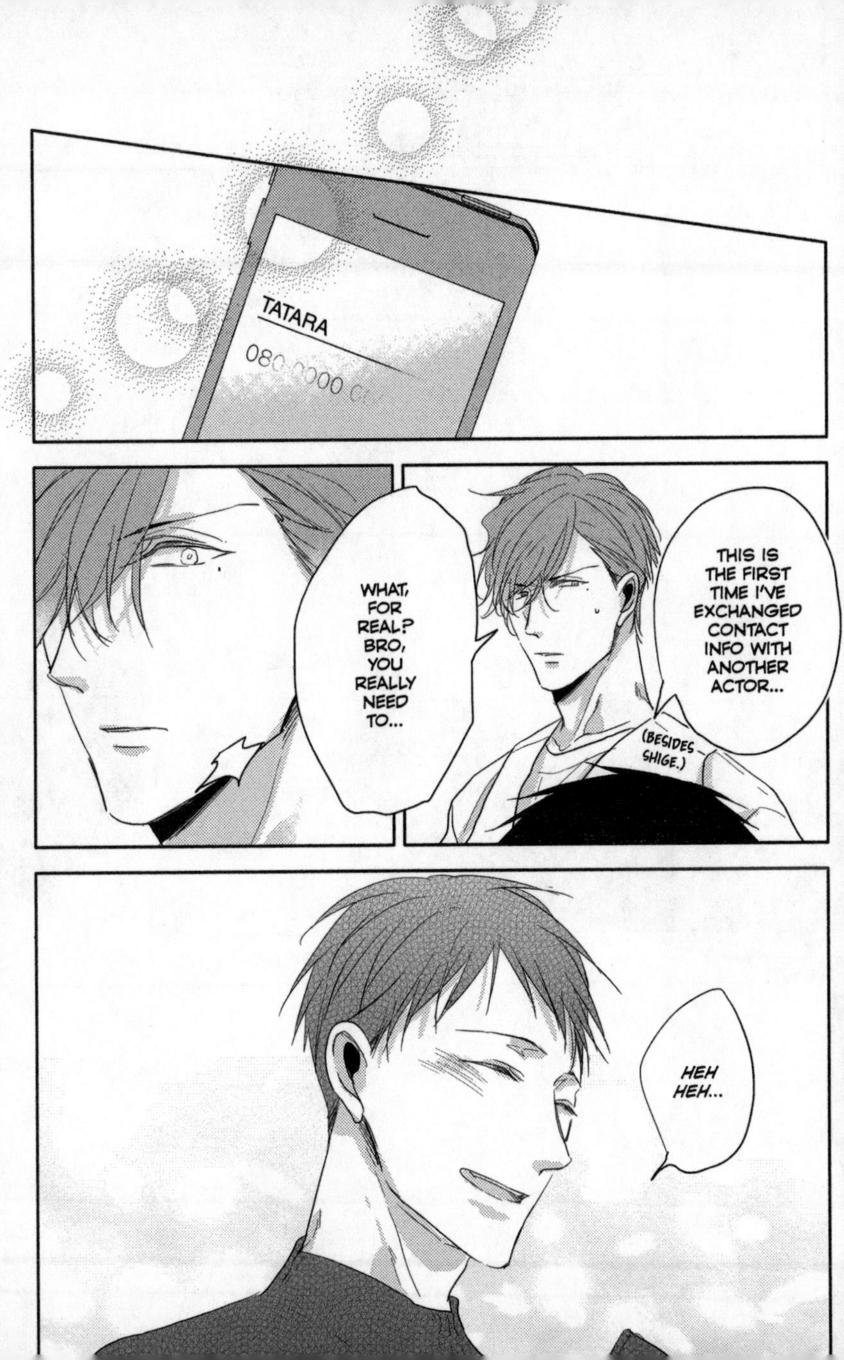
TATARA
080-0000
THIS IS THE FIRST TIME I'VE EXCHANGED CONTACT INFO WITH ANOTHER ACTOR...
(BESIDES SHIGE.)
WHAT, FOR REAL? BRO, YOU REALLY NEED TO...
HEH HEH...

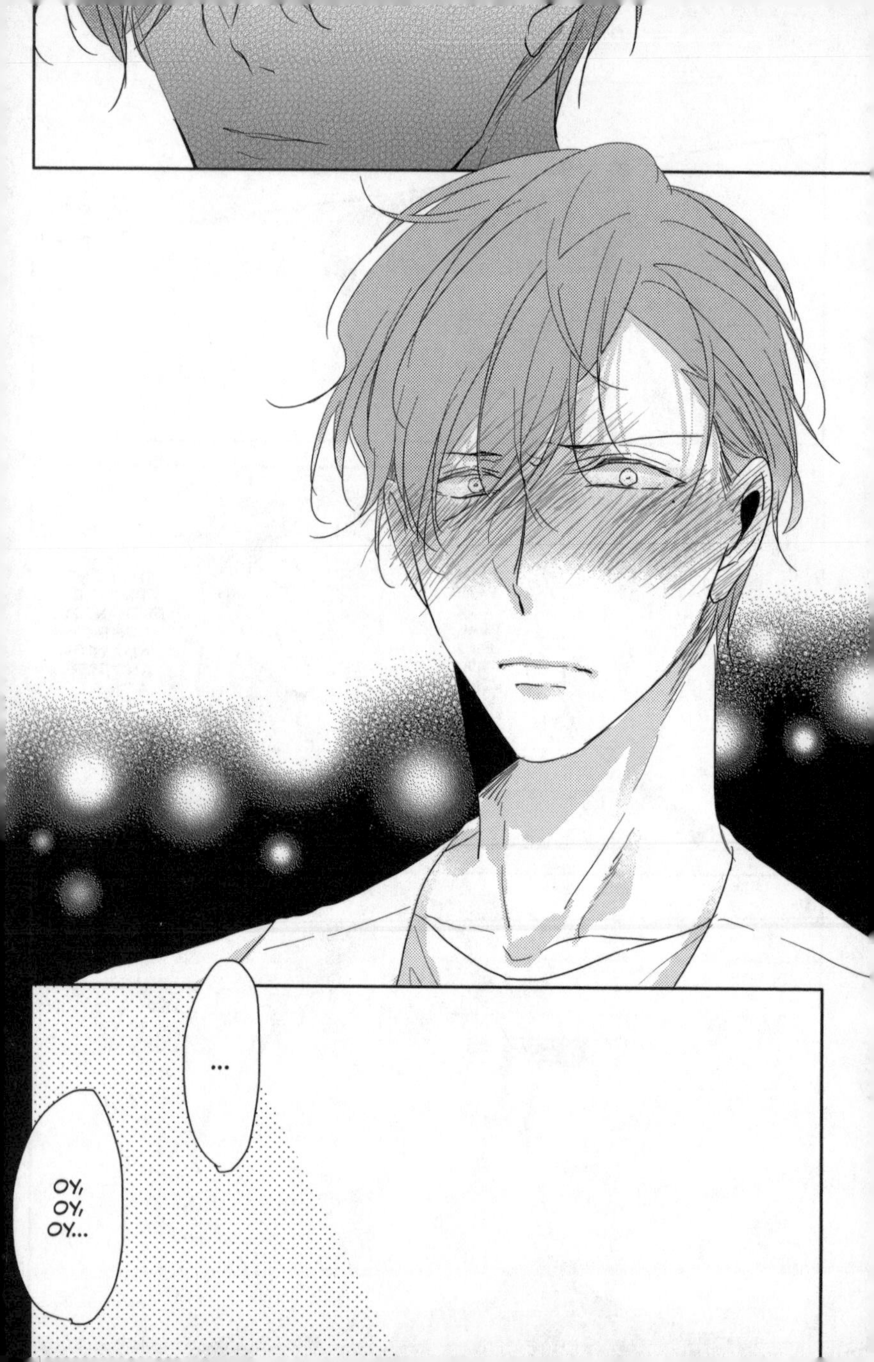
...
OY, OY, OY...

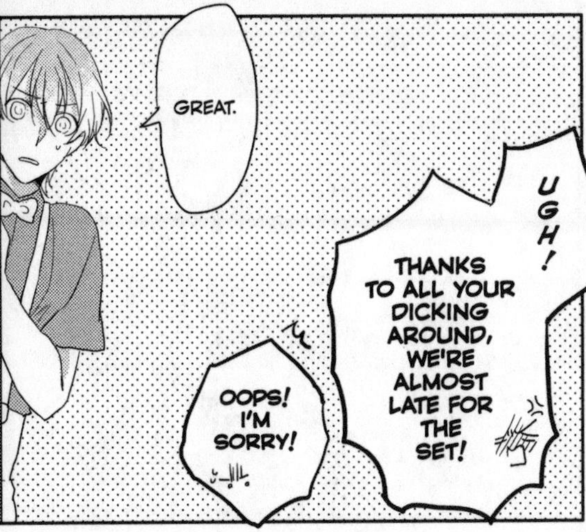
UGH!
THANKS TO ALL YOUR DICKING AROUND, WE'RE ALMOST LATE FOR THE SET!
OOPS! I'M SORRY!
GREAT.
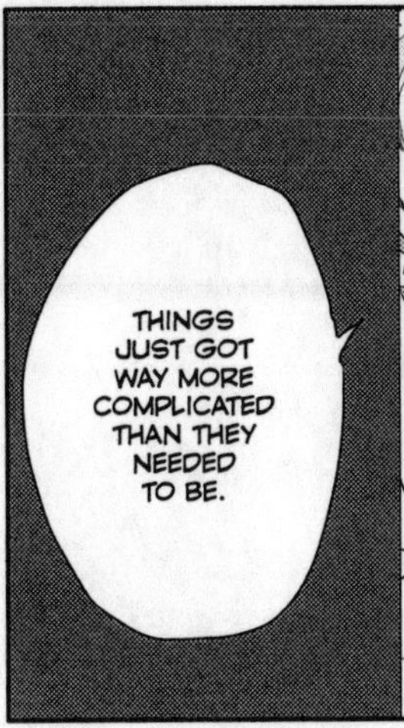
THINGS JUST GOT WAY MORE COMPLICATED THAN THEY NEEDED TO BE.
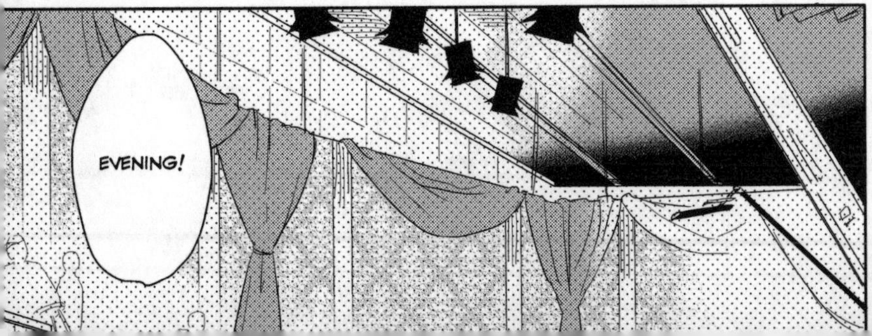
EVENING!

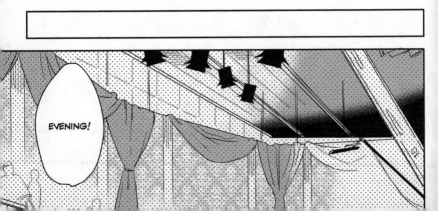

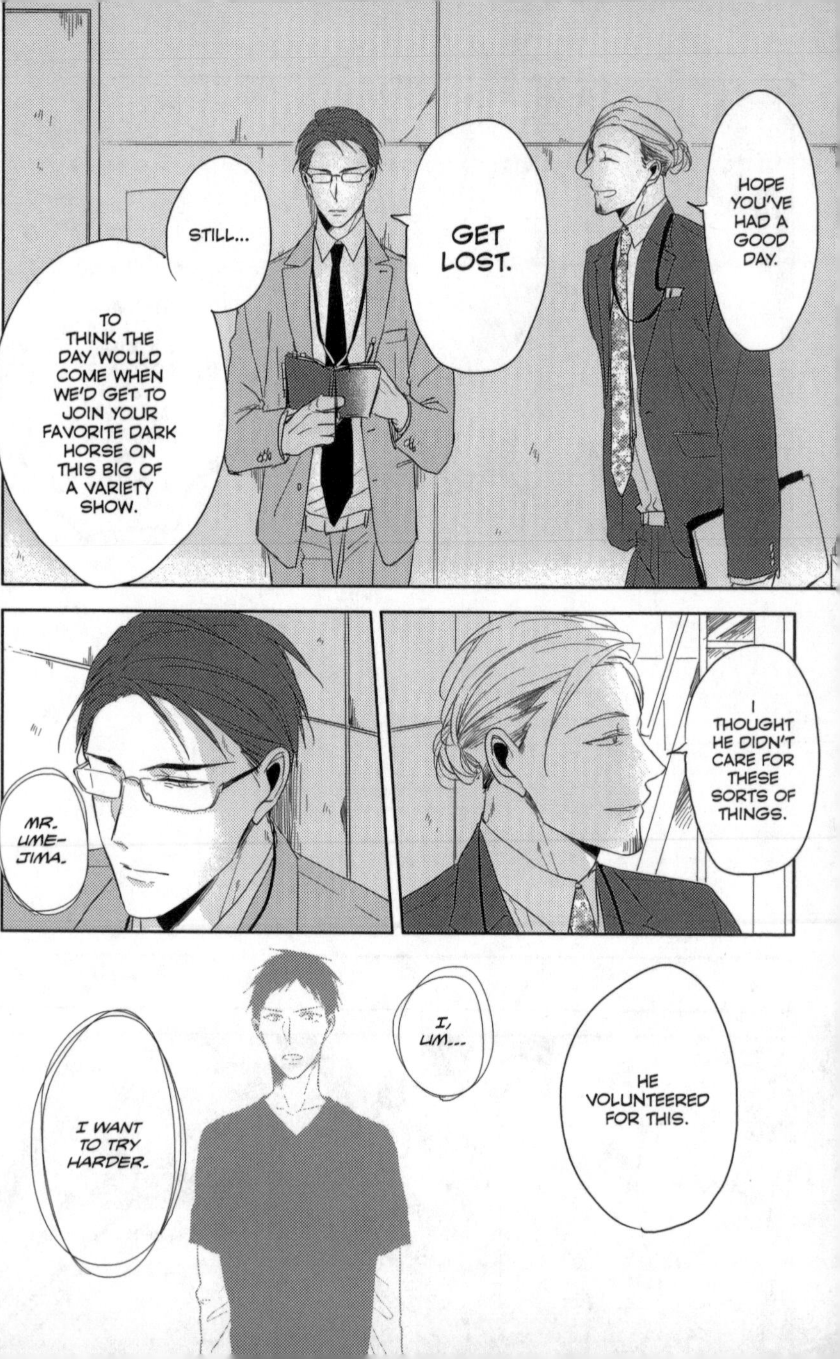
HOPE YOU'VE HAD A GOOD DAY.
GET LOST.
STILL...
TO THINK THE DAY WOULD COME WHEN WE'D GET TO JOIN YOUR FAVORITE DARK HORSE ON THIS BIG OF A VARIETY SHOW.
I THOUGHT HE DIDN'T CARE FOR THESE SORTS OF THINGS.
MR. UME-JIMA.
HE VOLUNTEERED FOR THIS.
I, UM...
I WANT TO TRY HARDER.

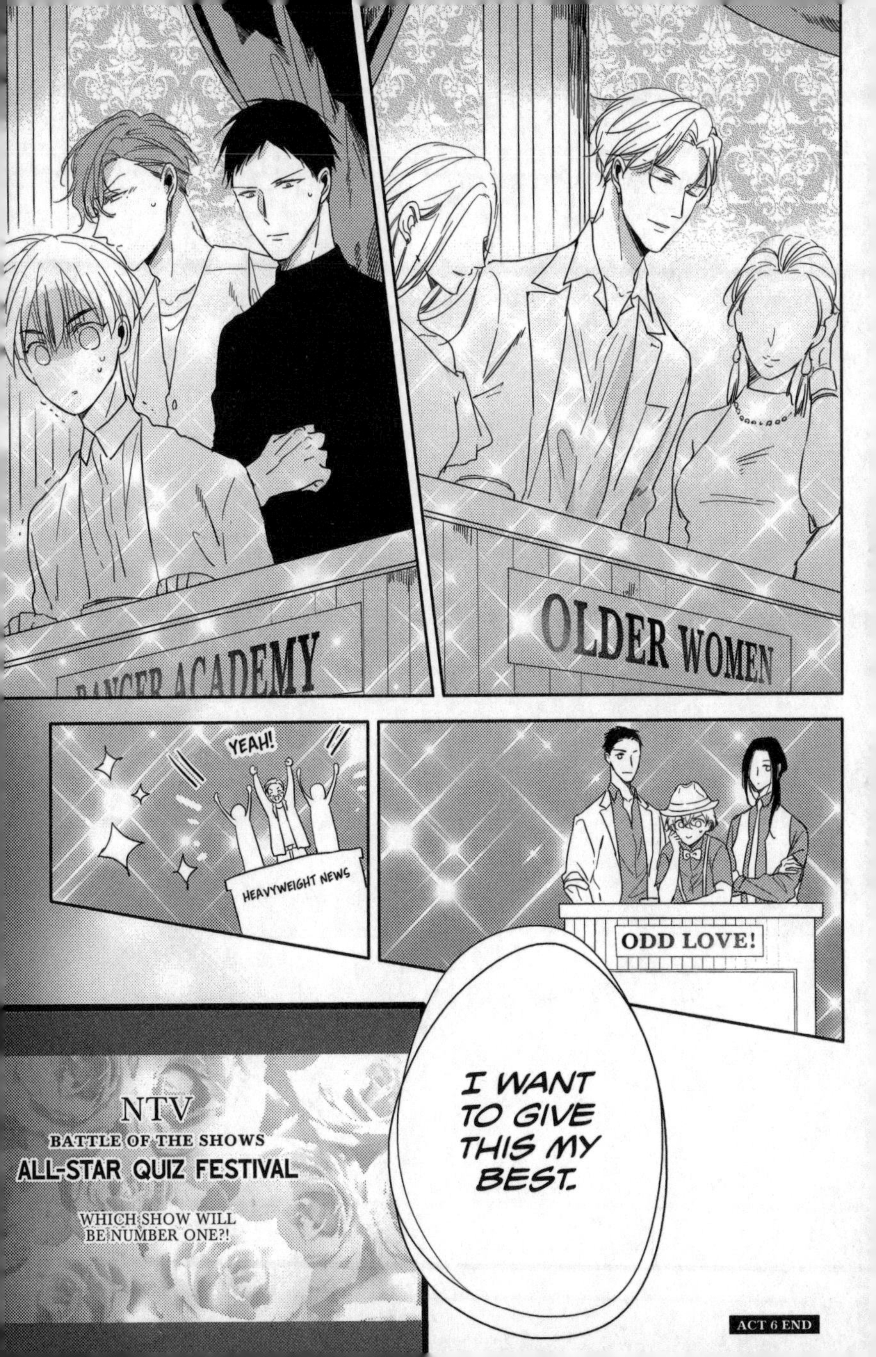
OLDER WOMEN
RANGER ACADEMY
ODD LOVE!
YEAH!
HEAVYWEIGHT NEWS
I WANT TO GIVE THIS MY BEST.
NTV
BATTLE OF THE SHOWS
ALL-STAR QUIZ FESTIVAL
WHICH SHOW WILL BE NUMBER ONE?!
ACT 6 END

Black
or White

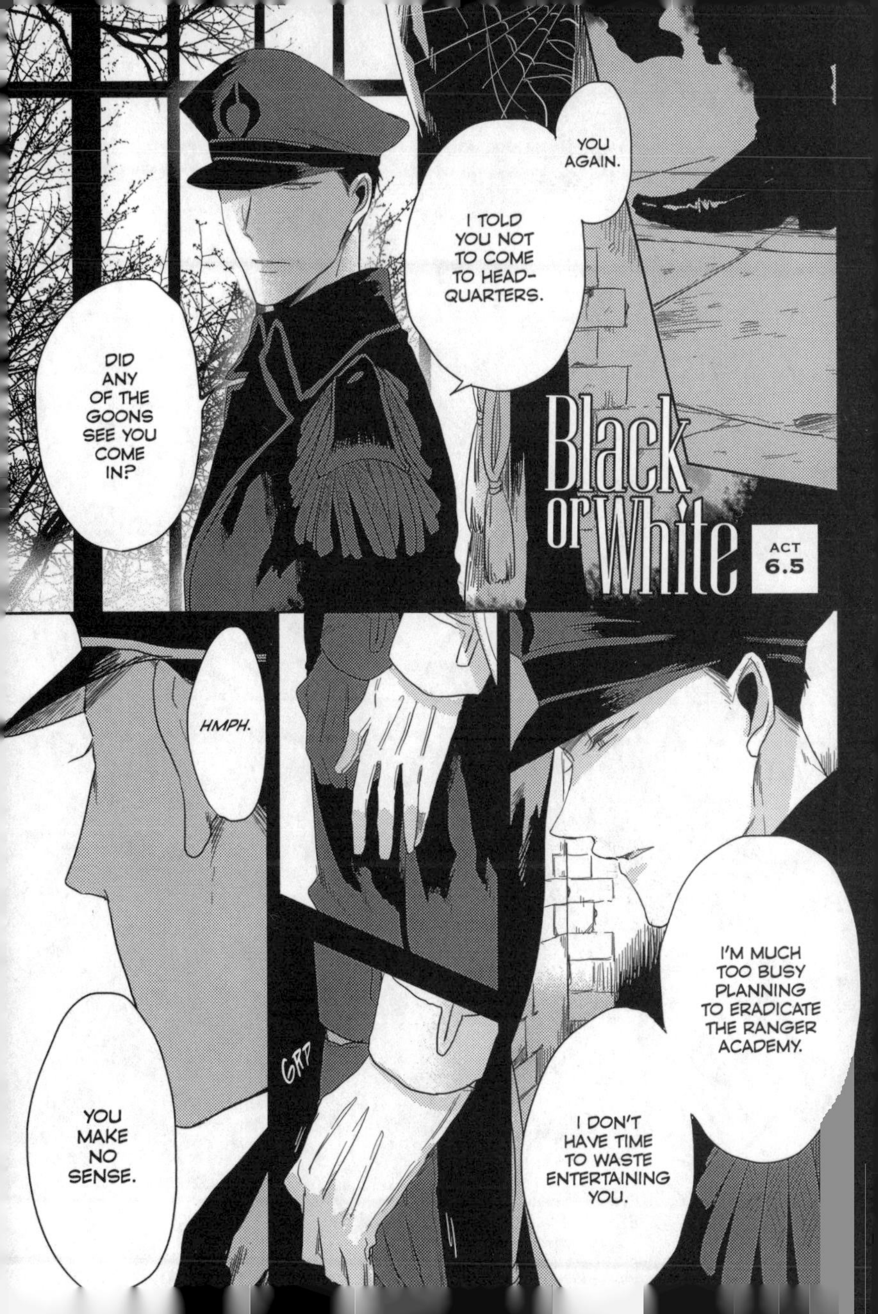
YOU AGAIN.
I TOLD YOU NOT TO COME TO HEAD-QUARTERS.
Black or White
ACT 6.5
DID ANY OF THE GOONS SEE YOU COME IN?
I'M MUCH TOO BUSY PLANNING TO ERADICATE THE RANGER ACADEMY.
I DON'T HAVE TIME TO WASTE ENTERTAINING YOU.
GRP
HMPH.
YOU MAKE NO SENSE.

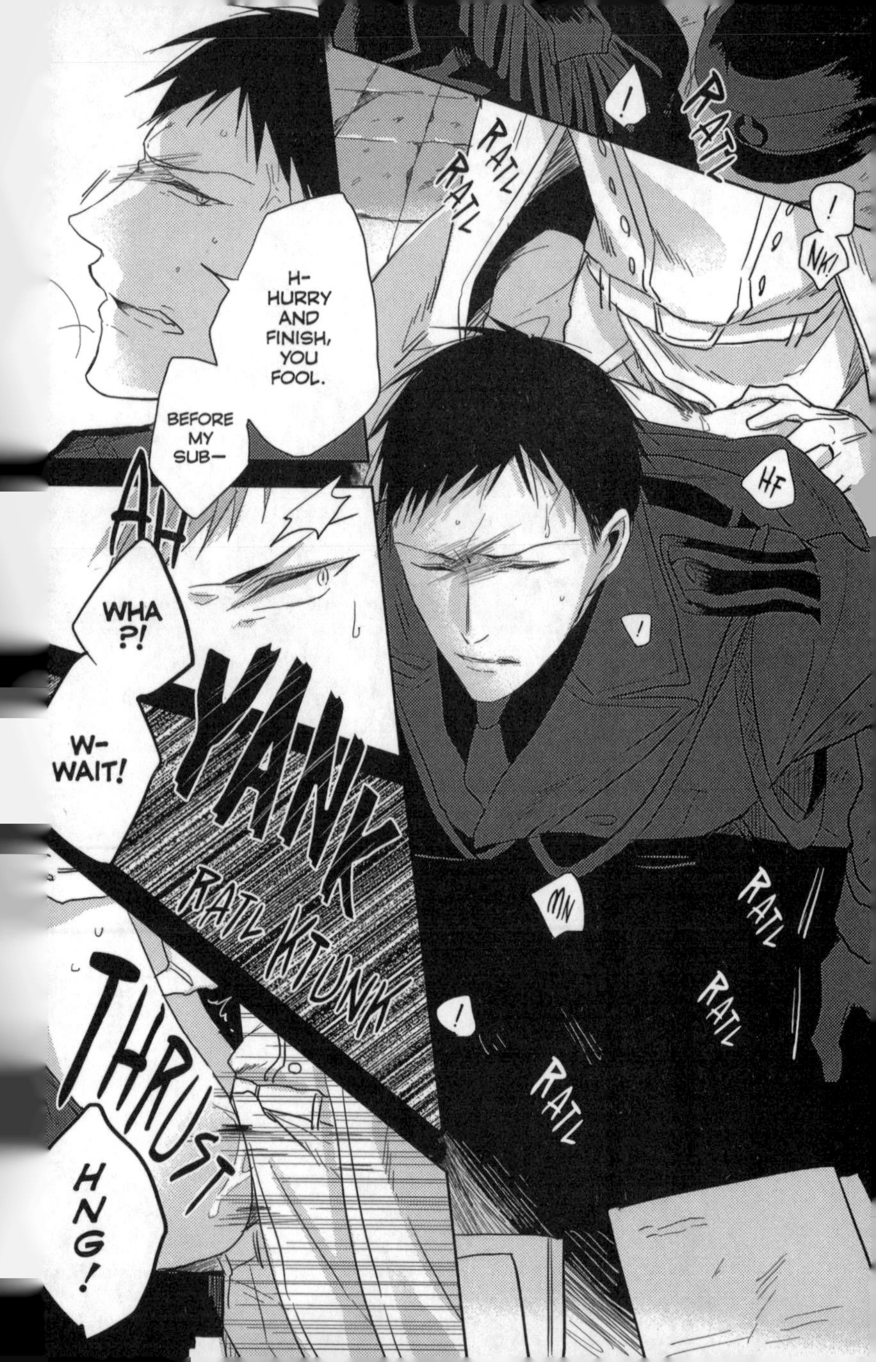

RATL
!
RATL
RATL
!
NK!
H-
HURRY
AND
FINISH,
YOU
FOOL.
BEFORE
MY
SUB—
HF
!
MN
RATL
RATL
RATL
!
AH
WHA
?!
YANK
W-
WAIT!
RATL KTUNK
THRUST
HNG!

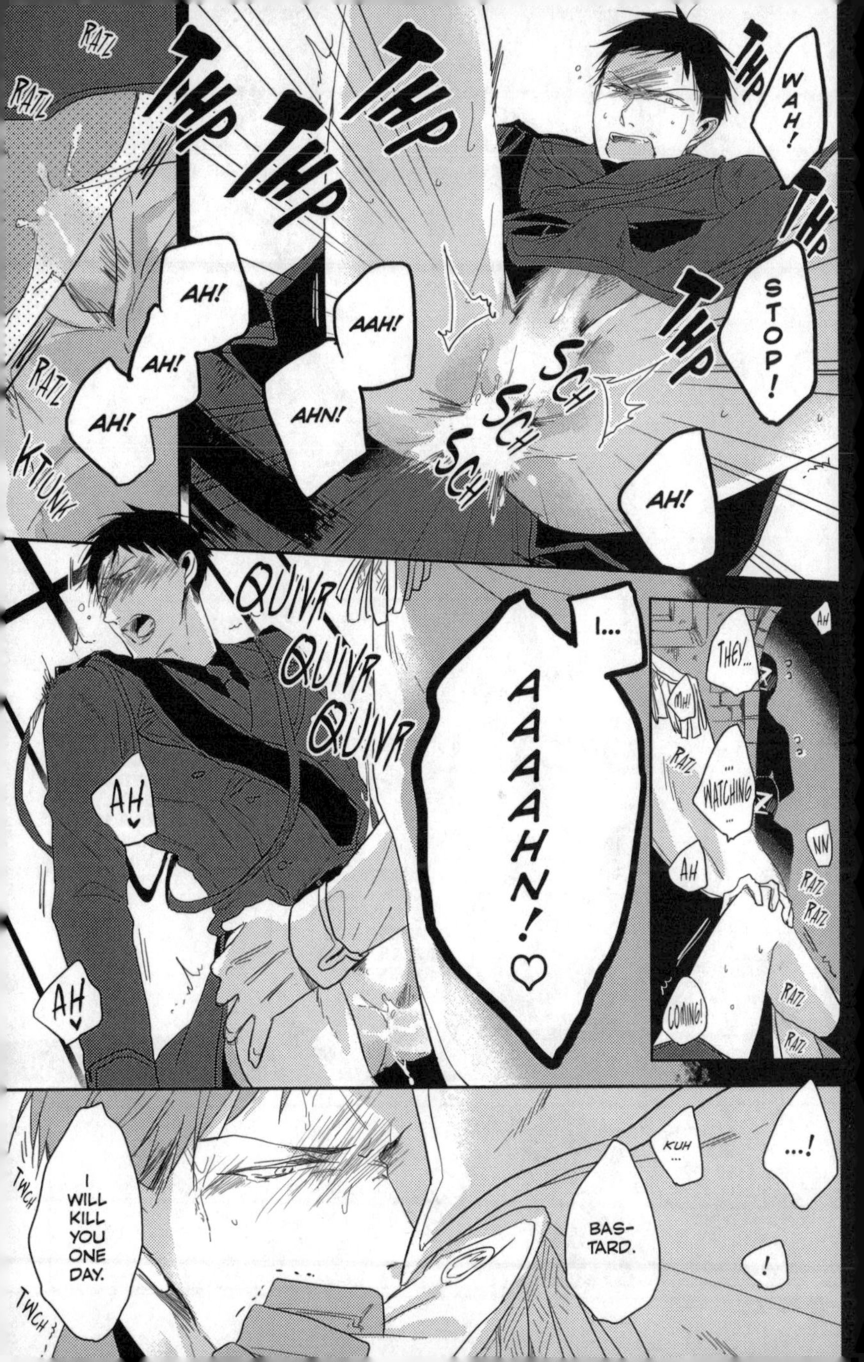
THP
WAH!
THP
THP
STOP!
THP
AH!
SCH
SCH
SCH
AAH!
AHN!
THP
THP
THP
THP
AH!
AH!
AH!
RATZ
RATZ
RATZ
KTUNK
AH
THEY...
MH!
RATZ
... WATCHING ...
NN
RATZ
RATZ
AH
COMING!
RATZ
RATZ
I...
AAAAAHN!♡
QUIVR
QUIVR
QUIVR
AH♥
AH♥
...!
!
KUH ...
BAS-TARD.
I WILL KILL YOU ONE DAY.
TWCH
TWCH

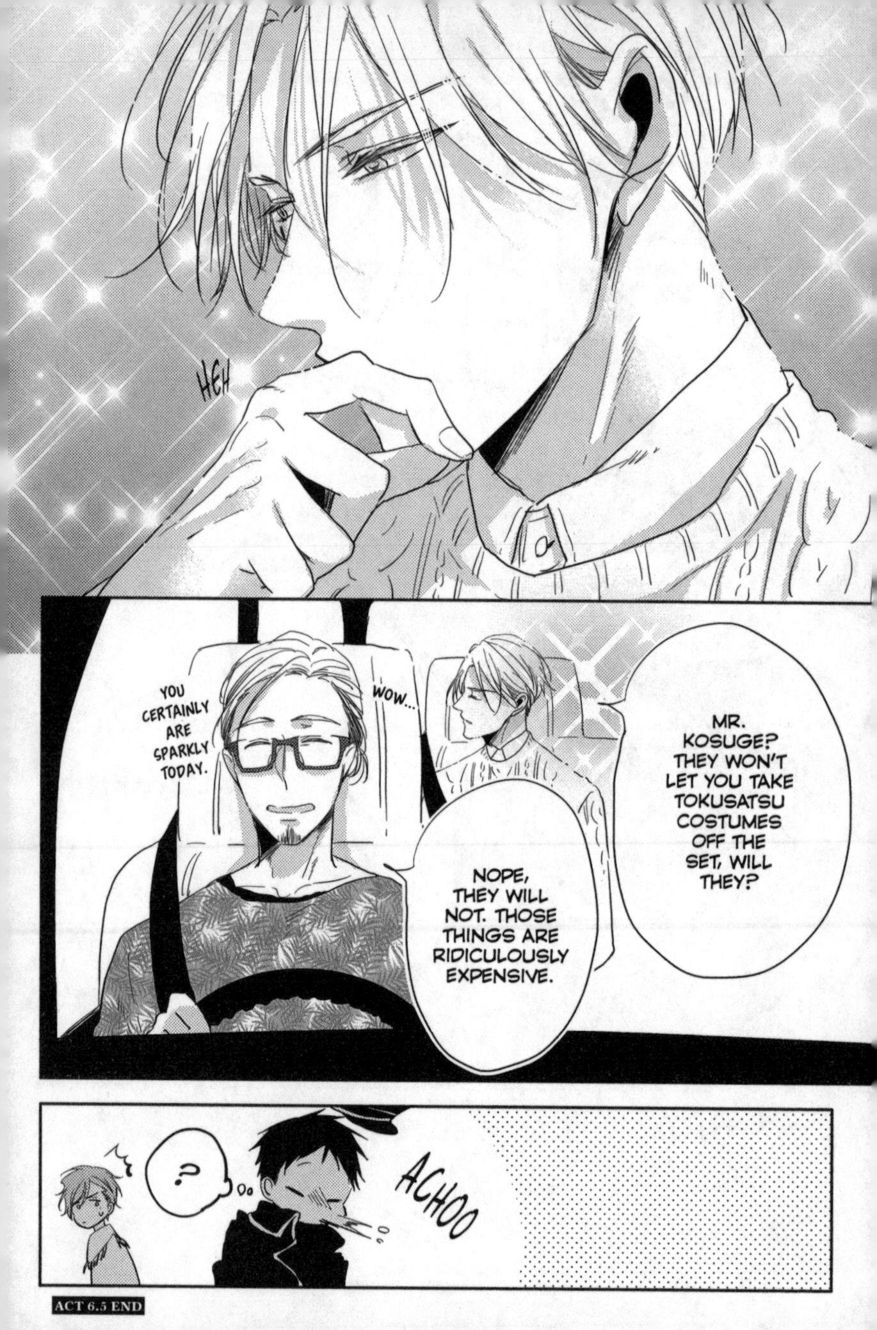
HEH
MR. KOSUGE? THEY WON'T LET YOU TAKE TOKUSATSU COSTUMES OFF THE SET, WILL THEY?
NOPE, THEY WILL NOT. THOSE THINGS ARE RIDICULOUSLY EXPENSIVE.
WOW...
YOU CERTAINLY ARE SPARKLY TODAY.
ACHOO
?

ACT 6.5 END

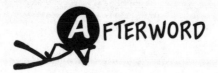

AFTERWORD

HELLO, I'M SACHIMO, AND BOY DOES IT FEEL LIKE VOLUME 1 CAME OUT ONLY YESTERDAY. WHAT, IT DIDN'T?

I'M DOING MY BEST TO PUMP OUT THE CHAPTERS AT A RAPID PACE WHILE STILL ALLOWING THE STORY TO DEVELOP AT A NATURAL ONE.

THIS VOLUME'S BONUS STORY IS A SWEET LITTLE SEX SCENE THAT COULD NEVER, EVER HAPPEN IN THE MAIN STORY...BUT IS TOTALLY POSSIBLE IN A SIDE STORY! I HAD A BLAST DRAWING IT.

I HOPE TO SEE YOU NEXT VOLUME!

さちも.

SACHIMO

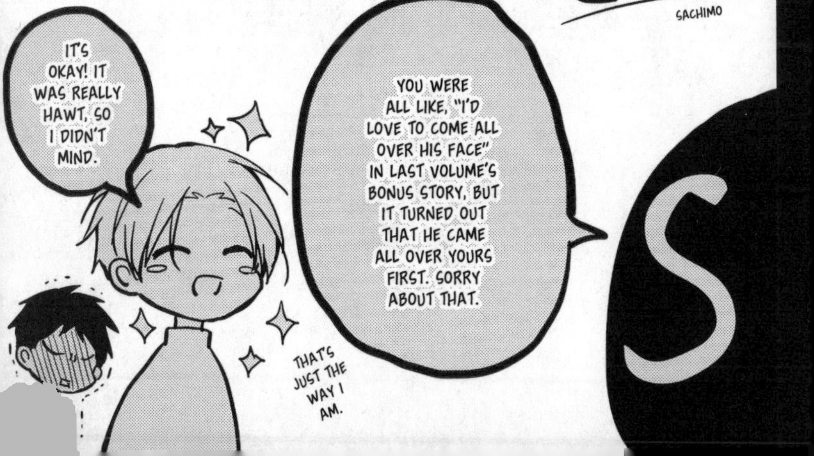
YOU WERE ALL LIKE, "I'D LOVE TO COME ALL OVER HIS FACE" IN LAST VOLUME'S BONUS STORY, BUT IT TURNED OUT THAT HE CAME ALL OVER YOURS FIRST. SORRY ABOUT THAT.
IT'S OKAY! IT WAS REALLY HAWT, SO I DIDN'T MIND.
THAT'S JUST THE WAY I AM.
S

About the Author

Sachimo
DOB August 17
Blood Type O
Born in Saitama Prefecture

Black or White
Volume 2
SuBLime Manga Edition

Story and Art by **Sachimo**

Translation—**Adrienne Beck**
Touch-Up Art and Lettering—**Deborah Fisher**
Cover and Graphic Design—**Shawn Carrico**
Editor—**Jennifer LeBlanc**

BLACK or WHITE Vol. 2
© Sachimo 2018
First published in Japan in 2018 by KADOKAWA CORPORATION, Tokyo.
English translation rights arranged with KADOKAWA CORPORATION, Tokyo.

ASUKA
COMICS
CL_X

Printed in the U.S.A.

Published by SuBLime Manga
P.O. Box 77010
San Francisco, CA 94107

10 9 8 7 6 5 4 3 2 1
First printing, December 2021

SuBLimeManga.com

For more information

on all our products, along with the most up-to-date news on releases, series announcements, and contests, please visit us at:

SuBLimeManga.com

twitter.com/**SuBLimeManga**

facebook.com/**SuBLimeManga**

instagram.com/**SuBLimeManga**

SuBLimeManga.tumblr.com

SUBLIME
MANGA